Secrets of the Lotus

Secrets of the Lotus

Studies in Buddhist Meditation

EDITED BY
Donald K. Swearer

The Macmillan Company, New York, New York
Collier-Macmillan Limited, London

The Macmillan Company
866 Third Avenue, New York, N.Y. 10022
Collier-Macmillan Canada Ltd., Toronto, Ontario

Library of Congress Catalog Card Number: 75-150068
First Macmillan Paperbacks Edition 1971

PRINTED IN THE UNITED STATES OF AMERICA

Acknowledgments

The editor's indebtedness to Chao Khun Sobhana Dhammasudhi and the Reverend Eshin Nishimura goes without saying. Neither the experiment in Buddhist meditation nor this volume would have been possible without them. The Venerable Dhammasudhi initially went to England to serve as head priest at the Buddhapadīpa Temple in London. Responding to the strong interest in Buddhist meditation and with the support of some of his followers, he established a Vipassanā Centre in Hindhead, Surrey, a London suburb. He is the author of *Insight Meditation, The Real Way to Awakening* and *Beneficial Factors of Meditation* and has lectured widely in this country and on the continent. The Reverend Nishimura is currently a research scholar in religion at the Institute for Religion, Hanazona College, Kyoto, as well as serving a Rinzai temple in neighboring Shiga-ken. He has completed his studies for the Ph.D. in religion at Kyoto University and for two years (1956–1958) was a student of Shibayama Roshi at Nanzen-ji in Kyoto. Before his visit to this country in 1969 he had spent a year at Pendle Hill, the Quaker study center in Wallingford, Pennsylvania, and he was at Carleton College, Northfield, Minnesota, during the winter quarter of 1971.

The editor is particularly honored to be able to include

Mumon Yamada Roshi's lectures on the *Zazen-gi*. Yamada Roshi is the Zen master of Shofuku-ji Zen monastery near Kobe, Japan, and is also president of Hanazona College. A student of *zazen* for more than forty years, he has written many books on Zen in Japanese although his exposure to an English-speaking audience has been limited.

Encouragement and support have come from several sources. The editor wishes to express his special appreciation to Nyāṇaponika Thera of Kandy, Ceylon, for introducing him to the practice of *satipaṭṭhāna* and to the Reverend Shohaku Kobori, Abbot of Ryuko-in, Daitoku-ji, Kyoto, Japan, for spending many hours with him discussing Zen and *zazen*. Professor Kenneth Morgan of Colgate University, whose interest in the study of Asian religions is unmatched in this country, provided essential financial support for the experimental workshop in Buddhist meditation.

Grateful acknowledgment is made to the Buddhist Publication Society, Kandy, Ceylon, for permission to quote from *The Way of Mindfulness* and to Kheminda Thera of Vajirārāma, Colombo, Ceylon, for permission to quote from *The Path of Freedom*.

Finally, a special thanks to those students who participated in the Buddhist meditation experiment and who through their interest, dedication and enthusiasm (not to mention sore legs and backs!) made the project so worthwhile and exciting.

Contents

Preface

Buddhism is one of the world's most ubiquitous religions. Originating in northern India in the sixth century B.C., by the beginning of the Christian era it had already found its way to parts of Southeast Asia and across Central Asia to China. It eventually spread to Japan by way of Korea, and much earlier, at the western borders of the country of its origin, may have had a more profound impact on Greek thought than historical sources have so far revealed. Nor is Buddhism only important historically. Some claim that Buddhism now offers the most viable spiritual option of all the great world religions.

This option is not one characterized primarily by a set of rituals or elaborate dogma but by a unique world view and a distinctive way or path. Buddhism offers, on the one hand, a radical critique of the human situation; on the other, it optimistically affirms that a man can find a solution to the human problem by his own efforts. It promises no easy panaceas, however. The way is well charted but it demands effort and self-discipline. Central to this way is the practice of meditation. It is this focal aspect of the Buddhist way to which this book addresses itself.

Of all the forms of Buddhist practice none offers a better insight into the nature of the teachings of Buddhism than

meditation. True, there are Buddhist sects for which meditation is not crucial. There is no country touched by
Buddhism, however, where a meditation tradition did not
take root: Buddhism developed at a time when Yogic
forms of physical and mental discipline were originating
in northern India; the Buddhist traditions nurtured in
Ceylon and Southeast Asia have extolled meditation as
the primary means to realize the goal of Buddhism; and,
throughout East Asia Zen Buddhism, which always prized
the practice of meditation, has been one of the major
Buddhist sects. To understand Buddhist meditation, consequently, is to know much that is essential to the Buddhist tradition at large. It is our hope that *Secrets of the
Lotus* will make a significant contribution to that knowledge.

The idea for *Secrets of the Lotus* originated in January
1969. At that time an unusual workshop was held at
Oberlin College, Oberlin, Ohio—an experimental project
in Buddhist meditation. The workshop brought together a
Thai Buddhist meditation teacher, the Venerable Chao
Khun Sobhana Dhammasudhi, and a Zen priest, the Reverend Eshin Nishimura, to share in instructing a group of
twenty-eight students in the theory and practice of
satipaṭṭhāna and *zazen*, two forms of Buddhist meditation.
The workshop proved to be so successful a means of introducing students to the study of Buddhism that plans for
this book grew out of it. As originally envisaged, the book
would contain classical as well as contemporary interpretations of Buddhist meditation and a description of the meditation project itself. In this way it was hoped that the book
would be an interweaving of method with interpretation,
history with the existential Now.

Secrets of the Lotus is designed to meet a variety of
needs. Within its covers are classical meditation texts such
as the *Zazen-gi*, a brief instruction manual in Zen meditation, and selections from the *Vimuttimagga*, an important
but often overlooked treatise on meditation techniques in

the Theravāda Buddhist tradition. It also contains modern commentaries on enduring meditation manuals such as the chapter in exposition of the *Foundation of Mindfulness Sutta* and Mumon Yamada Roshi's lectures on the *Zazen-gi*. The book, furthermore, offers interpretations of the nature of Zen training and the practice of mindful awareness by two young priests, accomplished in the Buddhist traditions of Southeast and East Asia.

The materials contained in the volume were prepared by the Venerable Dhammasudhi, the Reverend Nishimura, and the editor. The Venerable Dhammasudhi wrote Chapters 1 and 2 and the Reverend Nishimura wrote Chapter 5. The latter also translated the materials in Chapters 6 and 7. Chapter 3, the Prologue and chapter introductions were contributed by the editor. Chapter 4 was excerpted from a recent translation of the *Vimuttimagga* published in Colombo, Ceylon. The editor is responsible for numerous stylistic changes in the contributed materials, but at no point was the substance intentionally altered. Although much of the technical terminology has been eliminated, some words in Pāli, Sanskrit and Japanese have been employed. The meaning of these terms is usually apparent in the text, but a glossary has been added for clarity and coherence. In general, it should be pointed out, Pāli terms (e.g. *dhamma*) have been used in the Theravāda section and Sanskrit (e.g. *dharma*) in the Zen section. Diacritical marks have been retained throughout.

Secrets of the Lotus makes a unique contribution to the growing field of materials dealing with Buddhism and Buddhist meditation appearing in English. In recent years a number of books on Buddhist meditation have appeared in print, but they have focused on either the Zen tradition (e.g. Philip Kapleau, *Three Pillars of Zen*) or the Theravāda tradition (e.g. Nyānaponika Thera, *The Heart of Buddhist Meditation*), or have been primarily a compilation of texts (e.g. Edward Conze, *Buddhist Meditation*). This volume, by way of contrast, discusses Buddhist medi-

tation within both Zen and Theravāda traditions by employing classical meditation texts and commentaries, contemporary interpretations and a description of a Buddhist
meditation experiment. Hopefully the book will prove to
be of value for those whose interest in Buddhism is just
beginning as well as those well-versed in the field.

DONALD K. SWEARER

Swarthmore College
August 1970

An Encounter With
Buddhist Meditation

Buddhism is becoming increasingly popular in the United States. Its popularity rests not only on the appeal it has among college students or the role it has played in influencing "hip" culture. It offers a serious religious option for many Westerners, and it may well prove to have a significant impact on Judaeo-Christian thought and practice. Alan Watts[1] exemplifies those whose thinking has been decisively influenced by Buddhism, and even as devout a Catholic mystic as Thomas Merton[2] was deeply involved in Buddhism before his untimely death in Asia while visiting Buddhist centers.

Because of its multifarious forms, the claim that Buddhism is gaining an audience in the West is highly ambiguous. The largest identifiable group of Buddhists in the United States constitutes the Buddhist Churches of America, a Jōdo Shin Shu body whose following is primarily among American citizens of Japanese descent. There are

[1] Alan Watts is a well-known author on subjects dealing with Asian religions. His best known books on Zen are *The Way of Zen* and *The Spirit of Zen*.
[2] Thomas Merton was a member of the Cistercian Order at Gesthemane, Kentucky, before his death. He is the author of *Zen and the Birds of Appetite* and *Mystics and Zen Masters* among other books.

also Chinese and Tibetan Buddhist groups concentrated on the east and west coasts and a Theravāda headquarters in Washington which has plans to establish centers in other metropolitan areas. Yet, among all the varieties of Buddhism one can find in America today and all the forms of Buddhist practice, no aspect of Buddhism has a stronger appeal than Buddhist meditation, especially among younger people. In large part, perhaps, this appeal may be theoretical or ideal, part of the intellectual discovery of the study of Asian religions; however, meditation is also being practiced at several centers in this country two of which are particularly well known. One is in Rochester, New York, headed by Philip Kapleau, compiler of the book, *Three Pillars of Zen*, and the other is outside of San Francisco where Zen meditation is taught by Suzuki Roshi.

Buddhist meditation is attractive for many reasons, to be sure. For some it offers a retreat from the chaos and complexity of today's world. For others it may serve as a means of introspective self-understanding; and, for still others it is the means for attempting seriously to grasp the truth of Buddhism. Buddhism attests to an absolute or ultimate truth transcending the discursive intellect. Although that truth is referred to in Buddhism by a number of terms, e.g., Nirvāṇa, Śūnyatā, Tathāta, the fact remains that the reality the terms denote transcends description. The ineffable nature of the ultimately real in Buddhism raises serious problems for the student of religion, not the least of which is how it is to be known or grasped. In the Judaeo-Christian tradition the same problem is resolved by such categories as revelation or theophany. In most Indian Buddhist traditions, however, the ultimately real is grasped only by some form of suprarational, nonrational or intuitive knowledge often referred to as "enlightenment."

Although some of the earliest Buddhist texts attest to the sudden acquisition of knowledge of the highest truth upon confronting the Buddha or "Enlightened One," most schools of Buddhism developed a program aimed at the realization of this truth. This is not to say that any particular school ever claimed the enlightenment experience itself was anything but ineffable or an immediate intuition; rather, that it became part of a formal procedure or training. Consequently, in some schools of Buddhism, notably the Theravāda, the realization of the ultimate was conceived as a gradual process; whereas in other schools, notably Rinzai Zen, the sudden and immediate nature of enlightenment was stressed.[3]

The ineffable nature of the enlightenment experience and also the means or way to its realization offer pedagogical problems for the teacher as well as for the student of Buddhism. Perhaps these problems are no more serious than those encountered when teaching about such ideas as Eckharts' notion of the Godhead or Luther's concept of faith. That is to say, there seems to come a point where the usual logical procedures of rational discourse fail to convey the reality connoted by the terms. Such a problem is a familiar one for the philosophy of religion, but it is also perplexing when studying religions as an historical phenomenon. It is possible, of course, to adopt a purely descriptive approach by pointing out the way in which the tradition has understood such expressions. Nirvāna, for example, is referred to many times in Buddhist texts in such terms as the "unbecome" or "unconstituted"—whatever they mean! Buddhist commentators have also discussed the term, and Western scholars have written volumes disagreeing with each other about the interpretation of Buddhist Nirvāna. When teaching about the nature of the ultimate truth or the ultimate reality in Buddhism, one exposes the student to the texts, the traditional commentarial exegesis and even the literature of Western

[3] There are many different Buddhist schools and sects throughout Asia. Generally speaking, Buddhism in Southeast Asia is referred to as Theravāda and in East Asia as Mahāyāna. Zen is a school of Mahāyāna Buddhism and within it Rinzai is one of the sects.

scholarship. Yet, when all is said and done, many a student has been known to raise the query, "But what is Nirvāna?"

The means or method of attaining the ultimate, in this case a program of meditation, offers a different type of problem. Buddhist meditational procedures described in various texts can be analyzed in a number of ways.

For example, they might be divided into three stages —preparation, illumination and new life—corresponding roughly to classical characterizations of the mystic path or in terms more appropriate to the Buddhist perspective, Buddhist meditation might be described as a movement from sensory attachment and bondage to control of the senses and eventually to total freedom. This dynamic process, in Theravāda Buddhism, takes place between two different realms, one labeled, *saṅkhata* (constructed or artificial), and the other, *asaṅkhata* (unconstructed or real). In the former sphere man is blinded by various sensory distortions, chief among them being the notions of permanence and selfhood. These distortions are overcome by getting at the root cause of misapprehension, namely, the sensory inputs. If the attachment of one's senses to sense objects is limited and controlled, there is some hope of being able to see things as they really are. These controlling factors are introduced through the structure of meditation practice, the use of analysis or thought problems (*koan* in the case of Rinzai Zen), and the development of awareness and insight.

The above brief description may be helpful to students reading Buddhist meditation texts; however, would it not be an important addition if, in conjunction with primary and secondary source reading in Buddhism, students had the opportunity to practice meditation under a trained teacher? When I was in Ceylon in 1967 studying Buddhist meditation with Nyāṇaponika Thera, just such an idea occurred to me. If my students in Asian religion courses could have the opportunity of learning about Buddhism through the experience of meditation, how much more clearly such cardinal teachings as *anicca* (impermanence), *anattā* (no-self) and Nirvāṇa would be perceived. The experience of meditation would not only help answer the kinds of questions a logical or descriptive answer fails to satisfy, the context of meditation would also provide an investigative medium highly appropriate to the historical tradition. When I returned to Oberlin College in September 1968, where I was then teaching, I set about trying to make my hopes become a reality. In 1969, the college embarked on a new educational experiment in which the month of January would be devoted to innovative projects. With college approval and additional financial support from an outside source, I began to organize a meditation workshop for the January term.

There was no doubt about student interest in the January Term Meditation Project, as it came to be called. With minimal publicity sixty-five students indicated their desire to participate. To limit the group to a more sizable number all the students were interviewed, and from them a smaller group of twenty-eight was selected. It was a diverse group. There were both men and women; some had considerable background in Asian religions, others, none at all; some were committed Christians and Jews, others professed no religious faith; and, finally, all four undergraduate classes were represented.

It was my intention to introduce the students to the Theravāda practice of *satipaṭṭhāna* and the Mahāyāna Zen practice of *zazen*. To accomplish this end, two meditation teachers were invited, one from Thailand and the other from Japan. The Thai Bhikkhu was Chao Khun Sobhana Dhammasudhi, meditation master at the Vipassanā Centre in Hindhead, Surrey, England. He had had the benefit of three years of teaching *satipaṭṭhāna* in the West. The Japanese priest was the Reverend Eshin Nishimura, a disciple of Shibayama Roshi (a noted teacher of *zazen*) who, in addition to his duties at his Rinzai temple outside of Kyoto, is also a teacher at Hanazona Buddhist University. Both teachers were competent in English and were familiar with Western philosophical, psychological and religious concepts.

The project began the fifth of January and lasted for four weeks. The schedule included two periods of daily meditation practice between 10:30 and 12:00 each morning and discussion groups twice weekly. In addition to these group meetings, the meditation teachers made themselves available to individual students throughout the day and evening. The students were also reading materials relevant to Buddhist meditation. In the Theravāda tradition they read the *Satipatthāna Sutta,* Nyānaponika Thera's *The Heart of Buddhist Meditation,* Chao Khun Sobhana Dhammasudhi's *Insight Meditation* and several articles. In the Zen tradition they read the *Mumonkan,* the *Prajñāpāramitā Hṛdaya Sūtra* with Hakuin's commentary in addition to other articles and books. The structure and content of the project embodied its two major purposes: to introduce the student to Buddhism through the practice and study of meditation and, on a more personal level, to experience the beneficial insights of disciplined mindfulness.

For the first two weeks of the project the Venerable Dhammasudhi instructed in Theravāda meditation practice. He began by teaching the students how to sit in the half-lotus or full lotus position and instructed them in *ānāpāna sati,* or breathing mindfulness. Sore backs and legs were gradually overcome, and they proved to be apt and serious pupils. The combination of meditation practice and the study of texts and written materials proved to be very fortuitous. The students gained new insights into the traditional doctrines of *anattā, anicca* and *dukkha.* The impact of the teaching of the impermanence of sentient existence struck many of them with compelling force as they discovered the difficulty of calming the mind.

Perhaps the fact that they had not grown up in a Buddhist tradition was to their advantage. They were freed from the cultural biases that condition the truth claims of any religion. They did not become converts to Buddhism but, some of them at least, may have gained deeper insights into the essence of Buddhism than many who call themselves Buddhists. For example, one of the participants in the group wrote of his experience:

> On the third day I was meditating alone in the evening, attempting awareness of impermanence. Following the arising, existing and passing away of each individual breath, I achieved for a period of time a balance between mindfully perceiving this impermanence and that of the pain of the full lotus position (which at other times was too great for me to bear). In this manner I sank deeper into a state of conscious, active peace. Suddenly I became aware of loud shouts and laughter in the hall outside my room; then came sounds of people running, and a door slammed; and silence was again as before. In this event was a realization of the object of meditation in the three worlds instantly before me, and as I became the utter truth of the impermanence of noise, of breathing, and pain, that self-conscious seer was no more.

There is a profound degree of insight in this testimony. As a teacher I cannot help but think that this particular student opened a window into the nature of Buddhism which probably would not have been opened in the classroom.

Of course, not everyone gained this kind of understanding either of Buddhism or of themselves. Yet, even the apparent failures are difficult to evaluate. One boy, who dropped out of the project, wrote, "My enthusiasm for Theravāda meditation is inversely proportional to my knowledge of it. The more I get into it, the more absurd it becomes . . . I enjoy my senses, my emotions, and my 'meaningless world.'" Yet, as his report reveals, he learned much about himself, and perhaps his mistake was to expect that his self-awareness would necessarily coincide with stipulated Buddhist doctrines. Such expectation is the destruction of a viable personal faith. Surely religious experience in its most profound sense cannot be adequately expressed in the form of language. Words may function either as a mirror or a veil of experience, but they are not the experience itself.

One of the great values of the project for many of the students was not only the knowledge they gained of Buddhism but of themselves. For several a self-confrontation resulted which, in the ordinary course of events, all too rarely takes place. I can think of one afternoon discussion group in which a girl exclaimed, "But I don't want to give up my Western understanding of myself!" This exclamation may not have been an expression of enlightenment, but it was a revelation of honest self-evaluation. In strict terms, this is not "mindful awareness" (*sati*) or "clear comprehension" (*sampajāna*). But in the dynamics of religious experience, who can say what kind of a label it should be given?

One emphasis throughout the month was the importance of the application of mindfulness. The Venerable Dhammasudhi and the Reverend Nishimura were both very concerned that students not think of the practice of mindfulness solely in terms of sitting meditation. They stressed the fact that mindfulness should be relevant to all one's activities. This aspect of meditation seemed to surprise some of the participants who had thought only in terms of a formally practiced religious discipline. One girl observed:

> This type of mindfulness gave me a new perspective in examining myself, calmly observing, and from this distance I gained some self-knowledge. For instance, I learned the kinds of things that occupy my mind; I observed that my head is filled with memories of odd little things, and with worries about often insignificant problems. I also realized that mindfulness of action is valuable, for when one is aware of the situation and the action, time is not wasted because it is lived in full.

Many of the students concurred with the opinion that meditation pointed to a more total or complete mode of life. It was for some an experience in gaining a new freedom, a liberation from bondage to misconception and misconstrued attachment.

The applicability of meditation to daily life was brought out by the Reverend Nishimura when he commented that the purpose of the project was not to make converts to Buddhism but to make the participants better human beings. "For some of you," he remarked, "it might mean that you will become better Christians or Jews as a result of this month." This broad tolerance and concern for the individual needs and backgrounds of the students involved typified the attitude of both meditation teachers and was an important aspect of the success of the project. It was the same kind of experience I, myself, had had in Ceylon under the tutelage of Nyāṇaponika Thera, and served to emphasize the potential of tolerant concern for individuals within Buddhism.

The two weeks of Theravāda meditation practice and study were followed by two weeks of Zen practice and study after the Rinzai tradition. For the latter, the students were required to place their mats in carefully aligned rows and pay strict attention to the exactness of their posture. The care with which they sat was reinforced by the "stick of mercy" which the Reverend Nishimura carried with him as he walked slowly up and down in front of the students. The rigorous regime of *zazen* meditation was one of the significant differences between the Theravāda and Mahāyāna approaches. One student noted that he found it difficult to accept the intrinsic value in the discipline itself implicit in the Rinzai approach and that it produced a dilemma of trying to choose between concentration and awareness.

One of the valuable benefits of conducting the last two weeks of the project along fairly strict *zazen* lines was the knowledge it provided of another Buddhist tradition. Students were able to acquire a feeling for the Zen approach to meditation which they were then able to compare and contrast with Theravāda *satipaṭṭhāna*. Some students favored one method over the other, but all participants, regardless of their preference, developed a degree of insight into the two traditions difficult to discover in any other manner. One group member, while observing that "... both Zen and Theravāda Buddhism are concerned with confronting, not escaping, life's problems, and . . . achieving a viewpoint that will enable us to carry on the activities of life wisely and even-mindedly," saw differences between the two in the structure of the meditation procedure, the manner of practicing Buddhism in daily affairs, the nature of the discipline and the relationship to Buddhist doctrine and the intellectual life. It is doubtful that this student would have been able to make such observations merely on the basis of reading. Although her academic study of Buddhism was important to the conclusions she reached, their authority rested largely on her experience.

The project was a success in more ways than I had anticipated. It fulfilled my expectations on the levels of both personal relevance and insight gained into the nature of Buddhism. I was not prepared, however, for the élan or esprit which developed among the group members. At a bon voyage dinner for the two meditation teachers, it was obvious that all participants were united by a spirit of mutual concern and respect. At that point, perhaps, we were all Buddhists, not in the sense that we wore a particular label, but to the extent that we had plumbed the depths of our humanity.

PART I

Theravāda Meditation

THERAVĀDA ("Teaching of the Elders") Buddhism is found today throughout Southeast Asia and Ceylon. It predominates in Burma, Thailand, Cambodia and Laos though there are small Muslim, Hindu and Christian minorities. Theravāda Buddhists form the majority of religious adherents in Ceylon and are a sizable minority in Vietnam. Theravāda Buddhism, as we know it today, is an outgrowth of sectarian developments in India which began as early as the reputed second Buddhist council held in northern India in the fourth century B.C. It is doctrinally consistent throughout Southeast Asia with the same canon of Pāli texts being accepted as orthodox by all major Theravāda groups. Within each country where the Theravāda tradition prevails, nevertheless, unique forms and practices have developed. Consequently, Thai Buddhism, Burmese Buddhism and Sinhalese Buddhism each has its characteristic stamp.

One of the universal features of Theravāda Buddhism, however, is the practice of meditation as the way par excellence of realizing the highest goal of Buddhism, namely, Nirvāna (or in the Pāli language of Theravāda

Buddhism, Nibbāna). Although it is true that only a small percentage of Buddhists, monk or layman, actually practice meditation, it was traditionally and is still today held up as the core of the ideal Buddhist way. It is for this reason that the institution of a celibate monkhood became so important. It offered the best environment in which to withdraw from the usual concerns of the mundane world for the pursuit of Nibbāna through study and meditation.

For the average Westerner the term meditation probably evokes the quiet contemplation of the beauties of nature or thoughtfully considering an innovative idea. In the Buddhist tradition, however, the term denotes a more precise method of mental and bodily training. Throughout the history of Buddhism a variety of meditation procedures have been developed; some simple in form, others being more baroque. This section attempts primarily to illustrate one of the unelaborated and unadorned forms of Buddhist meditation. It is the practice of *sati* or mindful awareness upon which many other types of Buddhist meditation depend.

1

Prolegomena to
Buddhist Meditation

*This chapter represents two discussions of insight medita-
tion practice (vipassanā) by Chao Khun Sobhana Dhammasudhi. The first part of the chapter, "Introduction to
Meditation" is taken from the Venerable Dhammasudhi's
book,* Insight Meditation, *published privately in 1965 and
revised in 1968. Although it is organized in terms of the
author's own understanding of the meaning of meditation,
the discussion is filled with the classical terms of Theravāda
Buddhism. The second part of the chapter, "The Dynamics
of Insight Meditation," is a talk the Venerable Dhammasudhi gave in England in the autumn of 1969. While
reflecting the basic point of view of the earlier material,
the reader will note that the presentation is in language
more appropriate to a Western audience less familiar with
the Buddhist Suttas or texts. The two sections together
offer an interpretation of Buddhist meditation from traditional as well as modern perspectives.*

Introduction to Meditation

Many people misunderstand meditation as an escape
from life or as mysticism. In reality, however, meditation
is mental development and not an escape from life at
all. In fact, one cannot escape from one's own life even if

one tried to do so. Whatever one sows and accumulates in life, one reaps the result. Life is not a thing by itself but a compound of things. It depends upon conditions which form its existence. When certain conditions come into combination, life is formed. As long as the conditions of life are not brought to an end, just so long does life exist and proceed. Therefore, there is no escape in any particular form.

As human creatures we need right understanding of the true nature of life. By right understanding our attitudes toward life may be directed in a correct and positive way. Right thought or the right way of thinking is based on understanding things as they really are. In order to understand life as it truly is, we need to practice meditation. That is to say, it is necessary and essential for us to develop our minds for the purpose of purification and penetration into truth, as well as for the attainment of perfection in life. Life is not a mysterious thing, but it is sometimes difficult to understand. Nevertheless, it is not beyond the ability and intelligence of those who have eyes to see and minds to reason. All that is necessary is simply making the effort with firm and strong purpose to achieve the goal. No one obtains anything without putting forth some effort. Life is something to be known and understood, not to be ignored. Perfect happiness in life can be attained here and now on this earth.

What do Buddhists mean when they speak of meditation? The chief meaning of meditation is to contemplate reality. The word, "contemplate," means to observe, to understand things as they are, to penetrate into the true nature of things. Whatsoever one comes across or experiences in daily life one should notice, looking upon it to "see" what it is. One should attempt further to know how that thing comes into being and how it passes away. That is, the arising or cause of anything seen, heard or thought about should be clearly comprehended. Being vigilant and observing things according to their real nature, whether physical or mental phenomena, bring about this understanding. Everyone of us has the faculties of ear, nose, tongue, skin and mind. Our duty is to develop these six sense-faculties by way of contemplation and observation. We use the five physical faculties as instruments for contemplating the world outside, while the sixth one, the mind-faculty, is available for the world of ideas and thoughts. Reality is found within and not outside these faculties.

Another meaning of meditation is to remove resentment. Resentment is the destructive side of life, both material and mental, and is the dominant obstacle to spiritual progress and mental culture. The function of meditation practice is to get rid of, or at least to suppress, any form of resentment. There are two basic ways to remove resentment. The first is to be aware of it at the very moment of its occurrence. The moment we take notice of it, resentment will be kept in control. With controlling power we are able to find the proper reasons for what ought to be done and what ought not to be done. This controlling power is gradually increased by way of keen awareness and mindfulness of the present moment, sentiments, emotions and other states of mind. The second way of removing resentment is to cultivate and develop loving-kindness and compassion toward all living beings, toward any person one likes or dislikes, even an enemy or a foe. One has to be friendly toward oneself and also learn to love others. To love means to extend and expand without limitation friendliness and goodwill through action, speech and thought. At the moment resentment arises in one's mind, it should be considered as an evil and unwholesome thing and as something to be put aside. Then one should quickly meditate on loving-kindness and compassion, thinking: may I and the other person be well and happy, free from resentment and enmity; May I and the other person be friendly and live in concord; may we be safe and sound in our lives; may we love each other as a mother loves her only child.

To make the mind tranquil is another essential function of meditation practice. The mind generally is flickering and fickle, difficult to guard and control. It is like a fish drawn from its watery abode and thrown upon land. Obviously, such a fish will flutter and roll on the land so long as strength and circumstances allow. The wise man is able to train and straighten that sort of mind "just as a fletcher makes straight his arrow." In the world of desire the mind runs away and roams about, according to its fancy, in the sphere of sense-objects. It does not rest content with any present object. At this level of consciousness one is disturbed, dismayed and quite often disappointed. It is rare to be happy and peaceful.

The restless mind might also be compared to a boat on a sea tossed by the waves and stirred by the wind. The boat tosses up and down and sways from side to side. It does not rest for a moment. Disturbed and uneasy like that boat is the untrained mind. But, when the mind is properly trained and kept in control, one becomes tranquil and peaceful. The calm mind is still and quiet, alert and aware. Such calmness results from the practice of meditation. It is a happiness appropriately called peace of mind. We are all aware that passions or defilements, as waves of life, overwhelm and dominate people, pressing them down into the realm of deception and delusion so that they are unable to rise up to the sphere of happiness-in-truth. Such people submerge themselves into the unreal world of delusive sense-pleasure. Such uncontrolled responses are doomed to disaster for the only way to attain perfect happiness in the present life is to shun the passions and purify mental defilements and impurities.

In order to fulfill the aim of meditation it is quite important for us to discard hindrances that stand in the way. These are lustful desire, ill will, sloth and torpor, rest-

lessness and worry, uncertainty or skeptical doubt, ignorance, absence of joy and bliss, and all unwholesome
things. These hindrances retard and prevent one from
deep understanding of reality and from attaining the
highest perfection or the final goal of life. To abandon
and eliminate these hindrances we have to cultivate and
develop such noble qualities as insight into truth, unlimited love, brightness of mind, imperturbability, analysis
and investigation of doctrines, knowledge of wisdom-love,
gladness and all wholesome things.

It is interesting to note that meditation practice lies
mainly in equalizing the controlling faculties of mind.
These are of five kinds, namely, faith, energy, mindfulness,
concentration and wisdom. The first pair, faith and wisdom, should be developed together equally. A man with
too much faith but insufficient wisdom will become blind
and foolish; however, one who possesses too much knowledge without a balancing faith will be hardhearted and
will still be beyond the attainment of full perfection. These
two men will not be able to accomplish their goal. But a
man whose faith is based on wisdom will reach his final
destination in life because faith leads to the search for
truth while wisdom functions to realize the truth.

True faith or confidence is the basis of enthusiasm,
rapture, tranquillity and happiness which support concentration. Based on a concentrated mind is the understanding of things as they really are. With confidence and
wisdom one can practice mindfulness effectively. It is
mindfulness that brings about the balance of faith and
wisdom. Mindfulness also equalizes energy and concentration, the second pair of the controlling faculties of the
mind. Too much energy makes the mind distracted and it
becomes restless; while strong concentration without energy produces drowsiness, depression and indolence.

A further meaning of meditation is to seek to gain freedom of mind and so attain complete liberation. Freedom,
as it is used here, is the opposite of free will. So long as

there is will, freedom cannot exist. Will, itself, is conditioned by selfish desire, attachment, ignorance of truth and so on. Everything exists in a condition of interdependence and interrelatedness. Nothing exists independent of its own conditions and conditioning. One who speaks of free will in the sense of a will which is independent and free from conditions speaks of an unreal entity. Such a person is deluded and ignorant. Freedom, rather than meaning free will, means freedom *from* the will.

Freedom, in the sense referred to above, means to cleanse one's mind of impurities and disturbances as well as to liberate oneself from any fetters and defilements leading to the realization of ultimate truth and the attainment of tranquillity, peacefulness of mind and perfect happiness. This freedom may be spoken of as being in five stages—freedom of parts, freedom of suppression, freedom of eradication, freedom of tranquillity and freedom of liberation.

The first stage of freedom is attained through the practice of penetrative concentration which forms insight meditation (*vipassanā*). By means of practice one penetrates into the true nature of things through keen awareness and observation. Freedom of suppression, the second stage, can be gained through the state of mental absorptions (*jhāna*). At these two levels latent tendencies are not yet removed and rooted out, but they are under control. One will dwell freely and peacefully so long as the power of concentration and meditative attainment are maintained and gradually increased. Reaching the third stage, freedom of eradication, one becomes completely free from evil and unwholesome states of mind, destroying the root causes of demeritorious deeds. The heart is purified and the mind liberated. No selfish desire remains. The idea of self or "I" having independent existence is absolutely eradicated. One becomes free from any doubt and lives independently clinging to nothing in the world. Craving or thirst (*taṇhā*) in any form becomes extinguished and ceases. This is true freedom. The fourth stage is freedom of tranquillity which arises as a consequence of the third. The liberated one stands above the gravitation of mundane circumstances, but because of his compassion and unlimited love toward the suffering world, he unselfishly devotes himself to helping all beings reach liberation. Free, indeed, is he who attains to tranquillity. For him what was to be known has been known; what was to be done has been done. His burden has been laid down and his task is accomplished. Freedom of liberation is the final aim in life. He is free from all concepts of freedom. At this stage things neither exist nor do they not exist. This kind of freedom goes beyond existence and nonexistence. The unliberated being cannot know it, just as a man standing at the foot of the mountain is not able to see a person at the summit. This complete liberation of mind with wisdom can be attained through meditation practice only.

To acquire liberation, the appropriate means are necessary. A man wandering afar and seeking after liberation with appropriate means cannot gain it. Likewise liberation is not reached by one who ignores it and wrongly acknowledges it. It is fortunate, indeed, that meditation, as the true means leading to liberation is taught in the East and is gradually being introduced to the West at the present time.

The Dynamics of Insight Meditation

Buddhism is becoming popular in the Western world. Because Buddhism differs from Western religions, Westerners expect something different from Buddhists. The Buddhist way of living, is, therefore, very important, not only to Buddhists themselves but to those in the West. If Buddhism is for peace, love and understanding, then Buddhists must endeavor to live according to those precepts of the Buddha's teaching. The world urgently needs these qualities. The world is a community; and if its members cannot generate peace, love and understanding among themselves, then the world will remain in a state of chaos, unrest and disharmony. Our biggest task, consequently, is to bring Buddhist qualities into the world; but this cannot be done unless we are aware of these qualities within ourselves—peace in our minds, love in our hearts, and understanding.

The aim of education, according to the Buddhist point of view, is to realize our latent potentialities. As we know, human beings as small children live in a certain kind of harmony, largely void of conscious awareness. Later we lose that harmony. Though we struggle to regain it, our efforts do not succeed in bringing about our original state. We are able to achieve only *concepts* of harmony through our intellect. The intellect, in fact, creates a dichotomy, a separation of fact and concept. To realize harmony we have to go beyond the static concepts of the intellect.

Life is essentially a dynamic process. It is not something static or stagnant. Life is living and moving every second. You will remember that the Buddha compared life with a mountain river which flows continuously, never stopping for a moment. If we think about rivers, however, we will see their tendency is to flow toward the wider and deeper, not the narrower and shallower. The true nature of life is like that too, flowing on until it reaches the depths of being where it finally ceases to flow. The cessation of flowing is called Nirvāṇa, or as we say in Pāli, Nibbāna, the ceasing of all conditioned states.

Given the nature of our mundane existence, how can we cope with the dynamic process of life? If we try to cling to the static, occupying ourselves with the old, using the knowledge of yesterday or last year, the new cannot be seen and understood. We must let ourselves move and flow with the dynamic of life, but we must do so wisely and intelligently. Our mind cannot be occupied and burdened with objects, conceptual knowledge and beliefs. It needs freedom to approach and look at life-in-process.

Without this freedom the mind will lack genuine intelligence. If you observe the mind, you will see how it tends to create problems unnecessarily. All suffering arises through the inventions and reactions of the mind. There are many destructive elements in the mind, often on a deep level, which continually affect the quality of our lives, clouding the mind with stupidity.

One of the main aims of Buddhist meditation is to be free from stupidity and ignorance. It is not possible, however, simply to say: "I am now going to make my mind free," and to succeed. You may wish to fulfill an idea, but remain unaware of the conditions preventing action; and, when failure results, you feel frustration, disappointment and dismay. These feelings all arise from a mind which separates ideas from action, conceptualization from actualization.

How can the mind stop its negative creations? It is not easy or quick to achieve, but it is a task all human beings must accomplish to attain peace. Unless we are aware of how the mind creates suffering, how devious and tricky it is, we shall not be able to see the possibility of its transformation. We have to understand our own mind in all its aspects—not only the conscious, but also the unconscious mind. We have to penetrate to its deeper layers, to discover latent tendencies or factors underlying its conscious level. How do we do this? You may say it is necessary to go into deep meditation in order to reach this level, but, in fact, you can see the symptoms of all latent tendencies in your daily activities and expressions, both verbal and physical, and in the many facets of your behavior. All arise from latent factors within the unconscious mind. Therefore, if we become aware of our mental and physical behavior, especially in our interaction with different people, we shall be able to look beyond our explicit activities to the implicit influences which have their source in the unconscious mind.

To accomplish this end, attention is always required. Without attention, it is not possible for us to understand ourselves or to explore in any depth the gamut of our experiences. We have to be serious about what we are doing; yet, this seriousness must be free from tension. To be serious is to give full attention to what is before you, to what is happening. When your whole heart is there, tension is not distracting your energies into fear or confusion, and you can experience calmness and enjoyment while remaining attentive. There is no room for negative tendencies to step in or interfere. In this state watching things can be an interesting and pleasant activity without rigidity but also without expectation. Where there is expectation, there is fear. When you hope for a result, there is some degree of fear of not getting it; or if you succeed in gaining it, there is a fear of losing it. So, fear is a subtle but active element within expectation. Most of us, however, cannot live without hope. Enlightened people can because real living is in the present, finding fulfillment without hopes and fears for the future. In the present, there can be full clarity of mind which is one of the highest characteristics of a free being. If you are clear in mind, sensitive to your work and your environment, understanding and love will grow bringing about right action and radical change within you without planning and hoping. Expectation is an obstacle to action because it involves ideas about the future which create a gap between us and present action. When we indulge in hoping, we are building up a resistance to what is at this moment and trying to escape into what should be. This resistance blocks the flow of dynamic living.

In real living, we need not only attention but awareness and watchfulness. These three factors are equally important. When exercising attention, we often appear silent and still. How does this differ from stagnation, or a kind of mental death? It is different because you are closing the doors of only the superficial mind while leaving open the doors of intuitive insight which shows the truth of what you are attending to. Stagnation can occur when these doors are not open, thus blocking all the levels of the mind instead of allowing them to flow on more and more profoundly to extinction.

When we are totally attentive, our consciousness becomes more extensive giving us a wider, deeper, and purer vision because the ignorance and stupidity of the conditioned mind do not intervene. Only then can the intuitive insight flow, and we come into closer contact with the truth. I do not mean to imply a rejection of the intellect which is indispensable when dealing with factual aspects of life. But it is not dynamic; it cannot lead us to realization, peace, and full understanding.

If we can come into contact with intuitive insight, we shall develop more capacity for meaningful work and for living. Dead feelings of depression or frustration experienced by most people are lifted from the mind, thereby leaving a fresher state of consciousness. If problems arise in the mind, we should bring our awareness to bear on them to slow down their growth, and to be able to watch them more objectively free from preconceived ideas or knowledge. Understanding will, then, gradually arise, and the reality of the situation reveal itself.

If you try to solve problems through intellectual functions only, while you may be able to perceive many possible solutions, you will remain full of uncertainty, confusion and doubt. Some people, when in doubt, turn to learned or experienced people for an answer. For the mind to gain in real intelligence, however, it must look at its own tendencies to find its own answer with the encouragement of a teacher but not his answers. The mind must explore its own doubt by careful observation instead of requesting ready-made answers from other people.

Studying the life story of the Buddha, you will notice

that he said the Tathāgatas[1] only point out the way. The mission of a teacher is to inspire the quest and encourage followers to discover the truth for themselves. Also, you will see in the *Kālāma Sutta* that the Buddha taught people to be free from blind obedience to authority, even to religious texts. If we become dependent upon authority, we grow weak in intelligence and lose the freedom to act. Buddhism invites strong investigation and examination and encourages freedom to discover the truth of whatever is encountered. We should not just let things pass by or accept what others say, nor should we simply reject everything. The Buddha said that even his own words should be examined carefully. He was a frank teacher who opened himself to everything.

If we are going to flow, we must remain open. If we are narrow in our views or in our hearts, we become static and get stuck in the mire! To flow with attention, awareness and watchfulness there will be periods of silence, tranquillity and joy in which suffering disappears. At these times, problems might arise, but we do not suffer from them because we have objective understanding. Although this state of mind will pass, the knowledge that it is ever possible will give us patience.

When watching the breathing process in meditation, have you ever noticed that there are three things going on together: in-breathing, out-breathing, and pausing? Without a pause between in- and out-breathing, there is no breath. This pattern can be seen in all aspects of life. As the Buddha said, there is arising, falling away, and there is existing or a kind of pause when compared with the other two processes. Breathing is essential in life, and it is important for us to breathe properly. If we watch our respiration in meditation, our breathing will regulate itself, going in and out smoothly and deeply. Some people may

[1] The term, Tathāgata, is a title given to fully realized persons, those who have "crossed the farther shore" and have reached Nibbāna (Nirvāṇa). The Buddha is called a Tathāgata.

have practiced counting the breaths. What is the purpose of this? It is a means of focusing initial attention and calming down excitement. If you had to speak in front of a large audience, you might feel nervous. In this situation many people take a deep breath to prepare themselves to speak calmly and fluently. Here is an example of a superficial benefit obtained from a short breathing exercise. If, however, we practice awareness with regard to breathing, we can develop far deeper awareness. We can even stop thinking for a time, becoming free from all ideas and distractions and thus coming into a state of tranquillity. At an extreme point we can become as nothing, without breathing or body-consciousness or mind. At this stage the breathing has not really stopped but is completely even and undisturbed. Because the whole being is permeated with complete awareness, there is no concern for the breathing, body or mind. They are superficial compared with that other experience, the "treasure" that is the goal of our quest.

Before coming to that goal we have to "see" the three factors of arising, existing and falling away. Otherwise it is not possible to become completely objective. We have to shut the door to the old and open the door to what is new, the doors to positive, creative energy within us. Body and mind are nothing without energy—in fact they are both forms of energy. Desires, hatred, all feelings are energy which, if not expended in the right way, can be dangerous. Correctly directed bodily and mental energy is essential to the realization of the way.

Love is energy but by giving this energy to desire—wanting more, having more, becoming more—it is harmful since there is no end to having or becoming. If, on the other hand, energy is expressed as love and understanding in living, we become more perfect. Why do we become tired worrying about a problem? Because energy is dissipated and is no longer available for constructive effort. But, if something undesirable occurs in life and you give energy to being aware of it, rather than merely worrying about it, you will not feel tired. You can even begin to enjoy watching such problems as the mind becomes clearly focused upon the sources of mental ignorance and stupidity.

Seeing the truth brings about peace, happiness and understanding. This is the dynamic way of living; and if we pursue life using attention, watchfulness and awareness, it is not beyond our reach to achieve these goals. With the flow of intuitive insight, we shall open the doors to a truly creative life.

2

Discourses on Mindfulness

The contents of this chapter represent fourteen lectures delivered by Chao Khun Sobhana Dhammasudhi after meditation sessions at the Buddhapadīpa Temple, London, England, in the fall of 1968. These lectures were also used by the Venerable Dhammasudhi in January 1969 during his meditation instruction at Oberlin College (see Prologue). While they have been edited for clarity, no attempt has been made to modify the sometimes rambling or repetitive style typical of an informal talk, and also typical of more extemporaneous Buddhist teaching methods, both traditional and contemporary.

The fourteen talks all focus on the theme of the development of mindfulness; however, there is an implicit direction in them, just as there is in the practice of Theravāda meditation itself, toward the realization of complete understanding. Consequently the reader would be benefited by visualizing the lectures progressing through three similar but distinct phases roughly categorized as awareness (sati), understanding (viññāna) and wisdom (paññā). These stages point toward the movement in the progress of Buddhist meditation from the conscious awareness of all internal and external factors to the final realization of the true nature of things.

* * *

Attention and Concentration

For beginners in meditation the main problem is how
to keep the mind under control. We have been trained
that to think is to reason about things, to understand
reality by accumulating more and more information about
it. In meditation practice, however, we must not think but
be aware of the thinking process. This is very different.
If we *think about* meditation—the up and down movements of breathing, feelings and sensations—we are not
meditating. Rather, we are conforming to the desires and
states of our mind. Such conformity lacks the power of
objective attention and awareness.

Controlling power arises when we can look and act
directly. The majority of the time we react to things
according to previously accumulated ideas, views, opinions,
and knowledge. It is a rare moment when we can look and
act directly, without conforming to preconceived notions.
When we confront the mind with its ideas, knowledge and
views, it seems to possess us and shape our world. But if
we try to look at the mind with full attention, without
putting any views into it, leaving everything aside and
simply open ourselves to observe the mind—at that moment controlling power comes into our being. It arises
through the effort to be aware rather than to submit to our
prior mental conditioning. Such awareness is the process
of meditation. Two important aspects of this process are
concentration and attention.

Concentration is a translation of the Pāli term *samādhi,*
which literally means "stability of mind," or "stabilized
mind." In concentration a person focuses the mind on one
point, a particular object set before the mind. Suppose you
are looking at a Buddha image, trying to keep your mind
on the Buddha's face, head, and whole body with all its
parts. You look at it with open eyes, trying to remember
all the details. You then close your eyes and see the image

even with the eyes closed. If you forget anything, you open your eyes and look again, trying to capture the whole picture of the Buddha in your mind. You try and try to keep the whole picture of the Buddha in your mind. By trying time and again to keep your mind on the image, you are attempting to focus your concentration. Such concentration is, however, quite superficial because there is dependence upon the object. Your mind cannot leave the particular object. The moment you lose it, frustration and disappointment arise. Such dependence inevitably means that the level of concentration is superficial. When you are truly independent, you enter into the depth of existence and are able to live with a free mind.

This deeper concentration is referred to in Pāli as the state of *jhāna*, or "meditative absorption." By entering into the first meditative absorption there is concentration of mind together with five cooperating mental states described as application of thought, investigative thinking, rapturous joy, happiness (peace) and unification or one-pointedness of mind. Application of thought is the ability to direct the mind toward an object and not allow it to run astray or to wander. Such mental ability demands repeated effort. Investigative thinking complements application of thought. It enables the individual to see the whole picture, the forest as well as the trees. Through investigation in this deeper sense one becomes rapturous, happy, and one with the object. Nevertheless, the feeling, "I am one with the object," presupposes that there is still an "I"—an indication that the goal is not yet won.

When the meditator comes to the second stage of jhānic absorption, the two mental states of application of thought and investigative thinking die away. There is only rapture, happiness, and one-pointedness. In the profound quiet of the third meditative absorption rapturous joy fades away leaving only happiness in the sense of peace with one-pointedness of mind operating. Finally, if the meditator succeeds in reaching the fourth meditative absorption, he is freed from both happiness and unhappiness. There is no physical or mental sensation, only equanimity and mindfulness.

In the fourth *jhāna* the meditator is indifferent, free from desire in the sense of its negation, but there still may be an unconscious attachment to the object of concentration. Genuine mindfulness and insight may result, but there is the danger that one may become attached to the state of equanimity and peacefulness itself. For this reason, as well as because of the difficulty of the jhānic path, the way of attention and awareness has much to commend itself.

What is the meaning of attention? Attention is the way of *sati*, or insight, not the way of *samādhi*, or concentration. Insight means seeing the truth in wisdom. Attention is the process of observing things carefully, closely and deeply. In attention there is interest. That is, the meditator is interested in something with the sole purpose of understanding it. There is no desire, craving, and attachment, but there is awareness. Accompanying awareness is a clear comprehension of the object and process of understanding. Attention, awareness and understanding or comprehending are the most important factors for developing insight into the true nature of reality. In attention, there is a love of doing, of hearing, of listening or of understanding. The quiet moments of awareness reveal to the meditator just how distrait he ordinarily is and how much unnecessary energy is expended in his life. By realizing the false as the false in life, one can come to understand the truth as the truth. Without realizing the false, one cannot realize the true. It is not sufficient to realize only the idea of the truth and not the truth iself. We cannot work merely with ideas in order to come to true understanding. We must see things as they really are. We must look and act— not cogitate and react!

In this process of attention, awareness is present. When we are fully aware of mental states or anything going on inside or outside of us, we can see ourselves as we really are. We have a mirror with us all the time, the mirror of the mind which can reflect anything as an object of awareness. In attention the meditator looks not only at the object as object, but is aware of both the process of the mind reflecting the object and of the object itself. Concentration is a different matter. It can see only one thing, only the object and not the process of the mind reacting to it. In attention, which sees both together, we have a mirror showing us how to respond to both internal and external objects.

All things should be observed without interpretation, without explaining the object or the process. When looking with clarity and alertness there is no dullness. The dull mind is confused. It gets caught up in things. It gets stuck and not knowing which way to go or how to move becomes frustrated and anxious. But in the process of attention there is always clarity, alertness and total awakeness because the mind is open, and one is gradually freed from his previous mental conditioning and preconceptions.

This freedom leads to a new way. It is new because it completely transcends the old patterns of life. Through attention one opens up the controlling power of meditation. It is a power based on seeing things as they really are. There are no questions at this final stage. We may ask, "How will I know when I reach quietness?" But when we really arrive at quietness, such a question will not exist.

Constant Awareness and Clarity of Acting

Awareness differs from concentration because in the popularly accepted sense concentration is a process of exclusion, of focusing the mind intensively upon a particular object without concern for anything else. Insight meditation practice demands concentration but not as a form of exclusion. Instead, it leads to expansion and penetration. At a certain level of meditation, when the

mind is tranquil, an expansion of consciousness occurs. It
is not something to be calculated but, rather, develops
spontaneously. In the Pāli texts this expanded consciousness is referred to as *appamāṇa* or unlimited awareness.
In such a state of consciousness one loses a sense of self-
isolation or separation.

Constant awareness aims not to gain a quantifiable
amount of knowledge, but to experience reality as it is.
Such awareness is the process of looking with full attention until one is able to see the true nature of things. It
is not a question of making a conscious effort to examine
the nature of an object; rather it arises spontaneously from
the process of awareness itself. That is why looking at
anything with complete attention or inclusive concentration is an integral part of awareness.

Up to a certain stage in meditation there is much difficulty in looking passively at the rise and fall of the physical
and mental processes and simply acknowledging them,
because the mind tries to interpret and explain everything
it encounters. The mind moves hither and yon stimulated
by the memories accumulated up to this point. Patience
at this level of meditation practice is absolutely essential.
Some people may feel themselves to be in the anguish of
great psychological pain. Such pain should not be re-
pressed. The mind will attempt to escape the dilemma in
which it finds itself; but to continue successfully in meditation, the fact of psychological suffering (*dukkha*) must
be acknowledged. Gradually the pain will ease, not because
you have sought to avoid it but because you have constantly observed it. In this way you are freed from mental
anguish. Persevering in the acknowledgment of psychological pain is an important aspect of meditation. It helps
plumb the depths of our own reality. It allows us to see
ourselves as we really are in the midst of what we take
to be the throes of mental anguish which dissolve through
the power of awareness. It is like seeing our face in a mirror. We cannot escape the reflection just as in meditation

we cannot escape the fact that we are conditioned beings. In this awareness comes release.

Constant awareness seems a rather passive thing compared with active life, but in reality it is active and creative. In meditation you sit quietly keeping a constant awareness of what is going on here and now. Your memories and thoughts will be like an unceasing stream welling up within you without any attempt to recall them. Let them come. Do not try to exorcise them. Such efforts will only lead to a greater preoccupation with your random thoughts. Simply be aware of them; understand them for what they are. See how they arise, how they operate within you, and how the mind reacts to them. Thus you will see not an isolated object but a process. Such awareness differs from mere concentration. It leads to clarity, alertness and awakening. Even if the mind becomes dull through desire for something, make every effort to be aware of the nature of this dullness.

With constant awareness in regard to seeing, touching, testing, tasting, smelling, hearing and thinking, you can understand yourself, in relationship to your ideas, emotions and sensations. Then you will be able to come to communion with Reality. Such communion is nothing but inward integration. All of us have problems of disintegration and disharmony. To overcome this condition we try to change things outwardly, to adjust ways of speaking and behaving, or to correct the external environment. But we make little effort to change our inner condition. Outer changes, however, do not bring changes of heart. In the end superficial alterations create more suffering because the mind clings to hoped for results while bringing about no self-transformation within.

Through meditation not directed toward a specific goal, inward change comes about gradually, and the problems of outward change and adjustment disappear. With self-understanding one is freed to live and act not arbitrarily but appropriately. Meditation changes inner qualities and outer actions because it leads to the understanding of falseness and unreality, truth and reality. By realizing the false, the untrue, the disharmony and disintegration within, one is enabled to come to communion with reality, to understand the truth.

In order to come into communion with truth, clarity of action is necessary. When you are walking, walk with clarity of perceiving and of consciousness; when you are speaking, speak with clarity of mind and a definite direction; when you are listening, have clarity about your aim. Why are you listening? In order to confirm your own ideas and views? Or are you genuinely willing to discover something new? Your aim and the intent of your understanding should be clear. Otherwise you will accept only that which is agreeable to your own background. Rather than basing agreement or disagreement on similarity or difference, seek to understand clearly. Such understanding transcends contradiction. Contradictions arise when you are unable to achieve the awareness and clarity of action which sees things as they really are without the bias imposed by your own self-interest. The desire for ego-enhancement limits the extent to which you can be genuinely free. By clarity of action based on objective awareness, one overcomes the contradictions arising from subject-object distinctions. The self or ego is transcended. There is no self at work or self acting. There is only working and acting as a consequence of clarity of consciousness and full awareness. As the Buddha has said: "What has been heard is just hearing; what has been seen is just seeing; what has been thought is just thinking." There is no subject or object of the acting.

The self prevents you from understanding this truth. You think of the self acting rather than the acting itself. You act according to preconceived ideas of who you are and what you want to become. You cling to the desire to achieve and suffer when it is not fulfilled. Such distinctions as self and goal separate you from communion with reality. Being conditioned by these ideas, you are unable to see the truth. By becoming aware we see things as they are in themselves. Only then can we commune with them unencumbered by those divisions which awareness alone can overcome.

Looking At and Going Into the Present

Looking at the present is essential in the practice of awareness or mindfulness, but to be able to do so is not easy. You can look at things with your eyes; yet, it is very difficult to see feelings and thoughts because the intellect tells you that the mind cannot be seen, that it is invisible. You may then say it is useless to look at the mind or that it is necessary to develop the third eye in order to see the mind, but I doubt whether the latter can be done.

How can you look at the mind? The mind is the process of thinking and remembering. The moment you start to meditate and pay attention to physical movements, the mind starts wandering about. You may say, "I must bring the mind back," but when it is brought back you must also be able to examine it. Such observation cannot be done with the naked eyes but only with awareness and full attention. The moment you study the mind, it slows down. If it is not carefully observed, however, it goes on roaming and seeking in order to satisfy its own desires. Slowing down the mind is necessary if mental awareness is to be developed. Caught in the ordinary rush of things, you are bound in a web of ignorance, confused, wanting this and that without success. It is far more beneficial to work quietly, consciously and knowingly. When a thought arises, examine it. You may say that the moment a thought is looked at it disappears. Why does it disappear, or is it lurking just beyond the fringe of your consciousness? By continually studying the mind you will come to understand the conditions operative in mental activities. The mind, it will be seen, is not a thing in itself but a compound of mental states.

The mind is ordinarily not quiet or still because it is influenced and conditioned by the many states conjoined with it. The most important of these states are desire and dullness (or delusion and confusion) which continually work in association with the mind. The mind is driven by the desire to satisfy itself. It is an insatiable drive which leaves us in a state of *dukkha* (suffering), a state in which the mind attaches itself to one object after another in a constant round of self-defining activities. This process goes on and on—dissatisfaction and suffering (*dukkha*) fed by the flames of desire.

What can we do to stop this process? The answer is so simple and yet so difficult to achieve. Look at the mind and its mental processes! Examine the condition of your thinking, of the arising and gradual passing away of your thoughts! Let all thoughts flow into your mind. Your duty is just to look at them objectively, to see them as they are. This initial stage will eventually lead to more profound levels of understanding. But, if at first you worry about the mind wandering or try to interpret what you are seeing you will create problems and confusion the mind will be unable to solve. By thinking in such a manner, you are really trying to control the mind, and this can only lead to difficulty, frustration and disappointment. It is not really difficult to understand the mind and its processes; however, through our ignorant ways we make it an almost insurmountable task.

In order to reach insight we only have to examine the mind closely, carefully, and passively without interpreting it as "conscious mind" or a mind of this or that state. Our task is to *look at* the mind, not *interpret* it! It is only seen from one angle, not as a whole, if we are always translating and explaining it. If you become completely aware of the mind, you will see how it operates, how it searches for things and what is the main cause for its search for gratification and for pleasure. We must understand the process of mental activity and conditioning as it is, not as theoretical knowledge or for any purpose other than itself. This is why the Buddha said, "Knowledge is the process of the accumulation of ideas, gathered from this place or that, from this or that learned man and is really a process of confusion." In meditation we do not use knowledge. Put it aside and meditation will become easier. Simply examine what is going on here and now within you, what presents itself to you and how you respond to it. Examining whatever arises is living in the present. Thinking about our observations is either remembrance or imagination and puts us in the past or the future. Memories belong to the past; imagination and speculation belong to the future. The present is between the two, where there is no thinking. It is simply looking passively, with full awareness and complete attention. Then we do not see things according to our ideas or interpretations, and we will have pure understanding or *paññā*—wisdom.

When we talk about wisdom, we ordinarily think it has something to do with discursive intellection whereas it really has no connection. Wisdom means pure understanding in the present, of reality in the here and now. It is impossible to accumulate it. The wise man has the ability to see the truth as the truth, and the false as the false. Not only that, he is capable of loving all beings without discrimination, as they really are, and, hence, has the power to eliminate suffering. Wisdom is developed through full awareness of the mind in the present.

The second stage of seeing things in the present as they really are is understood in Buddhist meditation as the process of investigation and full inquiry without doubt. This inquiry is part of the quest for reality itself and not an investigation in the logical or rational sense. By examining things as they present themselves to us, our perceptions gradually become refined to the point that we can enter more deeply into reality as it is. There is no question of *trying* to achieve the goal of going into things more deeply. We must simply go on examining, and then investigation will become more profound. Analysis will be part of this investigation but not analysis simply in the scientific or psychological sense. Buddhist analysis does not aim simply at description or for that matter at adjustment, but at transformation of being through the realization of things as they are.

At this initial stage in meditation we are simply trying to understand how to look at the present, the things going on within us—emotions, thoughts, processes of mind or physical activities, rising and falling. When we are able to observe everything immediately, there will then be no distraction or exclusion. All will be noted but without attachment or disturbance. We shall have attained peacefulness and calm.

Why are we suffering, frustrated, and depressed? The most important factor in this question is how we look at things we come across in life. Suffering does not depend upon the things themselves. You cannot blame the circumstances or the situations. If you know how to look at them, you will be free—without making comment, without criticism. To be enslaved to the criticizing mind is to be in trouble. But if you learn how to truly observe things, whether pleasant or unpleasant, you will be free and will then know the best way to deal with problems, conflicts or anything that might arise. Look passively and you will understand; with understanding all problems are resolved, and you can live happily and peacefully.

The Power of Passive Watchfulness

In the practice of *satipaṭṭhāna*, or mindfulness, it is very important for the students of meditation to silently and passively watch everything that is going on in the bodily and mental processes. Such observation produces power, not in a worldly but in a spiritual sense. Indeed, the concentration associated with meditative watchfulness evokes an extraordinary psychic strength. When the mind is perfectly focused on something, a new kind of power is at work. It is not unlike the concentration of the power of the sun on a single point through the refraction of a magnifying glass. Or it might be likened to the power that would burn the retina of the eye if one stared at the sun. When you concentrate the mind on a particular object, you are developing the power to achieve your highest aim. The force produced through mindfulness provides the necessary combustive energy for self-transcendence. In a general sense we speak of the achievements of thoroughness and attentiveness. Passive watchfulness in the area of meditation enjoys even greater consequences.

Just as the student or the businessman hopes for some degree of success, those who meditate also wish to succeed. Especially in relationship to others with whom they may be comparing themselves, they may hope to come out on top. Such a desire is badly misguided. It is the product of ego-delusion, the quest for a power over others. The power of attentive watchfulness associated with the quest for truth is, paradoxically, powerless. That is, the power of passive watchfulness does not lead to the conquest of others but to the conquest of self. It is a creative energy essential for enlightenment. Or, perhaps it would be more appropriately called re-creative energy for it is the power of new being. Creative energy plays a very important role in the process of meditation aimed at achieving enlightenment. This process, however, must not be accompanied by the desire for success or the desire to achieve higher and higher levels of meditation. In the desire to achieve such ends, conflict arises; and in this conflict there is *dukkha* or suffering. Desire is the active cause of *dukkha* as Buddhism teaches. If there is a desire for self-enhancement, the practice of meditation will be much more difficult. On the one hand you want to achieve higher levels of meditation, while on the other you are held back because you must fight against conflict within yourself, conflict caused by desire. Many more difficulties arise until in the end you cannot meditate. Numerous negative states come into being, and your energy disappears. There is no power, no creative energy left. You just want to give up and run away from what you are doing. The mind becomes confused and muddled. There is no longer any clarity, no alertness, no awakening.

The question we must now ask is whether passive watchfulness can produce power, that is, re-creative energy. Why is it so necessary for us to observe or watch things passively? In the active process of doing anything there is usually a purposive idea we are seeking to actualize. Consequently our orientation is toward the idea or the intention rather than toward objective reality. Our purposive suppositions, therefore, cause us to *react* to our surroundings in certain set patterns rather than to *act* openly in any given situation. This is not the right way to come into contact with reality or to maintain peace within because in this reactive process the personality, the idea of "me" or "self," dominates our actions. Dominated by a preconception of self, we become exhausted trying to react to every set of circumstances in relationship to the self-notion. A state of frustrated inertia may result. For this reason the idea of self is the main obstacle to acquiring a state of quietness or to experiencing peace of mind. Such a condition is acquired by being passively alert to everything going on within us. All ideas of self must be put aside; the concept of "I" must not come into play in insight meditation. You must not be conscious of yourself practicing meditation; for when you are conscious of yourself doing something, it is not meditation but thinking of meditation, imagining something about to happen. In this manner it becomes impossible to live in the present.

In the *Satipaṭṭhāna Sutta* we are taught merely to watch the breathing processes but not to control the breath with the goal of self-enhancement. Focusing attention on the breathing is not calculated to gain something. It is, rather, only an exercise in watchfulness. Let the breath come in and go out naturally and normally. Your function is to watch passively the course of events without putting any idea, explanation or interpretation on the breathing or on the breath. By watching the breathing processes, you observe when the breath is deep or long, shallow or short. Gradually you understand it and see it just as it is. If you watch carefully, closely and passively, you arrive at an objective, detached understanding of events for what they are. There is no question of naming, "This is long breathing," or "This is short breathing," and there is no intention to control the breath. If by controlling the breath, tranquillity or peace should come into being that is only an emotional or physiological phenomenon. Genuine peace and tranquillity cannot be achieved by the method of breath control. If while observing the breathing processes, the sensation of calm or tranquillity comes into being, that sensation should be noticed. When the mind is silently watchful, anything coming into contact with the mind-sense is received and perceived very clearly and immediately. There is no reflective questioning of how to perceive these things. The mind is immediately receptive, clear and alert; and perceptions are accurately sharp. In this way you can directly understand the whole activity of the body through the breathing processes. The up and down movements of the breath become a mirror, as it were, in which you can become aware of things as they are.

An analogy to passive watchfulness might be the act of watching television. What do you see watching the television? You see the images and pictures appearing, and you have the feelings that arise with watching. Sometimes you may feel very excited, but you are not aware of yourself. The pictures on the television screen involve you, and you are "lost" in watching them. In other words, you do not see yourself or observe your mind and mental states reacting to the sequence of images. Can this act be called objective seeing? No! It is subjective seeing because you are interpreting the pictures seen according to your unobserved emotions of likes and dislikes. If, however, you try to watch the television by using it as a meditational mirror to observe your mind, mental states and emotions, then you become aware of the real "you" in the process of watching television. You see not only the pictures but you are also able to understand your states of enjoyment and amusement, fear, and anxiety.

The "I" may be very unhappy about losing the sense of emotional involvement in the television image, and you may say "How can I relax without a sense of 'me' having pleasure?" How fallacious! The real relaxation of the mind and the body is in the state of passive watchfulness. Try and see for yourself if this is not the case. If you passively watch the mind (note, for example, how your mind reacts to my talking), you can see the whole picture of what "you" are; and when the mind has reached a state of total passive watchfulness, it becomes very silent. At the threshold of silence there is still movement, but any stirring will be silent, quiet and smooth, allowing the state of clarity to grow wider and wider and the consciousness to become more and more extensive in all its aspects.

How can the mind come to that state of stillness which is the aim of meditation? When the mind reveals itself to you, contemplate it by passive watchfulness. From the moment you watch the mind it tends to stop moving, and the moment you lose your aim it starts moving again. Therefore your purpose must be maintained. Observe any state of mind—worry, anxiety, cogitation—without thinking about it, or trying to control it or without interpreting any thought. The effort to interpret and thereby control is the main obstacle to reaching a deeper level of meditation. The moment you give identity to what you are watching, ideas come into being. At that point you are thrust into a level removed from reality itself. In remaining at the level of things as they are, all concepts, names or words must be given up completely. In this manner the mind can remain silently watchful, and because of that, creative energy comes into being. All mental impurities are cut off through the power of understanding, thereby releasing creative energy. One who has experienced the state of passive watchfulness is deeply aware of the creative energy resulting from stillness and complete tranquillity.

I have observed many friends who come to do meditation under my guidance. Most of them have the same difficulties in entering into stillness and tranquillity and are unable to achieve full understanding. The main stumbling block is the desire to achieve. If you understand Buddhism clearly, you must agree with me that desire is the cause of suffering and conflict (*dukkha*); and *dukkha* embraces the mind, mental states, feelings, body, and bodily activities. Conflict manifests itself clearly if desire arises. Desire produces the concept of duality wherein there is the observer and the observed. There is separation within, and there is no harmony when there is division. Where there is no harmony, there is no integration. Then there is no possibility of understanding reality. All of this, however, must be left to you to see for yourself. Meditation is the means whereby one comes to "see" the truth about existence.

The Five Sense-Faculties and Feelings

The five sense-faculties are the body of insight meditation. They are all in us, may be experienced at any time, and should be understood clearly and precisely. The Buddha said in the *Samyutta Nikāya*:[1] "The followers of the Dhamma, the followers of the Buddha's teaching, must understand the five faculties as they really are." One must

[1] The *Samyutta Nikāya* or *Kindred Sayings* is a subsection of the *Sutta* or "dialogue" section of the Pāli canon of Theravāda Buddhism.

understand their arising or coming into being, their passing away or disappearing, the satisfaction or suffering inherent in them, and the freedom from them. Without freedom from them, it is impossible for anyone to abide in peace or to attain to the truth of enlightenment.

What are these five faculties? They are the faculties of ease, discomfort, joy, grief, and indifference but must be analyzed to be understood. As you know, the Buddha was a master of analysis and usually his teaching starts with analytical knowledge and only after that comes to integration or insight.

The faculties of ease and discomfort are bodily. When we experience things through the five physical senses, namely seeing, hearing, smelling, tasting and touching, we have either bodily ease and happiness, or bodily discomfort, pain and unhappiness. The faculties of joy and grief refer to mental ease, happiness or bliss, and mental unhappiness and suffering. These are experienced through mental contact. Such thoughts arise in the realm of ideation through the mind which in Buddhism is called the sixth sense. The last faculty is indifference. It may be experienced both through the five physical senses or through mental contact.

First we must analyze these five faculties in terms of feelings. The faculties of ease and joy are regarded as the pleasant feelings; the faculties of discomfort and grief as the unpleasant feelings; a neither pleasant nor unpleasant feeling characterizes the faculty of indifference. Thus, from these five faculties arise three types of feeling state.

What then is the difference between faculties and feelings? Faculty in Pāli is *indriya*, which means "the chief" or "the lord." The faculties of ease and discomfort, as we have seen, arise only through the physical senses; the faculties of joy and grief only through the mind. Thus, for example, the faculty of ease could not arise through the mind, nor could the faculty of joy arise through the body. Feeling, on the other hand, means experiencing the contact between any of the six senses and their objects. For example, the hand might have contact with an external object from which could come a pleasant, unpleasant or neutral feeling; and through this the faculty of ease, discomfort or indifference would arise. This faculty would be called the "Faculty as Chief or Lord of the Senses."

When one is fully aware of the feelings, one sees and knows clearly whether they are pleasant, painful or neither. Through developed awareness, one understands how feelings arise, how they disappear, and sees them as they truly are at the moment of their occurrence. Thus one becomes steadfast, maintaining perfect equilibrium, neither excited nor depressed. This way leads to the mastery of the feelings.

In Buddhism everything is examined according to the Four Noble Truths. Thus to study life you must first know what it *is*, second how it *comes to be*, third how it *passes away*, and fourth the *practice* leading to its passing away. These are the Four Noble Truths, which must be understood simultaneously and not progressively. It is like understanding one thing in four ways. That is why the Buddha said that when we realize Nibbāna, the Four Noble Truths are comprehended all together at the same time, like the rising of the sun simultaneously dispersing darkness and giving light. When we understand the Four Noble Truths, we understand the whole truth. We are fully equipped to realize this truth in our daily life. The only necessary requisite is to have the right means for it to be realized or understood. There is no need to wait for enlightenment sitting in meditation at the temple or somewhere else. Nibbāna can be realized now and it can be described by applying the Four Noble Truths to the five faculties.

The faculty of discomfort is something all of us experience. When discomfort arises, the first step is simply to be aware, "That is bodily discomfort," that is, acknowledge it as it is. Then you must face the question, "How did it arise?" Nothing can arise without conditions, causes or constituent parts. These must be observed and understood. Third, you will gradually come to understand that discomfort is not permanent but disappears or passes away from moment to moment. Finally, if you maintain awareness of this conditioned process remaining indifferent or equanimous toward discomfort because you have understood it as it is, then you can stand aloof from evil conditions, unwholesome states of mind and from all disturbing things. Understanding the faculties presents several factors of meditation such as application of thought and investigation and then through these, rapture, delight, joy and serenity, or concentration of mind. These qualities free one from the faculty of discomfort.

By further practice we can remove the faculty of grief through cultivating rapture and delight, and because grief is very closely connected with the activity of mind, by calming down the application of thought and investigation. Later we progress to the removal of the faculties of ease and joy. Because we usually like happiness, we do not want to be free from it. In Buddhism, however, we are taught to be free from happiness also and not to cling to it since attachment denies the individual the attainment of perfect peace. The way to remove happiness is to be detached from rapture, joy and delight through disinterested alertness. What is the meaning of disinterestedness? It is to remain equanimous, indifferent and neutral toward all things. We must not be interested in anything apart from the object set before the mind, and even to that object we must not be attached or cling. We notice it but remain free even from the reaction of happiness or joy. It is not that happiness and joy do not exist for us. Rather, in our acknowledgment of it, we are set free from preoccupation with it.

In the end, even the faculty of indifference has to be transcended. We free ourselves from everything in Buddhism! In order to have perfect peace we have to be free from indifference because it can cause pleasure and pain later on. In order to transcend indifference it is very important to pass beyond the state of "neither perception nor nonperception" and attain the cessation of perception and feeling. In maintaining equilibrium, equanimity can arise—the equanimity of utter purity. When you experience this state, you will see that it is not happiness or peace as we understand it in daily life. It is quite different, but since we have no words to give it, we call it perfect happiness or perfect peace. This is the highest state of meditation practice and spiritual attainment. When you come to this state, perception and feeling have completely ceased. You do not cease to be or die. You still live, and consciousness still functions smoothly and gently, but it cannot be perceived because ordinary sensory perception has been transcended. You cannot feel it because feeling has "cooled." By the attainment to the cessation of perception and feeling you are completely free from the faculty of indifference. This is the highest peace.

This is our way—the way of awareness and insight. Through this practice you can understand all the five faculties and free yourself from attachment to any one of them because you come to know them as they are. Awareness and insight grow together at the same time, and through insight all things are integrated. At the highest peak of attainment, you overcome all things and come to oneness. Oneness is allness because it is the state of perfection. This is not allness in the sense of all things collected in ordinary life, but rather that all things come to perfection and you are perfected at that unique moment.

The Stilling of the Mind

Experiences in meditation are not the same for all meditators. Since everyone is conditioned, his own *kamma* [past actions] experiences will be in accordance with *kamma*, with what has been accumulated in life. We must not expect the same experiences as others, but with the realization of truth there is the same understanding. The same understanding, however, will have different expressions because the way in which people express themselves depends upon their experiences, the backgrounds of their lives. Language usage conforms to certain patterns of life and society, which invariably leads to different ways of expressing truth. That is why the Buddha warned us not to get stuck in words. Language is a poor means for describing truth. Words are not the truth itself, and to think they are is to remain on a superficial level. Even religious people believe language adequately describes the truth, but at best words only point the way to the truth.

Regarding the stilling of the mind, I have asked you to see whether the mind can be quieted and how it can reach this state. If it cannot be stilled, you must discover the reasons. Such knowledge is not to be gained from books or from other people. Rather, the best way is to see the truth for oneself, and to do so we must apply some analysis.

What is the mind? Everyone of us has a mind, but what is it? We speak about the Western mind, the Eastern mind; and perhaps if there were human beings on Mars, there would be a Martian mind! The mind is a concept, a collective term for consciousness and mental states, including perceptions, feelings and tendencies both unconscious as well as conscious. Superficially speaking, the mind is the product of time, education, training, and of *kamma-vipāka*, the law of action and reaction, cause and result. Each individual has a different mind because of the law of *kamma*, the accumulation of life experience. Mental contents are accumulated in life, as well as different aspects of mind developed. But the mind always has the same *function* of recognizing, perceiving, understanding and thinking. These activities are universal to all forms of mind.

These functions are conditioned by different tendencies or states depending on the background, education, status and age of the person concerned. Consequently, the mind of a child is different from that of an adult. A child is not conscious of his own patterns because he depends upon the ethos established by his parents' mindset and others who surround him. Even adults are often unconscious of their own mental states because they lack a way of becoming conscious of them. As a result they cannot attain peace. The mind is so conditioned that it cannot be free.

When you are listening to me, your mind is still conditioned to some extent by your previous knowledge and beliefs and by your thinking processes. It is not really free to understand. It always moves, seeking something else. It always interprets, looking for explanations. There is no quietness for such a mind. Is there an end to searching? It appears not. The mind strives for satisfaction and gratification. Yet, it remains unsatisfied by anything it comes across. It is enslaved by desire, craving and thirst; hence, there is no peace.

It is of utmost importance in meditation practice for all of us to be aware from moment to moment. Unless the mind is aware of itself, it cannot come to stillness. Some people say that they are aware, but it is doubtful if they are actually aware, or whether they merely *think* they are aware. Sometimes we convince ourselves that we are aware when we really only think we are aware. In awareness, there is no thinking, only complete attention given to the process or object. Awareness in the sense of total or complete attention produces comprehension and understanding. In your waking life when full attention is given to anything, understanding arises. But when attention is weak, or only partial attention is given, comprehension is seriously limited. Most of us live our lives in partial levels of understanding because we lack the ability of full attention.

You may then ask, who is really aware? So long as there is self-consciousness, consciousness of the subject, then there is no awareness in the real sense. Real awareness has no subject. The notion of a subject comes into being through the connections of unconscious contents in the world of the mind. We look at things subjectively because of ego consciousness. At first the ego is the object of consciousness. Later it becomes more complex with greater energy until it comes to dominate all the thoughts and activities of the individual. Observe how children come to understand things in their lives. At first, a child thinks of himself as a third person—that is, the ego as the object of consciousness. As he grows up, he refers to himself in the first person, hence reflecting the growing power of the ego as subject-agent.

It is important to be free from the ego because the ego is an imaginary entity produced out of the contents of the mind. That is why, the moment we come to stillness and awareness, ego consciousness drops away. There is neither subject nor object—only peace remains and truth shines forth. We then see that the ego is the creation of unconscious mental associations and is, therefore, not real.

In awareness of the mind we must first understand by what the mind is conditioned. All consciousness has one or two states arising together. Consciousness does not arise independently without mental states. That is why the Buddha in referring to consciousness said, "When the mind is lustful or with attachment, hatred, delusion, or confusion, one must know the mind itself and the states arising with it." Without full awareness we cannot know nor imagine the real state of mind since ordinarily we know only the conditioning symptoms or mental states. These symptoms of delusion, hatred and confusion bring about frustration and unhappiness if there is attachment to them.

People ask, "What can we do, when we know the mind's attachments?" If you are fully aware of the mind's attachments, you will know what to do. Do not try to project or obtain the answer before knowing it through genuine awareness. When you are fully aware of the mind's confusion, then you will know how to deal with it. Be fully aware and gradually the mind will become clear.

If you look for an answer, the result will be to play with ideas, a distraction which will lead you astray. If this happens, do not become discouraged but simply be aware of the mind's distraction.

To become aware of the mind distracted is to come to realize the causes for distraction; however, it is also to come to realize how the mind reaches a state of concentration. Such knowledge which accompanies the stilled and concentrated mind leads to expansion and liberation. The mind is enlarged in the sense that it is freed from conditions. Such enlightenment-freedom is a noetic state. You do not need confirmation of your enlightenment. If you do, you are still in doubt and not yet enlightened! For he who is enlightened, there is no doubt.

The only way to deal with the mind and mental states is through the development of true awareness. The practice of meditation is to make us aware, from moment to moment, "seeing" everything which arises or goes on within us. Only in this manner can we come into contact with the unconscious contents of mind. These, as we know, cause many problems in life. People appear to be able to carry on life smoothly on a superficial level, but within the mind there may be many psychic disturbances. Material things can provide comfort and satisfaction in life, but they cannot guarantee happiness. Often we imagine or pretend we are happy, but we are not really so. If unconscious psychic disturbances are at the source of our problems, it might appear that to become conscious of them would lead to further unhappiness. How fallacious! Such a notion is but a projection of the imagination with no basis in the actual awareness of these disturbances. In truth, full awareness of unconscious disturbances enables one to erase them. They are cut off by understanding, by wisdom.

Wisdom will take away all disturbances. Fear arises because of ignorance and lack of understanding. Ignorance always causes fear. You have fear because of illusion, because of ego-consciousness. When you have gone beyond the vain limits of the ego, there is no fear or insecurity. With the warmth of an open heart, you will feel secure, work happily and live a peaceful life.

In Buddhism, there is a form of knowledge referred to as the "Third Degree of Knowledge" acquired or developed through meditation. This knowledge involves the examination and understanding of all the unconscious contents on the mind, i.e., the root cause of human problems. This does not mean that all unconscious elements are disturbances. There are creative as well as destructive unconscious factors within us. When we come fully into contact with all aspects of our inner self, we can remove what we do not want and cultivate what is good. Yet, even when what is good has been fully developed, we must be free from it. We are only truly free when we transcend both good and evil and all other dichotomies. For this reason for the enlightened ones, especially the *arahants*, or Perfected Ones, there is no *bhavānga*, i.e., no becoming or life continuity of consciousness. In the perfected person guarded by complete awareness every moment, no unconscious remnants remain, hence, eliminating the motive power of becoming. Only on the attainment of that point of enlightenment is the unconscious completely at one with the conscious.

We know very little about ourselves. We know about the body, about the five aggregates of material forces, feelings, perceptions, tendencies and consciousness, but what of the unconscious contents—the accumulated elements still within us? Without full understanding of these, enlightenment cannot be attained. For this reason enlightenment is said to be within rather than without. Enlightenment is not found under a tree or in the forest. It is found within you. Of course a quiet place and a "good friend" are helpful. A meditation instructor is called a good friend, one who does not impose anything on you but who will help you along the way. When the mind is still, you will understand all these things. This knowledge does not come from books, but from a quiet mind—a mind free from all conditions.

Insight and Detachment

The system of Buddhist meditation we are practicing is called insight meditation. Those of you who have been with us know what insight is, but sometimes the word is misleading because it assumes different meanings according to your background and degree of understanding. In discussing the meaning of insight, I am not intending to add just another definition to the ones you already have. Leave aside all the meanings you may have accumulated. Otherwise it will not be possible to understand the Buddhist conception of the word.

The real meaning of insight is seeing in wisdom the truth as the truth. When you see things with the naked eye, your vision of them is not blocked. Similarly, if you see the truth in wisdom, there is no doubt, no confusion, no illusion. There is perfect awareness, alertness and clarity. Otherwise, there is no seeing, only imagining and speculating.

In that kind of seeing there is no seer, no consciousness of a person who sees, no separate entity that sees. This is very important. If you think you see, then it is not real seeing, only perception; and in perception there is always the perceiver and the object perceived. Consequently, mere sense perception cannot be trusted because it may be distorted and perverted according to unconscious conditions and mental states.

There are fundamentally two functions of insight. The first one is penetration, piercing the walls of ignorance. Without penetrating the walls of ignorance, you cannot see reality. It is like the parable of the blind man touching the elephant but unable to identify it completely. Penetration is a crucial function of insight because only by rooting out our ignorance can ignorance be removed.

The second function of insight is called "cutting off." Insight cuts off impurities, defilements and all unwholesome states of mind. No person destroys these defilements. Rather, unwholesome states are cut off by the power of insight. In order to realize truth completely both functions of insight are essential and should go hand in hand. Some people fear the consequences of the cutting-off function of insight. They erroneously believe that the self may be harmed. The fallacy of this belief, of course, is that no self exists as a separate entity. Indeed, it is this false concept of self that is cut off by insight. In other words, insight allows us to see things as they are rather than as they have been incorrectly ideated.

Insight has different levels of which three may be distinguished. First there is the insight of the Supreme Buddha, the fully enlightened one, the one who has discovered the truth by himself. This level is called the insight into the all or the all-seeing. This means the Buddha developed perfection in all its aspects and can, therefore, see all things very clearly and perfectly.

The second level of insight belongs to the Silent Buddha who attains enlightenment through his own efforts and intelligence but lacks that quality required for teaching people. His insight is deep enough to cut off all impurities and penetrate into reality just as the Supreme Buddha, but he cannot explain clearly what he has seen and understood. His insight lacks the quality of a teacher.

The third level of insight belongs to disciples, the followers of the Buddha. Those who attain enlightenment can clearly see the truth as the truth, but not as directly as the Buddha understands it. This is due to the perfection required for enlightenment which makes the Buddha's understanding deeper than that of his followers. Sāriputta, one of the Buddha's disciples, was reputed to possess great wisdom so that many people compared him with the Buddha. But his understanding was not that of the Buddha's even though it came very near.

Should anyone of us attain enlightenment, it will be on that level attained by the Buddha's followers because we are on the path taught by the Buddha. We accumulate knowledge. We do not go into direct discovery or devote ourselves completely to meditation without asking for instruction or advice from anyone else. That is why our insight is weak compared with that of the Buddha. But this does not matter. What matters is to attain an understanding of reality, to attain enlightenment. This is the essential thing.

Now the question arises, how can insight arise? Insight arises when awareness or mindfulness is fully established. In fact, we do not aim to develop insight but awareness or watchfulness, which is the factor leading to insight. If you are fully aware of your mental states and all contents of the mind, you will understand them for what they are. You will realize the condition of things: how this comes into being, how that passes away. You will see both the appearing and disappearing of all phenomena whether physical or mental.

The only way to reach such understanding is to establish awareness. The moment you are fully aware of what is going on in the present, you will understand the real nature of things and processes. No one can tell you about reality. That is why enlightenment must be attained by yourself. You cannot be told, for the full meaning of insight is in personal experience. Insight is not remembering, thinking, or perceiving, but experiencing.

It is difficult for us to be aware of ourselves because of the obstacle created by our idea of the "self," the "I am." Here is the main hindrance to the practice of awareness. At the beginning stage of meditation, you may say, "I am meditating," "I am being aware of this." "I" means the self, which always interferes with meditation practice. But when awareness becomes full and complete, the self disappears. In the self there is desire, expectation, speculation, imagination, thinking. The self is a bundle of all these things and is the chief block to the practice of awareness.

It is very important for us to understand the processes of the self, of "you" and "me." When you understand the processes of thinking, feeling and existing, then awareness will become strong. If you have the feeling of being lost or ashamed for having done something wrong, then there is no awareness, only the concomitant emotion which arises and dominates you. But by applying awareness to this emotion, you can gain controlling power over it. Such awareness leads to insight into the true nature of things. In meditation practice, therefore, it is imperative not to be carried away by the self.

Insight and understanding are always coupled with detachment. Ordinarily life is characterized by attachment because we are afraid of losing the security of permanence in life. Consequently we attach ourselves to our possessions, to what we hope to acquire. Since attachment characterizes the attitude of most people, detachment appears to be a negative state. In fact, however, it is quite the opposite. When you are *attached* to something, the mind is really in a *negative* state of not wanting to understand the real nature of things. To be possessed by the innate tendency to grasp is to destroy creativity. But with detachment, especially from pleasant or unpleasant feelings and from all active states of mind, you are truly creative. You are freed because you understand things as they really are. Clarity of understanding is not just knowing that something should be done this way or that way. Such understanding is merely technique. The understanding accompanying detachment, however, offers more than technical knowledge. It plumbs the deepest reaches of human existence.

A detached mind, born of understanding reality, is a

creative mind. It is free to work to its full capacity. The attached mind is limited and develops a wide range of problems stemming from the pursuit of "self"-interest. By contrast the detached mind's power has destroyed the illusion of self-interest. The Buddha said, "Of all conditioned and nonconditioned things, detachment is the best." To work with an acquisitive mind is very different from working with a detached mind. The acquisitive mind becomes the victim of what it does not get. It believes its state of being depends on what it acquires. The detached mind, however, is characterized by calmness, peacefulness and steadiness, possessing an inner equilibrium not distraught about achieving things. With detachment—liberation within—everything is achieved without effort. It is not a state of laziness or inertia in which nothing is done, but a profoundly creative state in which everything can be done.

Understanding the Conditioning Process

One of the important things in meditation practice is to be free from anxiety of any kind, even anxiety with regard to time. If you simply do your best without thinking about time, you can work much better. You may think it is very difficult to do anything without anxiety, but you will discover that being aware of anxiety whenever it arises will later free you from it. So long as you know, "This is the robber," he will not harm you. If you do not know the robber, however, you may be injured.

In meditation you have observed the arising and falling of the breathing process. As it is said in the *Satipaṭṭhāna Sutta*, the Discourse on Mindfulness, with any object being observed the meditator must be able to see its origination and dissolution and the appearing and disappearing of the object and the subject. Such observation will lead to the realization, "This object or event exists only momentarily." Physical processes have the nature of coming into being and passing away from moment to moment, as do states of mind or mental contents, regardless of the presence or absence of awareness. Recognizing this fact leads to the understanding of truth and freedom.

Given this fact, how does the body or the mind continue to exist? Is it possible for them to cease? We may say that the body will come to an end when it is very old and cannot carry on its functions, but is it possible for the mind to cease? Stopping mental processes is very difficult, and many people believe it to be impossible; however, the question of arresting the mind is not a matter of belief or disbelief, but of seeing for oneself. Opinions based on believing or disbelieving have no meaning in regard to the truth, but only offer a psychological value. "Clear seeing," or direct realization of the truth, is more meaningful. Meditation, seen as direct realization, is a method not for running away from things as they are, but for real living. Meditation is part and parcel of life and cannot be separated from it.

In reality you have meditated many times. Real meditation has no form or system. Buddhist meditation is not a system, but a way of living, or, it is better to say, a way of doing. The Buddha never gave any techniques for developing meditation or training the mind, but he gave instructions about training ourselves. The "how" of the Buddha is not a technique. He simply stated that you must be aware of the body, the feelings, mental states and phenomena. It must be done directly without relying on techniques. If anyone asked me for techniques, I would find it difficult to provide a program. But, when one realizes one's own hindrances, he will be able to meditate. The best advice is to keep on training yourself in awareness practice, day by day, night by night, and then everything can come. Do not worry about your difficulties and obstructions. We all have such problems, but they should become a part of your meditation practice rather than a block to it. By approaching conflicts mindfully, we will find a solution to them.

In this quest it is imperative to understand our conditions. How many things condition you in life? Do you want to exist? Do you want to become something else or remain the same person? The process of becoming and of continuity is what we call life. Without it there is no existence or nonexistence. The process of becoming characterizes all aspects of life. The breathing process rises and falls every moment without ceasing. If it stops, we say that we die. But there is a possibility of going beyond the perception of breathing processes without dying—it is simply the *concept* of "I" which disappears. At that point contact with reality comes into being. In that contact the concepts of life and death have no meaning. It may be called "dying within" because we die to memories, thoughts, feelings, and perceptions. "I" is not the truth but a concept existing only in the mind. For this reason you can go beyond it, beyond the process of becoming and continuity.

So long as there is becoming and continuity there is a craving for existence, for becoming, and there is attachment. You cling to life and do not want to die. Craving and attachment come into being through sensory contact and resultant feelings. In fact, life in general is a plethora of contacts. Indeed, it may be described as a series of experienced events. Without events there is no life, and so long as the process of becoming is conditioned by craving, attachment, feeling and contact, the body, mind and mental states must go on. When the process of becoming ceases, however, there is a complete cessation of conditions, sensory contacts and responses. This is called Nibbāna. Nibbāna is found when one breaks through the process of becoming and continuity, or the vicious circle of life-death-rebirth.

The process of becoming and continuity ties beings to *saṁsāra*, the circle of existence. We are born only to die and resume life again in this Wheel of Becoming. This process, in fact, occurs every moment, but because we do not attend to it, we do not see or understand this process. Our mind is engaged instead in many activities in the world outside, so that we forget the world within. In the practice of breathing exercises, watching the rising and falling of the abdomen, we come to see very clearly the momentary nature of our physical being. Furthermore, we are able to distinguish mental from physical processes, although in either case there is only the process of becoming. We are aware of nothing permanent, and by this analytical knowledge we are able to overcome false ideas (i.e. the concept of a self). Overcoming false views is the first step of insight.

If one only knows these processes theoretically, without seeing them for oneself, the knowledge acquired cannot help one to be sure of the truth. Such study begins in certainty and ends in confusion because information is based on accumulated abstractions which may make logical sense but lack existential validity. In meditation, however, one "sees" the physical and mental processes directly and the relationships between them from moment to moment with an eye undistorted by attachments. Without mental processes the physical processes cannot exist, and without the physical processes the mental processes cannot function. From this insight we come to another step: the realization of conditionality. How are these processes interconnected? What is the cause of their continuation? At this step in insight you will have a glimpse into the nature of the conditionality of things. You will realize through your own seeing that you are a conditioned being and also a conditioning being.

With the realization of one's real state, freedom from attachment to the conditioning process is attained. Understanding conditionality enables one to live with conditions, whether pleasant or unpleasant. The capacity to live with and thereby transcend any condition in life is part of a more complete understanding of the nature of things, including oneself. A Buddhist does not try to escape from life; rather, he penetrates through its illusory nature, hence gaining the ability to live with anything life offers. With this ability, you have genuine freedom by understanding what you are and should be. Lacking this understanding of the conditioning process, one cannot live calmly or happily in the face of frustrations and troubles. For the most part we become upset and lose our equilibrium in the midst of problems. We know, theoretically, that we should remain calm but we cannot. Meditation holds out to us the promise of being able to cope with unpleasantness and unhappiness. In sum, meditation offers to give meaning and purpose to our lives.

Two things are essential to bear in mind. The first is understanding or clarity of perceiving anything with which we come into contact. The second is freedom or liberation, in the sense of not being caught up or conditioned by anything. The only way to achieve these two goals is through constant awareness with enough courage to see everything within us, whether pleasurable or otherwise. We must not expect to see only the good or beautiful in life. Meditation provides a training ground for facing all aspects of our situation. It enables us to overcome the anxious expectation of gaining the pot of gold at the end of the rainbow. With this acknowledgment we overcome a good deal of misery. Keeping full awareness, we can experience everything: material events, feelings within, other people's actions, or ideas and opinions which conflict with our own. We shall see all such things continuously arise and pass away. They arise because of conditions and then disappear. Seeing the nature of arising and ceasing in all events, the mind will be liberated by understanding the conditioning processes—both within and without.

Recognizing Hindrances

To be able to see one's own hindrances or obstacles to meditation practice is very important. What is the main obstruction to meditation? If we can say it in one word, it must be *self*—nothing more than that. Self is the main obstacle to any progress, especially spiritual progress. You may say that in material progress the more you have the more you will become. But this notion of progress is really nonprogress since it results in envy, competition, jealousy and suffering.

You may say that it is impossible to do anything without the concept of a self since achievement, success, advancement or progress all seem to presuppose such a notion. In meditation you may say, "*I* am meditating. *I* want to be peaceful, *I* desire stillness." If these statements mean you are working for the self, peace will be beyond your grasp. Sometimes, when you achieve quietness for a short period, you are so satisfied with the experience that you become attached to it. The next time you sit, you expect a similar experience to occur; and when it does not, you feel depressed and unhappy. Such a result occurs because you have failed to see your efforts in any terms other than *self*-ish.

To be free from the self is mandatory for a full life. Although it may not be part of our present view, we can live without self, happily and peacefully, still working and taking part in social life. Indeed, to overcome self-preoccupation is the only way to guarantee that one can achieve genuine peace and happiness. You will remember I have always said that a good moment for meditation is the moment you are in a state of suffering. In the moment of suffering, you can clearly perceive yourself reacting to a situation; hence, awareness of the nature of the self is acute. With fully developed awareness, that is, seeing events for what they really are, trouble and happiness cease to have meaning. In the state of true awareness when hindrances are overcome one reaches inner liberation where only freedom is meaningful.

How can we achieve this state of inner liberation? Paradoxically, we must remove all hindrances by not making aggressive efforts to clear them away. Such an attempt, without fully developed awareness and without awareness understanding, will merely create more problems and more hindrances. According to Buddhism, there are two ways of removing obstacles. One is the way of entering into meditative absorption, the *jhāna* state, wherein you can be free from hindrances. In such states, however, hindrances are only suppressed, not rooted out, and they will arise again upon coming out of the meditative absorption. The second way is by understanding hindrances clearly the moment they appear. Here is the way of insight. The *Satipaṭṭhāna Sutta* teaches us about the way of insight. That *Sutta* given to the monks by the Buddha came from his own experience. Everyone can have a similar experience.

In this *Sutta* five hindrances are mentioned; and although more may be specified, these five offer a comprehensive typology. The first hindrance to meditation progress is sense-desire, including seeking gratification or enjoyment through the imagination or mind. Any satisfaction or pleasure gained through the senses, especially the mind-sense, plays a very active role in life and even more so in meditation. In beginning meditation the mind seeks happiness and peace, wanting to enjoy the spiritual life and the inner world. Such sense-desire as this can be clearly observed in meditation. It is the nature of the superficial mind never to be satisfied with anything. Therefore, the search goes on forever unless the hindrance of sense-desire is removed. Sense-desire can be removed by vigilant watchfulness at the very moment the mind wanders and seeks anything. Note the arousal of desire, and examine it closely and carefully. Such arresting examination will bring about a cessation of sense-desire. The mind will gain a new clarity, and the dullness of conditioned thought will be overcome. Alertness characterizes the person for whom the conditions behind the mind are no longer ignored.

In insight meditation it is important that our attention not be confined to one object. In this system, rather, we must see the whole process of an event. Such perspective is not a state of distraction but one of lucidity. Our life is not, in fact, characterized by isolated events. When we talk about the mind, for example, we do not mean only the mind but the many conditions and states connected with it. To understand fully is to experience the truth in its wholeness, not merely to remember isolated truths you were once taught. The problem with equating the truth with memory, or, for that matter, with any conceptual scheme or manner of ideation, is that it may deceive you. In your concern to ideate or intellectualize your experience, you may fail to look at what is really happening within you, with clarity of mind and alertness. As soon as you try to name the insightful experience, a little dullness arises. The name does not matter. What is important, however, is to "see" things as they really are. Knowing what is going on, there is no need to label it or to repeat it in words.

The second hindrance is ill will, repugnance, or hatred. This refers to the violent mind, agitated states within. We must be able to recognize violence within us and why we do things violently. Violence within is often a motivating force. Hatred and violence are forms of harmful consciousness. Sometimes memories arise of someone injuring you, and the memory of the event provokes you to seek revenge. At those very moments the ego is exceptionally strong. What can we do to combat such states? Focus attention on them by applying full awareness to discover why the mind wants revenge, why it is violent. Through such direct understanding of violent states, you will come to know what to do about them. The way of insight is, first, to look at and to see, to be fully aware of what is going on and how it comes about, how it operates and how it fades away. All these things must be comprehended through keen awareness and with clarity, without projection or the veil of conceptualization. The thinking process may become the main obstacle to the awareness of reality, because in itself it provides only a limited pattern. Being aware of things in order to understand them for what they are, is action without ideas, dullness or confusion. In insight the mind is always clear and free. Only such a mind can begin to approach reality.

Another hindrance is the condition of sloth and torpor, or sleepiness. For the first few days during a period of intensive meditation, people at the meditation center often have difficulty with tiredness. It may be physical or mental fatigue, or sometimes it is both. In the case of the third hindrance, however, we do not mean physical fatigue but mental laziness, when the mind is in a state of inertia. In this state the mind does not want to work and makes you think, "I am very tired." The "I" is sleepy. To overcome this sense of exhaustion we must look and see whether it is mental or physical. The first step of insight is distinguishing the mind from the body, the mental process from the physical process. Tiredness may, indeed, be a physical condition, but we have to see whether or not it is so by observing it. When your fatigue is understood through observation, tiredness disappears. For myself, when I feel tired and meditate, physical fatigue disappears quickly and I become alert. This phenomenon is very natural in meditation. That is why I ask our friends who feel tired in meditation to observe closely the distinction between mental and physical processes. It is not a matter of acquiring knowledge—you do not need any information—only watch closely and clearly, and your understanding will dispel your sense of torpor.

Restlessness and worry are the fourth difficult hindrance. Only by attaining to Arahantship, the final stage of realization, can this hindrance be removed. Why is the mind restless? Why is it worried? Because you lack peace. Restlessness can be compared to dust blown and scattered in many directions. In meditation, many things within us which have been accumulated in life rise up, and people tend to run away because they are afraid to review the vicious circle of life. It is good when disturbing things arise, for you can then observe and distinguish them clearly. Everything accumulated in life must be brought to the surface in order to understand them; otherwise you cannot come to the full realization of truth.

Some meditators will have disturbing feelings arising at this stage and, if he or she is not strong, not brave, there will be a wish to escape quickly. This reaction is natural in meditation; it is also natural in daily life. In daily life, however, you do not notice it so much because you are so busy with external things that inner disturbances remain unconscious. You feel that outward affairs appear to be going on quite smoothly and you are happy with them; but if inner disturbances are seething within, you cannot have peace.

In the last analysis it is impossible to rest content with the sensate or superficial values of life. Through inward observation and contemplation we are made aware of the disturbing elements within us. We really do not need to seek them out. They will find us, perhaps at those moments we least suspect them.

You may say, "I listened to the Chao Khun's talk about inner disturbances, and now I must watch out for them." Do not try to create such feelings artificially. The reality of these inner disturbing tendencies depend upon your *kamma* accumulated throughout your life. They emerge from within, not from without. What we call Māra[2] in

2 Māra is a mythological personification of the power of the world of the senses. In this capacity he tempted the future Buddha to give up his quest for enlightenment and submit to him much like Satan tempts Jesus in the Book of Matthew.

Buddhism, the "Evil Tempter," is not something outside yourself—it is within. Māra as a sign of a psychological reality is useful to spiritual progress. Without Māra, the Buddha would not have attained to enlightenment. When the Buddha was tempted by Māra, his reply was very interesting. He said, "Māra! I know you. You cannot do anything with me." He was a little frightened when he was strongly tempted the night before his enlightenment. But when the Buddha knew, "This is Māra," he was able to continue his meditation and attained enlightenment. We should not regard Māra, the sign of the restless temptations of the sensate world, as something obstructing our spiritual progress. Rather, when we are aware of these inner disturbances, we are enabled to confront them directly with the conscious mind. They no longer function as subterranean images confining our view of reality.

The last hindrance is skeptical, or defensive, doubt. Doubt is easy to overcome. It arises when the mind is confused. The moment you have doubt, stop, sit still and examine the doubtful mind. Gradually doubt can be resolved by careful observation. Do not rationalize the subject or try to find a solution. The answer will reveal itself when the mind is quiet. An answer arrived at intellectually will be part of the subject of doubt! When you look for an answer, you create ideas to explain something. That is no answer. A mental creation is not the way to solve problems on the way to enlightenment.

Analytical Knowledge

According to Buddhist teachings, the first step of insight is analytical knowledge or the objective understanding of the physical and mental processes. We cannot say that things exist or that nothing exists, because the existence of anything is characterized by coming into being and passing away, appearance and disappearance. We seem to see the *continuity* of appearance or disappearance, however, and therefore make such claims as, "This exists." Such perceptions arise as a consequence of the recognition of similarity through comparison. The same factor applies to meditation as well, only here the mature meditator penetrates through the facade of sameness and stability to the nature of the dynamic of the mental and physical processes.

This first step of insight is essential in order to understand life. Life simply is not a static entity; it is a living and moving process. Sometimes we call it a process of becoming or a process of continuity. Life is a collective term for processes. We cannot touch life as an entity existing inside or outside of us. What we call mind is certainly not an entity. Can you touch the mind? Even in deep meditation you still see variations going on—in the initial silence or in the beginning prelude to stillness. But, where is the mover? There is no mover to be perceived. Consequently Buddhism claims that the mind is not an entity. False ideas of "self" produce the principal misconception of life for everyone. What is a "self"? Does it exist as a separate entity? Can you discover it in meditation, or in other forms of experience? You believe you are "Mr. this," or "Mrs. that," because people call you by a name given you by your parents. You simply accept such concepts without question, but the real "you" might well be very different from "Mr. this" or "Mrs. that." Who is the real you? What you are and what you should be are different things. For this reason we experience contradictions and conflicts. When you know what you really are, however, such conflict is resolved.

How can we know what we really are if we do not meditate? To meditate is not just to sit quietly, doing nothing but hoping for the best. Such an activity is just *thinking* about meditation. *To meditate is to put an end to mere hope.* You must not expect anything or hope for anything, for otherwise you will fail to meditate. Hopes and expectations are among the main obstacles to the progress of insight in spiritual life. Can we live without

our hopes? Yes, we can live very happily and quite successfully in life without them. Expectations produce an
illusory world of a never-never land always in the future.
It is better to live life to the full in the present, from
moment to moment. You may have plans for your life, but
they must be flexible. They should not be too fixed or
definite, because all things are changeable. You must be
able to adapt, able to bend without breaking, because
things continue to change in the phenomenal world.

These are not just words, but one of the truisms of life.
I think there is evidence for saying that most people do
not really live—they just exist. We exist in the world, the
world of business or the world of religion, and are confused
by existing in so many realms of experience. We meet with
vicissitudes in life; we are disturbed, unhappy, or pleased
with things experienced in life. Such is existence. But
living is different from existence. In living, one is alive
to *all* the circumstances of life unhampered by labels or
defensive reactions which cut us off from much that we
experience. Above all, such total aliveness or awareness
demands that we accept the changing facets of life with
their falseness and unreality.

To live is to have full awareness of everything all the
time. By being aware and mindful, one has freedom,
clarity, alertness and wakefulness. Anything which comes
into your ken is understood for what it is including a
profound self-understanding. Such understanding enables
you to deal with everything peacefully and happily because your inner world is purified and free from disturbances. There is equilibrium within and peace without
attachment. If you become attached to peace, you are no
longer at peace but diverted to thinking about peace.

Analytical knowledge is the way to freedom with regard
to external events. If external things or experiences are
analyzed into their aspects of coming and going, arising
and passing away, then seen as passing events, we will be
led to freedom from attachment. But if we are unable to

analyze physical and mental changes or experiences in life, we cannot achieve clarity and will be bound to satisfactions and pleasures, or unhappiness and sorrow. To be free in the sense of not being bound to ordinary things in life does not mean that there is nothing pleasurable in life. Actually, you can experience everything that is not harmful either to yourself or to other people. The essential thing is liberation within. In this way you can serenely observe discomfort, ease, or anything going on in the internal or external world.

In meditation, analytical knowledge is very useful when the mind is slack. When attaining to some stages of meditation, a relaxed state of mind arises before passing into peace and tranquillity. At those levels of meditation where a person feels very peaceful he may get stuck, as it were, and the mind may not want to go any further. Thinking, "I am peaceful now," the mind becomes lazy and lax before it has reached the end. In order to overcome these tendencies the only thing to do is to investigate, to look into the nature of peace or the relaxed state of mind. When one starts to examine this condition, the power of analysis will be able to determine whether you are experiencing real peace or merely a creation of mind, i.e., deep peace or superficial peace. Investigating with the intention to understand the slackened state of mind, that state disappears and clarity arises. You can then go deeper and deeper into the state or condition of peace, rather than experiencing only temporarily a sense of ease or relaxedness. In this way investigation will help you overcome diverting side paths on the way to Nibbāna.

Analytical knowledge is essential in deep meditation, but I use the word "knowledge" in the sense of understanding through spontaneous analysis of mind and body (*nāma-rūpa*). Deeper still, analytical knowledge can reach full conviction regarding the idea of self. You can obtain analytical information through books, texts and various studies, but it is of a superficial kind. Analytical knowledge acquired through insight meditation practice, however, is much deeper. Analytical knowledge of this kind was emphasized by the Buddha himself. The Buddha never urged the monks or lay followers to try to analyze things merely through the intellect. He said "Meditate, Bhikkhus, and investigate the true nature of things."

From our experiences in meditation we can say definitely that the analytical knowledge acquired through insight is the only kind for removing the false idea of self, the main obstacle to be overcome before attaining enlightenment. Enlightenment cannot be gained while one has the wrong idea of self. As described in the Buddhist texts, on gaining the first glimpse of enlightenment the idea of the self is removed along with attachment to all kinds of outward and vain ceremonies and rituals. At this stage, however, the individual is not entirely free from doubt. He must still develop another step of insight called insight into conditioned genesis (*paṭicca samuppāda*). On attaining that stage of insight, doubt is removed completely. It is not essential to *learn* about the self before experiencing the reality within us. If you do not understand the Buddhist teaching of non-self (*anattā*), just leave it and get on with your meditation work of awareness-practice. Understanding will come. Do not worry about the question and become unnecessarily disturbed.

Buddhist analytical knowledge divides individuals into five aggregates or component parts. Intelligent people can see the five aggregates clearly in meditation, but all people can at least perceive themselves in terms of physical and mental processes, or what the Scriptures call *nāma-rūpa*. It should be understood here that the Buddha discussed the five aggregates with intelligent people only, whereas to ordinary people he talked about the general components of mind and body. Any individual can analyze himself into physical and mental processes without great difficulty. To analyze oneself into the five aggregates, however, requires penetrating intelligence.

The five aggregates were clearly delineated by the Buddha and the great disciples. First there is the physical body, its functions and activities. Feelings, perceptions, mental formations (habit tendencies or impulses) and consciousness complete the five aggregates, labeled the "self" according to conventional concepts, although not according to ultimate truth. When we analyze the supposed self into these five aggregates, we cannot find a controlling self in any one of them. Why? Because each one of the five aggregates has the nature of continuous arising and passing away. In meditation practice, as the Buddha emphasized in the *Satipaṭṭhāna Sutta*, one must know, "This is body; this is physical movement; how it comes into being and how it passes away." One has to understand three things with regard to each aggregate: what it is, how it comes to be and how it dies away or ceases. If one cannot observe these three aspects of the bodily and mental processes, one will not understand the nature of the "self."

When a feeling arises, for instance, we have to notice whether it is pleasant, unpleasant, or neutral, and how it comes into being by trying to understand the conditions giving rise to it. Without full awareness, the aggregate of feeling cannot be understood. In looking at how it passes away, we try to realize the nature of all things—that they have the habit of ceasing. Events cannot exist forever; they must cease. This ceasing is the nature of all things. Things or events have a moment-to-moment existence. Nothing is unchanging or everlasting, and this fact must be directly realized by yourself. Anyone can realize this truth, for it is not difficult; however, one must be free from the influence of all kinds of secondhand knowledge. As long as the mind is conditioned by supplied information, by beliefs and ephemeral life-conditions, the real nature of existence cannot be understood. One must open the mind, let it expand and see completely so as to understand.

You need to analyze each aggregate into its three essential phases—what it is, how it arises, and how it passes away—in the true spirit of *satipaṭṭhāna*, or detached awareness, and in this way you will understand yourself. You, yourself, are no different from the physical and mental processes, including consciousness, which you are analyzing. What are you, apart from this? The five aggregates embrace all things comprising you, and "you" arise only through the combination of these five.

Impact Through the Senses

As human beings we are fully equipped with sense organs which enable us to communicate with both the world outside and the world within. Awareness of the presence of these senses is essential to the practice of Buddhist meditation. One should know that Buddhist meditation is not only sitting quietly, but practicing to be aware of all the things we come across and experience in life. Whenever any of the senses is active, whether auditory, visual, tactile, olfactory or mental, we should be aware of it; full awareness of any sensory activity is meditation. In meditation practice sensory input is limited, hence easing awareness of sensory activity. For this reason formal meditation provides a training ground for the development of awareness in all aspects of life.

Buddhist meditation is always directed toward life, not away from it. You do not have to retire from the world or enter a monastery to practice meditation. You can live in the world and do meditation through observing the senses. In this way awareness will be maintained and increased.

I have entitled this talk "Impact Through the Senses" because the essential thing in the awareness of the sense organs of seeing, hearing, touching, tasting, smelling, and thinking is to be conscious of the impression or fetter arising from the contact of the sense organ with its object.

First, we should be aware there is an internal sense organ, an external object, and contact between the two. Because consciousness is present when the external and internal come into contact, an impression arises. This impression is a fetter (*saṁyojana*) or defilement binding you to what you are seeing, hearing, touching, tasting, smelling, or thinking. Your attention is caught, or trapped, as it were.

This teaching regarding the senses was not formed as a theory but developed through the Buddha's observation and awareness. The Buddha was aware not only of external things but also of internal processes. If we are fully aware of the sense of seeing, for example, we perceive no more than the eye-sensitivity, the visible form, consciousness, contact and attention. Such knowledge arises through meditation and demands that one put aside intellectual theories. The only requirement on the practical side is for you to give full attention to the sensory processes. When your full attention is given to hearing— not only the sound heard but also the subject who is hearing with all the conditions and states of that subject— several consequences follow. Awareness-understanding based on truly objective analytical knowledge is one result. Moreover, when you give full attention to the senses, they become tranquil because there is no distraction or selective exclusion.

In this process of sensory awareness there is no self who hears or sees. No one can prove there is a self-entity aware of seeing and hearing. There is, however, wholeness of seeing and hearing. The idea of self is one of the fetters which tie us to the lower (sense) world. The self idea is sometimes referred to as *sakkāya-diṭṭhi*. *Diṭṭhi* in this usage means false idea or false view. It contrasts with the term *sammā-diṭṭhi* which means full understanding. The "self" can be an idea, or view, or subject and refers to oneself as a person who sees or hears. This notion of self is part of our common-sense perspective, but it rests on a superficial, conceptualized framework, and not on reality itself. Reality, itself, is without concepts or names.

When you hear, or see, or touch, there is a strong feeling of, "*I am* hearing, *I am* seeing, *I am* touching." At that particular moment it is very important for you to be aware of the "I am," how "I am" operates—*not to be "I am" but to be aware of "I am."* This is meditation. When you become "I am," you identify yourself with the "I," and then you have no power to see or understand because self-control or controlling power has been lost. When "I am" becomes too powerful, it instills in you a sense of agent so that you become interpreter, creator, liker, etc. But the moment you become aware of the "I" operating and reacting, you gain controlling power over seeing, hearing, touching, tasting, smelling, and thinking. Only through detached awareness is one free of self-identification. We may identify ourselves with the subject or the object. Although either is fallacious, it is usually the self or the subject identification which blinds us to things as they really are.

Apart from the false notion of self, you may also suffer from doubt. When you are hearing a talk such as this, for example, you may feel uncertainty, and a state of indecisiveness may arise in the mind. Be aware of such doubt. Perhaps it is the speaker who is causing the uncertainty, or perhaps it is arising from your own biases. Being aware of your doubt and the conditions of its arising will allow you to remain calm and free from anxiety. Without such self-consciousness you will be carried away by your doubt. Other traditional causes of illusion include attachment to ceremonies and rituals and other events of that kind, and the false belief that such ceremonies will guide one to Nibbāna. Attachment to any ceremony leads to unhappiness and bondage to the sensate world.

Two other psychological fetters which tend to dominate people's lives are desire for sensual pleasures and ill will, repugnance or hatred. When you see, hear, touch, taste, smell, or think of the things you like, or which satisfy your mind, a desire to possess them arises. Or if you come across unpleasant or undesirable situations, dislike, ill will, repugnance, anger and hatred results. Because pleasant or unpleasant situations and the reactions they produce cannot lead to lasting satisfaction, you experience disappointment and dismay, frustration and unhappiness. Only if you are fully aware of all these mental states arising through the senses can tranquillity be developed. The Buddha said, "You must train yourself to be tranquil in the mind and in the senses," and the one who has achieved enlightenment is always described as one who has tranquillity of the senses. Only with full awareness of the senses and the sensory processes can there be tranquillity.

You may ask, "How can we have pleasure and happiness in life if we are always aware of seeing, hearing, touching, tasting, smelling, and thinking?" What do you mean by happiness? What kind of happiness do you want? Changing happiness? Passing events? If these are your aims, you need not practice awareness; however, you will suffer from troubles and unhappiness when the happy conditions change. Happiness, in the true sense, is the stilling of mental formations. When there is no illusory fabrication or wishful expectation, then there is happiness. As soon as there is false mental creating, there is no real happiness.

On a higher level, if you gain a more refined attainment of meditation or spiritual life, you may become bound to the higher world, the world of deep meditation, if you like. Mental fetters can still arise at this level. For instance, if a person attains meditative absorptions (*jhāna*), the states of *jhāna* may lead to attachment to the fine psychic world or the objects of intense meditation. Sometimes when you come across beautiful or marvelous things in meditation, you want to stay with them. Becoming attached, you remain there and cannot progress because you are tied to that state of attainment. Sometimes, there is no mental object as a form but something extremely subtle and profound, a formless thing. This experience may be very wonderful; but without full awareness, you will become attached to it and stay there. Every time you sit in meditation, you will come as far as that state and remain with it. "Oh, I had a wonderful experience today!" You are proud of your attainment, but this is also a fetter.

Three more fetters bind us to this higher level or stage: the restless mind, spiritual pride and ignorance. The restless mind is very difficult to remove unless one attains to the final stage of enlightenment—Nibbāna. For this reason beginners or intermediate meditators should not be discouraged to find their mind wandering or being agitated. The thinking mind is ever restless but to worry makes it even more so. Your duty is to be aware of restlessness. When the mind wanders, you must observe it and understand the causes of its restlessness. Is it because the mind is seeking for satisfaction, more pleasure for itself, or for other reasons? We have to perceive the conditions of the restless mind. When watched, the mind becomes quiet. Without this awareness, however, it will carry you away to the far distance through imagination and daydreaming.

Spiritual pride, or pride at any level, often stems from the natural tendency toward comparison. We seem to be inevitably driven to see ourselves as superior, inferior or equal to others; however, such comparison need not exist at all. The pride of comparison is like building a house on a sandbank rather than on rock. It will inevitably cave in. Even people who attain to a high level of spiritual life still may have spiritual pride which becomes the main obstacle to their further progress. Spiritual attainment, as long as it is measured by comparison, is not the transcendental state of achievement, Nibbāna.

The fetter of ignorance is not understanding the truth, dullness of mind, or a sense of confusion or delusion. It does not mean lack of information. One may have a large store of knowledge but still be blinded by perceptual ignorance. Such a person does not see things as they really are, especially in regard to the self. He takes himself as the sole criterion of judgment and sees all things in relationship to his "self." Ignorance, particularly the illusion of self, is the final fetter to be removed. Awareness of ignorance with regard to seeing, hearing, touching, tasting, smelling and thinking is the most important step toward its removal. Clarity of perceiving things as they are removes confusion. Without confusion there is clarity and alertness. These qualities characterize full understanding, the opposite of ignorance.

To be attentive to all the fetters as they arise through the senses is to establish full awareness at the sense-doors. The result is the attainment of peace, understanding, and insight. It is worthwhile seeing, if we see with full awareness; it is worthwhile hearing, if we hear with full awareness. Meditation is living, indeed. It is not running away from life. Real life *is* meditation, the timeless living with complete joy and bliss.

Full Development of Enlightenment Factors

Enlightenment factors are very important in meditation. In fact, if one of them is missing, enlightenment cannot be achieved. The Buddha said that by practicing awareness, or mindfulness, *all* the factors of enlightenment will be fulfilled. We shall discuss these factors, but I should like you to try and experience some of these factors with me.

As you know, the meditation we practice is called insight meditation and is founded on awareness. The objects for this awareness are the body and bodily activities, feelings, mental states and mental contents. All are within us, and we do not have to look beyond the experiences and the faculties which we already have to practice insight meditation.

Bodily activities include breathing, walking, eating, resting, listening, talking, and so on. Feelings can be described in various ways but are usually classified as pleasant, unpleasant, or neither. There is also the mind with all its mental states; and when we perceive anything through the senses of hearing, seeing, touching, tasting, smelling or thinking, all the conditions of mind come into operation. Mental phenomena continually appear during the sitting practice of meditation as well as in daily life. Our task is to be aware of all bodily and mental activities, seeing them as they really are.

In Buddhism the factors of enlightenment are usually listed as seven: mindfulness, investigation of truth, energy, rapturous joy, tranquillity, concentration, and equanimity. They are not abstract concepts but are part of the being of every person and should be fully developed as aspects of the path to being fully enlightened. The first step is to know whether you have any one of the seven factors. Secondly, you have to know the nature of the arising of any one of the factors. The third step is to realize the full development and complete perfection of the seven factors. At that stage, we say one is a fully enlightened being. The seven factors of enlightenment are not difficult to talk about, but they are difficult to realize. In part, the difficulty is the psychological blocking that takes place whenever one strives to attain a goal. Yet, it is precisely such blocking that insight meditation aims to overcome.

The first factor of enlightenment is mindfulness. Mindfulness is the faculty of constantly looking at whatever arises which leads to the ability to see the nature of anything you observe. In such awareness, complete attention is given to the object, event or process with the passive watchfulness of genuine objectivity. Mindfulness is characterized by clarity and alertness and is the opposite of the mental states of dullness or listlessness, excitement or anxiety. In other words, in the state of mindfulness one has that perfect attentiveness when the clouds of feeling or ignorance, which so often blind us to things as they are, are swept away.

With mindfulness you have a mirror in which you not only see objects or events reflected, but your own reactions to them. In the perfect reflection of the mirror you acquire that self-knowledge which cannot be separated from the understanding of truth and falsity, purity and impurity, beauty and ugliness not only within you but within all things. With the eyes of mindfulness you will come to understand reality—the beauty of ugliness and the purity of impurity. Ultimately these distinctions are as meaningless as they are arbitrary, for they do not reflect reality itself, but our preconceived ideas conditioned by our training and background. Everything in the mundane world is relatively good and relatively bad, relatively true and relatively false. Who can state the absolutely good? The good *appears* good from the angle you look at it, but others may disagree with your judgment. Good or bad are concepts, and we have to go beyond concepts in order to understand the truth. Otherwise the mind is clouded by attitudes and opinions where ignorance is a powerful and unconscious factor.

When complete awareness is attained, there is no observer, and ideas and opinions are put aside because there is no opinion-forming self. Basically it is the ego from which our interpretations and explanations arise; and as that ego is illusory, the reflections resulting from it are bound to be illusory also. It is mindfulness which strips away all those conditioning factors which have gone toward creating the ego. Mindfulness is total nakedness where we and all things stand reflected before the eye of the perfectly reflecting mirror.

The second enlightenment factor is the investigation of truth. Once things are seen as they are, then we must begin a process of inquiry into what *is*. Surprisingly enough, this inquiry does not concern thinking but meditation. It is the quest for truth, the active search not for intellectual knowledge but for a new way of seeing and being. To understand what things really are is to see them in their state of constant change—how they arise, manifest themselves and pass away. Investigation of truth demands that we give up doubt, not that we may believe, but that we may pursue our inquiry without trying to prove or disprove some belief. Pure investigation is an inquiry pursued without comment or interpretation. It is not interested in establishing anything or proving one theory better than another. It is not an irrational condition, but a seeking to inquire without the distraction of thought-comments. The moment thought arises, the mind becomes distracted; and what really is, cannot be understood. Thinking is often very shallow, and when it disappears, reality appears.

What is reality? There is no definition because the mind is limited and cannot define the unlimited, the indefinable. Without the second factor of investigation, you will just sit quietly enjoying thoughts and memories which run on and on in the mind. If they flow very strongly or become unpleasant, you may become frightened, but with true awareness you will understand both your thoughts and your fears.

The third factor of enlightenment is energy. In order to pursue the investigation of truth, energy is required. Energy is cultivated in a variety of ways. Physical energy may be cultivated through the walking exercise taught to meditators in insight practice. You are not learning to walk; rather, you are learning to cultivate mindfulness and energy. When energy has been developed and stored, then you can sit with the body still and quiet. The body will not complain for its organs will be functioning properly.

Mental energy is a previous reservoir of power, but it wastes away in many forms of thought, emotional disturbances and depression. One of the main purposes of the practice of mindfulness is to conserve mental energy through the full awareness of all mental states. As awareness becomes more steady, energy becomes more powerful and creative. If the mind becomes lazy or inert during meditation, such indolence is a hindrance to spiritual progress. The meditation must become detached from such lax states in order for the power of mindfulness to become effective. Meditation is not a state of inert relaxation but of attentive energy.

The fourth factor of rapturous joy is directed by thinking since the first sensation of joy caused by physical factors brings into operation the application of thought. Yet, this is not thinking for its own sake but directing the mind toward particular objects and processes. Such thinking is not a distraction, but a direction of thought, a lifting of the mind to the object.

The investigation of truth, energy, and rapturous joy is necessary to overcome a sluggish mind, and it is not possible to cultivate the final three factors of tranquillity, concentration, and equanimity if the mind is slack. In other words, the mind must be properly trained and prepared if the higher fruits of meditation practice are to be attained. When the mind is so elevated, then tranquillity, concentration, and equanimity should be applied. Tranquillity and concentration are necessary complements to each other. From concentration, calmness arises just as laxness produces confusion. Tranquillity is a strong basis for the growth of insight. In a state of elation, the mind may become confused and led astray. You feel happy and the mind leads you to believe that you have gone far enough. When this happens, you cannot make any further progress.

Tranquillity not only means calmness of the physical body. In the Buddhist scriptures *kāya-passaddhi* (tranquillity of the body) is mentioned, but *kāya* here refers to feelings, perceptions, and mental formations. When all these become calm, tranquillity will be achieved and the body will be under control. Then composure, steadiness, and stability of feelings, perceptions, mental formations, and mind or consciousness results.

Of all the seven factors of enlightenment none is more important than equanimity. It is not a state of indifference or neutrality as some have translated the Pāli term. As a factor for enlightenment it has close connections with concentration and refers to the detached mind or the detached state of mind in the sense of liberation from all kinds of attachment. At this stage, the mind is free. The meditator has no concern for results or progress. At this point there is no differentiation between the meditator and the goal of his efforts. Once you have achieved freedom it is no longer meaningful in an ethical or psychological sense. You are simply not free. It is a state of being, in which there is no more attachment, distracting desires, fetters of pride or the "I" conceit. In sum, equanimity is perfect freedom.

The seven factors of enlightenment are not only an important part of group and private meditation but also of daily life and daily experience. You can cultivate them at any time. When the Buddha spoke of these seven factors, he did not mean that they only appear during intensive meditation. He said that in any circumstances one should be aware of them. Such constant attentiveness is demanded for genuine progress in insight into the truth.

Self-Discovery and the Realization of the Truth

The feeling of self is very strong in all people, but through the process of analysis during meditation, we come to understand that there is no self to be found. Through the conceptualization and projection of the mind, the belief in a self is created, and it is this belief which lies at the basis of their understanding of rebirth. Yet, we must ask ourselves if it is necessary to presuppose a self which is reborn when one dies? This question is beyond

rational explanation. Even the Buddha himself dismissed
it as not tending toward edification. One who asks such
a question lacks genuine insight so answering it is a waste
of time.

The best approach is to try and understand the process
of rebirth as it occurs from moment to moment and not as
a theoretical question. In that process of becoming and
continuity, is there a self? The teaching of rebirth may
appear fallacious to many people, but this is because they
fail to face the transient nature of their lives from day to
day. Seen from this perspective, rebirth becomes part of
the evanescent and fleeting nature of life the ignorant
man tries so hard to ignore. To believe in rebirth is not to
accept on faith the notion of a self which is reborn. Quite
the contrary, in Buddhism rebirth is seen as part of the
continuously fluctuating nature of existence as seen em-
pirically in the mirror of mindful attention.

Self-discovery does not mean the uncovering of an entity
or a "self" existing in a being, but the *full understanding*
of oneself, complete understanding of the five aggregates
which together form existence and becoming. Through
such self-understanding we come to perceive the greatest
good and the way to it, not simply for ourselves but for
others. For, while Buddhism stresses the individual nature
of self-discovery, its truth claims are universal.

The greatest problem for unenlightened people is the
problem of self. Think for a moment how many of your
activities are oriented to strengthening and defending the
self. For most of us the self provides the focal point for
everything we do. Consequently, for the greatest part of
our lives we never come to an understanding of truth, but
are continually subject to sorrow, misery, suffering, pleasure, pain and joy—all passing events and changing conditions.

The realization of truth can only be achieved through
self-discovery. Here the truth refers to the Four Noble

Truths in Buddhism. I should like to talk about these with you, in relation to *satipaṭṭhāna* or insight meditation practice. How can we *realize* the Four Noble Truths in meditation? Without fully realizing them, enlightenment cannot be achieved. As the Buddha said, the realization of the Four Noble Truths is like the rising of the sun, dispersing darkness and giving light at the same moment. The Four Noble Truths are realized at one and the same time, not separately. You cannot say that on one day you will realize the first noble truth of suffering, the next day the second and so on. That is not realization, but memorization— merely trying to recall what you have read and have been taught. It is only through the awareness of all aspects of life (*dhammānupassanā*) that we understand the Four Noble Truths completely. Meditators who have come to this understanding may not be able to express it to others, because the ability to explain differs from the ability to experience truth.

The first noble truth is *dukkha*, or suffering. What is *dukkha*? In the process of watching the up and down movement of the body, you will see the appearance and disappearance of bodily activities which belong to the noble truth of suffering. The occurrence of physical movement provides the conditions for its appearance and disappearance. This process of continuity, or becoming, never stops. Within it you can see the characteristic impermanence of life which gives rise to a feeling of suffering, because the process of appearing and disappearing never ceases. This may frighten you during meditation. Simply be aware of this fear. It is essential that awareness be applied to everything which arises. You can watch the appearance and disappearance of feelings, perceptions, tendencies, consciousness, or any mental and physical phenomena which arise. Without such application, awareness is not being practiced but only conceptual thinking, which never brings about the real understanding of truth.

When awareness becomes strong, you will see three phases of everything: its coming into being, its existing or prevailing and its ceasing. These characteristics apply to all phenomena and processes and belong to *dukkha*.

What is the second noble truth, the arising of suffering? Why does it come to be? There must be a cause, a condition working behind the flux of appearing, disappearing, and continuity. This cause is desire, or craving, which is the second noble truth of Buddhism. Without desire you will cease to exist as a person subject to the laws of becoming. Such a claim may be confusing and cause you to ask how enlightened people exist, if they have no desires. To live without craving means that the feeling of "I" ceases. The five aggregates at the basis of phenomenal life still continue, so physical existence goes on so long as the five aggregates have functions to carry out. With the appearance and disappearance of phenomena, you are usually dominated by the "I" concept: I am watching this, I am aware of this. "I am" plays a very active role; but the moment you lose the feeling of "I am" or "I," desire and craving disappear.

At that moment you will be able to see the third noble truth because all the conditioned processes are stilled, thereby quieting the incessant activity of the self. This is the cessation of *dukkha*, that particular moment when the realization of truth has been achieved and the person who attains it understands what it is. You may have heard Nibbāna described as "extinction without remainder." Indeed, it is the extinction of all conditioned states. There is no more movement, forming, or creating. No mind is moving or looking at anything.

And what is the path to this?—It is the fourth noble truth. The path is awareness, itself, initially involving concentration and effort. When the path is fully developed, however, there is no feeling of effort, concentration, or even of being aware. There is only the stillness of all processes, even the smallest vibration, and with it the complete understanding of the Four Noble Truths. When understanding is right and perfect, all things will be right and perfect.

Right understanding cannot be obtained from books or from speakers, but from seeing the truth for yourself through meditation. You may remember things that have been written in books you have read, or that have been spoken by people you have heard, but this is not complete knowledge, not the *sammā-diṭṭhi* of meditation. At the beginning, conceptual knowledge may inspire you to obtain the *sammā-diṭṭhi* of meditation; but the knowledge obtained in meditation must be judged as practical not merely conceptual. It aims at the total transformation of one's being, not simply intellectual certainty.

In meditation, if you observe your mental activities properly, you can see the never-ending search for satisfaction in enjoyment, imagination, and speculation characterizing the second noble truth, the arising of *dukkha*. This activity, stimulated by desire and attachment, must be observed clearly and deeply in meditation, or otherwise the Four Noble Truths will not be realized. Do not try to remember what the Four Noble Truths are! If you have no concepts of them in your mind, you may be unable to explain them, but you will be able to see them for what they are. Afterwards, you will be able to find words to express them, should you wish to do so. You will be able to explain how to realize the Four Noble Truths for themselves, for the flow of wisdom is the function of compassion and universal love. If you have not had much experience of meditation, you may not believe that the flow of wisdom goes on deep within us. Because the mind is preoccupied with the objects of the waking world, it often does not recognize its own profundity. The moment it becomes quiet, however, the flow of wisdom appears, and we are able to speak the truth. It is not a thinking process; rather, it is part of our new being.

Complete Understanding Here and Now

Complete understanding here and now is the highest result of meditation practice. It is the ultimate aim of every meditator. As it is said in the *Satipaṭṭhāna Sutta,* not to gain complete understanding here and now is not to attain the state of nonreturning, the guarantee that you will not return to the lower state of life and to the coming and going of the circle of rebirth.

How does complete understanding come? Before undertaking that subject, we should make clear the process of gaining knowledge in general. What is its basis? Belief is the basis of gaining knowledge whether scientific, religious or philosophical. All are based on belief in different forms. Rules and logic arise because of my belief. I accumulate knowledge because I believe it is true and useful. It makes me happy; I continue to accumulate it and am conditioned by it. If I am a scientist, I am conditioned by science. If I am a psychologist, I am conditioned by psychology. If I am a Buddhist, I am conditioned by the Buddhist religion and its traditions.

Because of the conditioning process we are prone to see things in terms of our suppositions and beliefs rather than seeing things in themselves, as they really are. The process of gaining knowledge based on belief is called *anubodha* in Pāli, meaning "understanding accordingly." It means to understand things according to your conditioning, training, tradition, background and upbringing which form your patterns of thinking. Is there "completion" to "knowing accordingly"? No. If you were reborn a hundred times, you would be unable to complete this kind of knowing. You may have many degrees in many subjects, but you will be unable to claim you have finished "knowing accordingly." There are many things you do not understand. Life is not very long—eighty or ninety years perhaps—and in order to complete "knowing accordingly," we need much more time. Real knowledge, however, cannot be calculated according to time. Even a person young in years may be truly wise.

Complete understanding is absolutely free from belief and ideas. Complete understanding means to see the whole, not just the part, to uncover the covered, to discover the undiscovered, to see the unseen. In that state there is no confusion or self-deception; no ignorance or delusion. If there is any uncertainty or doubt, it is peripheral. Of course, one who has genuine understanding may not know about many things in the world, but these are unessential —the concepts, speculations and beliefs which have kept men from seeing the truth about the nature of things. To try to know everything in the world is intellectual bondage. But it is essential to have complete understanding of truth —the truth of living, of communication, of relationships, of human existence and of yourself. There is no more to understand. With this understanding you can live and act rightly, perfectly. Right action may go against tradition and beliefs in some cases because these are not necessarily true. They may be logically true, or traditionally true; but in the sense of complete understanding the concepts of true or false, good or bad do not arise. There is no polarity, only wholeness. There is no comparison since it belongs to relative knowledge, not absolute knowing.

"Here and now" means from moment to moment. If there is complete understanding from moment to moment in living, you will not be deceived by anything. You can be master of all tendencies and mental states, with peace and happiness at any time, free from frustration and disquiet. No misery comes and no disappointment. Through complete understanding, you can see unpleasantness and sorrowful situations, but you yourself do not suffer.

The question arises: if you do not suffer, how can you understand suffering? You experience suffering before coming to understanding; you suffer many things in life and know what suffering is. Then, when you are enlightened, you are able to have compassion for suffering beings and understand their plight. Yet, you yourself are free. Through the depth of your understanding, you know how to react to each situation here and now, filled with dispassionate compassion for others.

Before coming to complete understanding, we may speculate, "What happens to a person who attains to enlightenment?" But such thoughts do not occur to the enlightened person. The way to enlightenment is not to ask such questions but to realize it, to see for yourself. Otherwise you will not be convinced and may become more confused by intellectual answers to your question. Sometimes even enlightened people cannot point the way to the truth without causing confusion. Hence, in many cases the Buddha remained silent in the face of such a question. He did not wish to add more confusion to those already confused.

The question about the nature of enlightenment is, in itself, not wrong. The point at issue is the intent with which it is asked. If you are seeking intellectual satisfaction, you are bound to be dissatisfied; however, if you know that your question really relates to what is beyond your understanding, you will be content to leave it. Many times the Buddha said, "Your question has gone beyond yourself," and this stopped people pursuing the subject merely theoretically. Questions should be asked, not to be resolved logically, but in order to gain right understanding. Better yet, we should not ask questions, but try to understand things through observation and awareness. You may put the question to yourself; and when the mind reaches the depth of stillness, understanding will emerge, giving you the real picture.

It is important for us to try and see the truth for ourselves in our daily life, not just in the period of sitting in meditation. Enlightenment can be obtained in daily affairs and activities, with the eyes open. In sitting meditation we close the eyes and we may say, "I have seen truth";

however, one needs to be able to see the truth with the eyes open as well. Otherwise, enlightenment has not really been attained. If it seems to be there only when the eyes are closed, then it would only be for those who retire from the world. But enlightenment is for everyone, in every form of life, if one knows how to gain it, how to live with it, in complete understanding here and now, at any moment, in any experience, in any activity of life.

How can this complete understanding here and now come to be? Only by full awareness, constant mindfulness —there is no other way, no miracle or revelation which can bring it about. To be continually aware of all activities of the physical body and of the mind, in relation to inner experiences and the world outside, is to be able to see the truth internally and externally. The truth within us and of the world outside is the undifferentiated. With constant awareness and clarity of acting, we can maintain complete understanding here and now.

"Here and now" does not refer to place or time, but the moment, a single moment which is unique, unrepresentable and unutterable. We live for twenty-four hours a day, fifty-two weeks a year, from moment to moment; and at every moment complete understanding may be there, living to the fullest without the limits imposed by conditioned existence. If you are afraid of losing your pattern of life, then your meditation practice will be in vain. If you are afraid to lose your self, then it will be impossible to gain the new self-without-self of complete understanding. Concentration is not sufficient. It must be accompanied by insight, the insight which has the power of making a new being. Ultimately such is the goal of Buddhist meditation.

3

The Foundation
of Mindfulness

In Theravāda Buddhism there are two fundamental types of meditation. One aims at the development of tranquillity (*samatha*) through the means of trance states, or meditative absorptions (*jhāna*); the other strives for insight (*vipassanā*) into the true nature of things. These two forms of meditation are by no means mutually exclusive; however, insight meditation has traditionally been considered the highest of the two forms. In particular, the revival of interest in meditation practice in Theravāda Buddhist countries (viz., Ceylon, Burma, Thailand) in the modern period has focused on insight practice.

Insight meditation has been summed up by the phrase, "Be mindful!" or being mindful of your own mind.[1] Two crucial assumptions are made in this definition: that genuine awareness or mindfulness will lead to enlightenment, or an understanding of things as they really are; and that one's ontic condition or state of being depends upon the mind—"Mind harbours all: the world of suffering and its origin, but also Ill's final cessation and the path to it."[2] Buddhist meditation, then, offers the hope of insight not only in the sense of new knowledge but of new being.

[1] Nyāṇaponika Thera, *The Heart of Buddhist Meditation* (London: Rider & Co., 1962), p. 79.
[2] *Ibid.*

The promise is the oft-heard phrase, "Know the truth and the truth will make you free." Knowledge and freedom presuppose each other; indeed, are necessary to each other for the very reason that "enlightenment" and "new being" are two sides of the same coin.

The heart of Buddhist meditation is the development of mindfulness, or awareness. The program of training in mindfulness is not arbitrary but is based on one of the most popular texts in the Theravāda, or Pāli, canon known as the *Satipaṭṭhāna Sutta*, or the text on the foundation, arousing, or setting up of mindfulness. Because of the significance of this text for all forms of Buddhist meditation, this chapter is an attempt to interpret some of its more salient aspects. Originally the editor intended to include only a translation of the Sutta to parallel the translation of the *Zazen-gi* (Chapter 6) with which it has much in common. However, since several English translations of the *Satipaṭṭhāna Sutta* are readily available, it was thought more helpful to provide a discussion of the text.[3]

The *Satipaṭṭhāna Sutta* is, in essence, a paradigm for the attainment of insight into the true nature of things through the vehicle of complete awareness (*sammāsati*). It offers a suggested program, at once both natural and logical, which anyone may profitably follow. There is nothing esoteric or magical about the practice of mindfulness. On the contrary, the Sutta epitomizes the Theravāda concern for concrete instruction or the practical application of the principles upon which Buddhist teachings are based. Unlike certain forms of Buddhist meditation, practice in mindfulness, or awareness, stresses simplicity in the extreme. No props are utilized. Chanting, visual symbols, or the burning of incense are all disavowed. Rather, medi-

[3] Acknowledgment is made to Soma Thera's translation of the *Satipaṭṭhāna Sutta* and commentary published as *The Way of Mindfulness* (Kandy, Ceylon: Buddhist Publication Society, 1967) and to Nyānaponika Thera's discussion of *satipaṭṭhāna* in *The Heart of Buddhist Meditation*.

tation subjects include the most commonplace of objects and events—breathing, the body, the feelings, consciousness, and mental objects. The utter unadorned nature of *satipaṭṭhāna* illustrates one of the principal convictions concerning the Buddhist ideal: that the senses (including the mind) must be transformed for the truth to be perceived.

One may claim, in the light of the above, that the *Satipaṭṭhāna Sutta* begins with the assumption of the deluded condition of the ordinary worldling. Man, in his usual state of being, is led fundamentally astray about the nature of things, in particular, the nature of his own existence. He inaccurately and incorrectly attributes to his own life and the world around him a permanence which, in fact, is not there. This belief results from ignorance (*avijjā*) which, in turn, is a product of sensory fallacies. The fundamental fallacy of sensory knowledge is that of permanence. Driven by an egocentric cluster of desires (e.g., greed, hatred, lust, ambition), the senses construct an artificial and unreal world. It is a world in which the "self" and "self"-satisfactions are of utmost importance. Threatened by anything which challenges place, status and position, the senses perpetuate the illusion of a world in which there are "selves" living in a world of "things" with the capacity of guaranteeing happiness and bliss. Because of this delusion men are driven by ambition to destroy other men, and nation wars against nation in order to establish position, or even a "permanent peace."

The Sutta assumes, then, that most of us live in an illusory or unreal world; not in the sense that the mundane or phenomenal world does not really exist but that it does not really exist *as we perceive it*. The purpose of *satipaṭṭhāna*, then, is to suggest a means or a way by which the true nature of things might be perceived. Such a task is not an easy one. Buddhist meditation is not mind-wandering reminiscing while contemplating a beautiful sunset. On the contrary, awareness meditation is a disciplined confrontation with the processes of life as they really are. It does not depend upon any outside stimuli, least of all the use of drugs. *Satipaṭṭhāna* minimizes or eliminates the sensory distortions controverting the truth about the nature of things. It aims to provide an objective understanding of self and world through an analytical method in a controlled environment. For the person who perseveres, the rewards of meditation are great; yet, one does not meditate to "gain" anything. One meditates simply to be able to "see" things as they are, and, hence, to *be* as one really is.

If you were to select one of the most natural occurrences for use as a meditation subject, what would you choose? Such a subject should be readily available, easily employed and appropriate to any set of circumstances. After some reflection you would probably agree that our breathing fits all these requirements, thereby making an ideal meditation subject. Indeed, in Indian religions the concept of breath has been an ubiquitous feature. In ancient mythological texts the breath was referred to as a cosmogonic element and, hence, endowed with creative force. It is no wonder that on an individual level in Indian Yogic traditions the breath should also be looked upon as possessing creative power. In Haṭha Yoga the disciplining of respiration (*prāṇāyāma*) is a specific exercise with the purpose of unifying the consciousness in order to penetrate levels of awareness unavailable to the ordinary man.[4] Buddhism, as part of the greater Indian religious tradition, is an inheritor of the important role of breath, especially in relationship to Yogic or meditative techniques. Frequent references are made to mindfulness of breathing (*ānāpānasati*) in Theravāda Buddhist texts; and an entire Sutta of the *Majjhima Nikāya* or *The Middle-Length Dialogues*, one group of texts within the Theravāda canon, is devoted to this subject.

[4] Mircea Eliade, *Yoga: Immortality and Freedom*, trans. Willard R. Trask (New York: Pantheon Books, 1958), p. 56.

The *Satipaṭṭhāna Sutta* begins, appropriately, with mindfulness of breathing. It is the specific exercise designed to produce awareness of the body and bodily processes. It is important to note that meditative awareness in Theravāda Buddhism does not utilize the abstract or general as a means of controlling the consciousness or producing insight. Rather, the concrete and specific provides the locus of mental training. Instruction in bodily awareness, consequently, does not begin with the vague assertion that the meditator should contemplate the nature of the body as a physical organism. The *Satipaṭṭhāna Sutta* instructs the monk (*bhikkhu*) to go to a quiet place, bend his legs in a crosswise position on his lap, keep his body erect and use his breath as a meditation object. "Mindful, he breathes in, and mindful he breathes out. He, thinking, 'I breathe in long,' understands when he is breathing in long; or thinking, 'I breathe in short,' he understands when he is breathing in short; or thinking, 'I breathe out short,' he understands when he is breathing out short."[5]

Consciousness of the breath through the simple exercise of attentiveness to long and short inhalations and exhalations produces a twofold result: a perception of the nature of the entire body and a calming of bodily activities. The incoming and outgoing of the breath accompanied by the rise and fall of the abdomen vividly illustrate the transient and fluctuating nature of the bodily organism. The activities of the body come into being and pass away time and again. There is obviously nothing inherently permanent about the physical body. Not only is there ongoing aging eventuating in death; each moment of conscious life is an ebb and flow process as seen in the rise and fall of the breath.

The awareness of the nature of the body accompanies a state of calmness resulting from the posture of detached observer. Think for a moment what the consequences

[5] *The Way of Mindfulness*, trans. Soma Thera (Kandy, Ceylon: Buddhist Publication Society, 1967), p. 1.

would be if every act you performed was done with conscious attention to every movement, feeling and thought. As the lectures in Chapter 2 by the Venerable Dhammasudhi make so clear, such consciousness is not a procedure of rational investigation and conceptualization but simple awareness of everything occurring internally and externally, a conscious noting-without-attachment of all mental and physical events.

As the Sutta on breathing mindfulness in the *Middle-Length Dialogues* makes evident, being aware of respiration and the mechanism of breathing is an exercise in and of itself; but also, as indicated here and in the *Satipaṭṭhāna Sutta*, attention to breathing is designed to lead the meditator to insight. In this regard, it is seen as the initial step of a regular program of training and development. In the *Ānāpānasati Sutta*, however, every aspect of the meditative process is accompanied by respiration mindfulness, or, it might be put the other way around. Thus, contemplating the body, feelings, mind or mental objects is accomplished as part of awareness of the breath. For example, "Experiencing the mind, I shall breathe in, thus he trains himself; experiencing the mind, I shall breathe out, thus he trains himself . . . Contemplating impermanence, I shall breathe in, thus he trains himself; contemplating impermanence, I shall breathe out, thus he trains himself . . ." etc.[6] In sum, the text states that the perfection of the four foundations of mindfulness (i.e., body, feelings, mind or consciousness and mental objects or ideas) is brought about through respiration mindfulness.

In the Sutta we are investigating, respiration mindfulness is only one aspect of other forms of bodily awareness. It is followed by even more analytical modes of observation in which every type of bodily activity is carefully scrutinized: "And further, O bhikkhus, when he is going, a bhikkhu understands: 'I am going'; when he is standing he

[6] *Mindfulness of Breathing*, trans. Ñāṇamoli Thera (2d ed.; Kandy, Ceylon: Buddhist Publication Society, 1964), p. 7.

understands: 'I am standing'; when he is sitting, he understands: 'I am sitting'; when he is lying down, he understands: 'I am lying down' or just as his body is disposed so he understands it."[7] The individual striving for insight is to clearly comprehend (*sampajāna*) every movement and act from "bending and stretching" to "wearing the shoulder cloak, the (other two) robes (and) the bowl" to "what is eaten, drunk, chewed and savoured."[8] In sum, nothing one does is to go unnoted or unobserved. Acts which for the average person are subconsciously motivated become part of one's conscious life. All physical activity is "understood" in the sense that it is subject to "bare awareness." Such scrutinizing does not mean that the mind endlessly involves itself in discovering reasons and motives for particular acts. Rather, the effort aims to eliminate the bondage of unreflective habituation through the development of a state of total, alert awareness.

Insight meditation, as we can see, places a high degree of confidence in the ability of the human mind to extract the individual from the throes of ignorance. Ignorance is attachment to sensory objects and a fundamental lack of understanding of the nature of sensate existence. According to the commentary on the *Satipaṭṭhāna Sutta*, true awareness of the body and all its activities leads to only one conclusion: "There is the body, but there is no being, no person, no woman, no man, no soul, nothing pertaining to a soul, no 'I,' nothing that is mine, no one, and nothing belonging to anyone."[9] And again in more poetic form:

> Just as a ship goes on by winds impelled,
> Just as a shaft goes by the bowstring's force,
> So goes this body in its forward course
> Full driven by the vibrant thrust of air,
> As to the puppet's back the dodge-thread's tied
> So to the body-doll the mind is joined

[7] *The Way of Mindfulness*, p. 2.
[8] *Ibid.*, p. 3.
[9] *Ibid.*, p. 51.

> And pulled by that the body moves, stands, sits.
> Where is the living being that can stand,
> Or walk, by force of its own inner strength,
> Without conditions that give it support?[10]

Insight meditation achieves, therefore, a full understanding of the conditions of existence. With that understanding the illusion of a self is eliminated.

From mindfulness of breathing and conscious awareness of all forms of bodily activity, insight meditation then moves to examine the body in terms of its constituent parts. Our Sutta admonishes the meditator to reflect upon the parts of the body from the soles of the feet to the crown of the head, and with an explicitness characteristic of our text delineates the body in terms of hair, nails, teeth, skin, flesh, sinews, bones, marrow, kidney, heart, liver, membranes, spleen, lungs, stomach, bowels, intestines; excrement, bile, phlegm, pus, blood, sweat, fat, tears, serum, saliva, mucus, synovic fluid, and urine. This list may offend some readers. Its purpose is, of course, not to paint an attractive picture of the body but to reinforce the notion that the body is but a collection of rather repulsive parts. What is there in the body worthy of attachment and desire?—nothing! The mindfulness of the monk is established with the thought that the body *simply exists*. In this manner "he lives independent and clings to naught in the world."[11]

The text establishes two mutually interdependent tendencies in regard to mindfulness of the body: the analytical nature of insightful awareness and the reduction of attachment. The first tendency develops beyond the mere examination of the traditional thirty-two bodily parts. The meditator is instructed to consider the body as a composite of the four primary material elements of earth, water, heat and air. This effort to reduce the body to component

[10] *Ibid.*, p. 56.
[11] *Ibid.*, p. 2.

elements is an integral part of Theravāda Buddhist psychology and philosophy. Other analyses of the psychophysical being include the five aggregates (body, sensation, perception, consciousness and volitional constituents) and the six sense bases (*āyatana*) not to mention the extensive analytical categorization found in Buddhist scholastic texts.[12]

The analytical process in which the meditator is involved while examining the body is itself training in controlling the mind. Definitions in this instance are limiting, not in a logical or linguistic sense, but as a mind-focusing exercise. It might be said that the *Satipaṭṭhāna Sutta* establishes a rigorous context for the mind rather than the usual one of undisciplined, uncontrolled and untrained mental responses to the human situation. Yet, the reduction of the individual to fundamental elements or constituent parts is primarily intended to eliminate ego attachment. If there is no ego or self, how can one be attached to it? The commentary elaborates this meaning with the following simile:

> Just as if some cow-butcher or a cow-butcher's apprentice, a man who works for his keep, having killed a cow and made it into parts, were sitting at a four-cross-road, just so, a bhikkhu reflects by way of the (bodily) modes (or parts), on the body, in any one of the four postures thus: "There are in this body the modes of extension (earth), cohesion (water), caloricity (heat) and oscillation (air)."
>
> The cow-butcher does not get rid of the cow-percept while feeding the cow, driving it to the place of slaughter, tying it and putting it up there, killing it, and even when seeing the dead carcase of the cow; not until he cuts it up and divides it into parts does the cow-percept disappear. To that butcher sitting (with the meat before him) after cutting up the cow, however, the cow-percept disappears, and the perception of flesh comes into being. To him there is not this thought: "I am selling the cow; these people are taking away the cow."

[12] See *Compendium of Philosophy*, trans. Shwe Zan Aung (London: Luzac & Co., 1963).

But to him, indeed, there occurs this thought: "I am selling flesh; these people indeed, are taking away flesh. . . ."[13]

Reduction of attachment to the body is furthered in the *Satipaṭṭhāna Sutta* by what are referred to as the eight cemetery contemplations. These are descriptive pictures of the body in varying degrees of decay and dissolution after death—certainly not a very happy thought! The directness of this portion of the text needs no elaboration:

> And further, O bhikkhus, if a bhikkhu, in whatever way, sees a body dead, one, two, or three days; swollen, blue, and festering, thrown into the charnel ground, he thinks of his own body thus: "Verily, this body of mine too is of the same nature as that body, is going to be like that body, and has not got past the condition of becoming like that body."[14]

The remaining cemetery contemplations speak of the body being eaten by animals, as a skeleton held together by fleshy remains and so on. Each of the descriptions varies slightly but consistently includes the refraining passages of internal and external contemplation of the body in terms of the cycle of origination and dissolution. Such contemplation aims at freeing the meditator from clinging to things in the world and producing a state of independence.

The term, "independence," which occurs again and again in the Sutta is a most appropriate one. To a profound degree the practice of Buddhist meditation aims to bring into reality a new state of being characterized by total freedom. The old condition of existence, by way of contrast, was one of bondage, or in the terminology of Buddhism, clinging and attachment to the things of the senses. It is in this context that the cemetery contemplations should be seen. In and of themselves they are repulsive, and, indeed, they are intended to be. They should, nevertheless, be read with the thought in mind that one of the "Four Sights" motivating Siddhartha Gautama to begin

[13] *The Way of Mindfulness*, p. 100.
[14] *Ibid.*, p. 5.

his spiritual pilgrimage was a dead man; and it should also be remembered that the famous Buddhist formula description of sentient existence, the cycle of dependent origination, concludes with old age and death. Thus it is that the concept of death prevails on many levels of Buddhist thought and should not be taken as especially startling in the context of *satipaṭṭhāna.*

The experience of death in Buddhism plays a dual role as it does in other religious traditions. There is, on the one hand, the notion that physical death is the characteristic par excellence of mundane existence. On the other hand, however, there is the idea that death is the entrance into new life. For example, one of the prime attributes of the initiatory *rite de passage* is the reenactment of a symbolic death scene prior to admittance to full membership into the tribe or society. Certainly the act of submersion in Christian baptism was intended to symbolize not only moral purification but also the dying of an old way of life and the entering into the new life of the church, the body of Christ. In the Buddhist tradition the use of the *Tibetan Book of the Dead* as a funeral breviary or the Zen notion of the "great death" experience prior to enlightenment offer further evidence of the positive role death plays in differing religious experiences around the world. In this regard it is significant to note that the *Satipaṭṭhāna Sutta,* while a manual for meditation, was also used as a death-bed discourse. Thus, although the text describes the death of the physical body in gruesome detail, the course of training the Sutta prescribes is one of death to the life of attachment and bondage and rebirth in a mode of existence characterized by perfect freedom.

Earlier we referred to the *Satipaṭṭhāna Sutta* as a paradigm for insight meditation practice. Within the body of the text itself, the elaboration of the mindfulness of the body which we have just outlined is something of an implicit model for other forms of awareness meditation. You will recall that these include awareness of the feelings, the mind or consciousness and mental objects or ideas. None of these receive the extensive treatment given to the mindfulness of the body, perhaps as we have suggested, because the form of mental investigation has already been established. The three remaining meditation subjects taken together constitute the noncorporeal or nonmaterial aspects of existence designated by the rubric, *nāma* (literally, name). Hence, one of the earliest references in the Pāli texts to the structure of individuality is *nāma-rūpa* (literally, name and form) or corporeality and noncorporeality. The term eventually comes to be identified with the formula of the five aggregates used to describe the components of a human being.

The contemplation of feeling (*vedanā*) is described by the commentary on the *Satipaṭṭhāna Sutta* as the easiest of the nonmaterial subjects of mindfulness. In the Sutta it is categorized into three kinds or classes: pleasurable, painful and neutral or neither pleasurable nor painful. The discourse in the commentary is worth quoting at some length:

. . . the Blessed One speaking of the nonmaterial or mental subject of meditation speaks by way of feeling. While expounding by way of sense-impression or consciousness the subject of meditation does not become clear. It seems dark. But by way of feeling it becomes clear. Why? Because of the clearness of the arising of feeling. Indeed the arising of pleasant or painful feeling is clear. When pleasant feeling arises spreading through and flowing over the whole body making one to utter the words: "Ah 'tis joy," it is like causing one to eat fresh clarified butter cooled in very cold water a hundred times after being melted again and again, also a hundred times; it is like causing one to be massaged with an emollient oil worth a hundred pieces; and it is like causing one to be cooled of a burning fever with a thousand pots of cold water.

When painful feeling arises spreading through and flowing over the whole body making one to bewail with the words, "Alas, what woe," it is like the applying on one of a heated ploughshare; it is like the sprinkling upon one of molten copper; and it is comparable to the hurling into dried grass and trees, in the forest, of bundles of wood firebrands.

Thus the arising of pleasant or painful feeling becomes clear, but the arising of neither-pleasant-nor-painful feeling is dark, and unclear.

The neither-pleasant-nor-painful feeling becomes clear to one who grasps it methodically thinking: "At the disappearance of pleasure and pain, by way of contrariety to the pleasant and the unpleasant, is the neutral neither-pleasant-nor-painful feeling."

To what is it comparable? To a deerhunter following the hoofmarks of a deer which midway having gone up a flat rock is fleeing. The hunter after seeing the hoofmarks on the hither and thither side of the rock, without seeing any trace in the middle, knows by inference: "Here the animal went up and, here, it went down; in the middle, on the flat rock, possibly it went through this part."

Like the hoofmark at the place of going up the arising of pleasurable feeling becomes clear. Like the hoofmark at the place of descent the arising of painful feeling becomes clear. Like the grasping through inference of the part traversed over the rock by the deer is the laying hold of the neither-pleasant-nor-painful feeling methodically with the thought: "At the disappearance of pleasure and pain, by way of contrariety to the pleasant and the unpleasant, is the neutral neither-pleasant-nor-painful feeling!"[15]

This lengthy exposition provides an insight into the nature of commentarial literature with its somewhat scholastic, analytic flavor and the extensive use of description, analogy and simile. It does not, however, provide much practical information in regard to the way in which the feelings might be used as a subject of mindfulness. A consistent interpretation by such meditation teachers as Chao Khun Sobhana Dhammasudhi is not to let feelings entering the consciousness become obstructive to attentive awareness. In order to overcome persistent, interruptive

[15] *Ibid.,* pp. 107–108.

feelings, it is sometimes necessary to use them as temporary meditation subjects themselves. As the Venerable Dhammasudhi frequently insists in his lectures, in insight meditation everything is to be understood for what it really is. Therefore, if a meditator is bothered by pleasurable or painful feelings, rather than trying to reject or dismiss them, he should become aware of what they are, their arising and passing away.

Such awareness of noncorporeal meditation subjects readily leads to a conclusion which forms an important part of Buddhist teaching, namely, the interdependence of mind and body. For example, as some of the student meditators report in the last chapter, they had a problem with meditation postures. Often the lotus or half-lotus position proved to be very painful, especially in the beginning days. Obviously, the feeling of pain was not an isolated or independent phenomenon but was directly related to discomfort in sitting in an unaccustomed posture for long periods of time. Some students discovered that being aware of the feeling of pain seemed miraculously to alleviate it or ease the source of pain. In ordinary parlance today we might refer to such a phenomenon as the power of mind over matter, but from the Buddhist viewpoint it is an illustration of the interdependence of the mental and the material. A familiar analogy employed by the commentator, Buddhaghosa, makes the point as follows:

. . . a man born blind and a stool-crawling cripple wanted to go somewhere. The blind man said to the cripple, "Look, I can do what should be done by legs, but I have no eyes with which to see what is rough and smooth." The cripple said, "Look, I can do what should be done by eyes, but I have no legs with which to go and come." The blind man was delighted, and he made the cripple climb upon his shoulder. Sitting on the blind man's shoulder, the cripple spoke thus, "Leave the left, take the right; leave the right, take the left."

Herein, the blind man has no efficient power; he is impotent; he cannot travel by his own efficient power, by his own strength. And the cripple has no efficient power; he is impotent; he cannot travel by his own efficient power, by his own strength. But there is nothing to prevent their going when they support each other. So too, mentality has no efficient power; it does not arise or occur in such and such functions by its own efficient power. But there is nothing to prevent their occurrence when they support each other.[16]

The interdependence of the mental and the material has more far-reaching consequences than the possibility of dispelling pain by being aware of the feeling of pain. It indicates the Buddhist concern for the whole man. To some, Buddhist meditation may seem, in its own way, to be overly cerebral. That is, it appears to be primarily mental training. Although such an interpretation is not without justification, it is also obvious that the successful meditator has been able to train his body to sit for long periods without undue discomfort. On a higher level, Buddhist meditation teachers both past and present insist that only a person of high moral character will be able to focus his attention and train his mind to a sufficient degree to gain true wisdom. Also and perhaps most significantly, the meditator who has gained genuine insight is a changed person. There is a definite moral dimension to the practice of insight meditation even though the state of enlightenment transcends moral categories. The freedom gained by one who has penetrated to the truth of the nature of things has an ontic significance with profound implications for a person's attitudes and the way he acts.

The third meditation subject discussed in the *Satipaṭ-ṭhāna Sutta* is *citta*—mind, consciousness or, perhaps, thought. Here the text follows a now familiar pattern of delineation:

[16] Buddhaghosa, *The Path of Purification*, trans. Ñāṇamoli Thera (Colombo, Ceylon: R. Semage, 1956), p. 691.

Here, O bhikkhus, a bhikkhu understands the consciousness with lust, as with lust; the consciousness without lust as without lust; the consciousness with hate, as with hate; the consciousness without hate as without hate; the consciousness with ignorance as with ignorance; the consciousness without ignorance as without ignorance; the shrunken state of consciousness as the shrunken state; the distracted state of consciousness as the distracted state; the state of consciousness become great as the state become great; the state of consciousness not become great as the state not become great; the state of consciousness with some other mental state superior to it as the state with something mentally higher; the state of consciousness with no other mental state superior to it as the state with nothing mentally higher; the quieted state of consciousness as the quiet state; the state of consciousness not quieted as the state not quieted; the freed state of consciousness as freed; and the unfreed state of consciousness as unfreed.[17]

The text does not say that the meditator who is aware of lust, hatred, ignorance, smallness, mental inferiority, agitation or bondage should feel guilty for such thoughts or that he should make an immediate effort to eliminate them through sheer dint of will. Indeed, to become embroiled in the agony of guilt for failing to think only the right thoughts is itself a form of attachment to be overcome. The Sutta simply instructs the meditator to be conscious of these negative qualities as well as of positive traits. From the Buddhist viewpoint the only way lust, hatred and ignorance can be overcome is through the awareness that they exist. True awareness has sufficient power to transcend them. This theme occurs frequently in the Venerable Dhammasudhi's lectures. To the Western man, such a claim may sound little different than the Christian affirmation that a man is saved through the saving power of faith. It must be remembered, however, that the Buddhist assertion about the power of awareness is made within the context of the practical discipline of attentive, insight meditation practice.

[17] *The Way of Mindfulness*, pp. 9–10.

The last section of the *Satipaṭṭhāna Sutta* deals with the topic of *dhamma*, one of the most elusive terms in Buddhism. In this context it carries the meaning of mental objects or, as translated by T. W. Rhys Davids, ideas. The ideas which the Sutta discusses in this rather lengthy section include some of the fundamental teachings of Theravāda Buddhism: the five *nivāraṇas*, or hindrances (i.e., sensuality, anger, sloth and torpor, agitation and worry, doubt), the five aggregates of grasping (i.e., material form, sensation, perception, volitional elements, consciousness), the *āyatanas*, or sense bases, the seven factors of enlightenment and the Four Noble Truths. In and of themselves these formulae offer a near synopsis of Buddhist teachings. In one sense, it is precisely the truth of these teachings which the Buddhist meditator comes to understand. Yet, in another sense, these teachings as stated are merely mental objects, ideas of which one is to be aware but to which one is not to be attached. If one achieves true insight, the ideas as formulated are not differentiated from the awareness of them. They are ultimately, therefore, not *dhamma* in the denotation of "mental objects" but *dhamma* as the truth. "Know the truth and the truth shall make you free." To know the truth in the fullest sense is to be the truth. It is not to know a set of propositions or to memorize a few formulae. Insight meditation aims at nothing less than making the truth and me one. It is not an easy task although some may have more aptitude and ability than others—or should we say, more intuitive insight.

The *Satipaṭṭhāna Sutta* sets forth a means to gain enlightenment. It does so through describing the application of *sati*, or awareness, to four aspects of human life—body, feelings, consciousness and ideas. The importance of this particular method can hardly be exaggerated, and its place in the Buddhist scheme of meditation training is forever guaranteed. For us, who merely read the text, there is no personal validation that its claims are true. Yet, the Buddha admonished his followers to accept no teaching, even his own, without testing; and we must be similarly admonished in order to test the truth of the Buddha's claim: "This is the only way, O Bhikkhus, for the purification of beings, for the overcoming of sorrow and lamentation, for the destruction of suffering and grief, for reaching the right path, for the attainment of Nibbāna, namely, the Four Arousings of mindfulness."[18]

[18] *Ibid.*, p. 1.

4

The Path of Freedom

The Satipaṭṭhāna Sutta *discussed in Chapter 3 is one of the bases upon which Buddhist meditation has been built. While the* Sutta *charts a general direction or way of progressing, its very brevity precludes presenting a detailed meditation map. Consequently, within the Theravāda tradition many more elaborate expositions have arisen. Some of them are explicitly meditation manuals. Others are part of a presentation of Buddhist doctrine often divided into the traditional stages of moral virtue* (sīla), *concentration* (samādhi) *and wisdom* (paññā) *where meditation techniques figure most prominently in the second stage.*

The *Path of Purity* (*Visuddhimagga*) by Buddhaghosa, the famous fifth century South Indian commentator, fits the second description. Less well known than the *Path of Purity*, but as a program for meditation perhaps even more valuable, is the *Path of Freedom* (*Vimuttimagga*) a Pāli text attributed to a certain Upatissa which has survived only in a Chinese translation thought to have been done in China in the fifth century A.D. There are many similarities between the two works and even the parallelism of the titles may not have been mere coincidence. Yet, by comparison, the *Path of Freedom* has the virtue of being less scholastic and, hence, more practical, brief and direct.

It is, as one Buddhist scholar put it, the product of a man for whom Buddhism was a way to be practiced rather than theorized about. For this reason the following excerpts from the *Vimuttimagga* have been selected as representative of a later and more detailed exposition of Theravāda meditation.

Due to the fact that the selections include only a fraction of the entire text a few introductory observations will be helpful at this point. The largest portion of the *Vimuttimagga* discusses meditation in terms of thirty-eight "subjects of meditation." It is presented in a dialogue type of format and ranges from the most abstract concepts of Theravāda thought (e.g. the plane of neither perception nor nonperception) to concrete instructions for constructing a *maṇḍala* or meditation circle on the ground and how to concentrate on objects of yellow, red and blue-green. Only briefly developed aspects in the *Satipaṭṭhāna Sutta* are greatly enlarged in the *Vimuttimagga*. Respiration mindfulness, for example, the beginning point of meditation in the *Satipaṭṭhāna Sutta* is elaborated into sixteen ways of mindfulness of respiration. Finally it should be mentioned that the selection included here on the "good friend" is illustrative of the crucial role played by the accomplished teacher or guide within the meditation traditions of Indian Buddhism.

* * *

What is meditation? It is to contemplate reality, to remove resentment, to make the mind happy, to discard hindrances, to gain freedom, to equalize, to arouse concentration skillfully, to dwell in right observation, to wish to arouse concentration and to aspire to acquire liberation.

Meaning of Concentration (*Samādhi*)

Concentration means that one has purity of mind, endeavors steadfastly, dwells with the truth having the benefit of tranquillity, and is not distracted. This is called concentration.

And again, it means not allowing one's mind to be bent by the strong wind of passion. It is comparable to the unflickering flame of the lamp behind the palace.

It is used in the Abhidhamma [see glossary] thus: "What fixes the mind right, causes it to be not dependent on anything, causes it to be unmoved, undisturbed, tranquilized and nonattached, rightens the faculty of concentration and the power of concentration, is called concentration."

Salient Characteristic [of Concentration]

What are its salient characteristic, function, manifestation and near cause? Dwelling of mind is its salient characteristic; overcoming of hatred is its function; tranquillity is its manifestation; nonassociation with defilement and the mind obtaining freedom are its near cause.

Who observes concentration? Namely, he who maintains the mind and the mental properties in a state of equilibrium. It is like the hand which holds a pair of scales evenly.

The even practice of mindfulness and energy is concentration. It is comparable to the evenness of oil in an oiled bowl. Equilibrated thought, like the equalized energy of four horses of a chariot, is concentration. It is like the attentiveness of a fletcher scrutinizing the straightness of a shaft.

Benefits Produced by Concentration

How many benefits can concentration produce? There are four benefits. What are the four? Pleasant dwelling in the happiness of truth in the present life; enjoyment of all objects through investigation; acquisition of worldly knowledge; the attainment of perfection.

What is "pleasant dwelling in the happiness of truth in the present life"? Namely, one acquires concentration and is freed from corruption. One's mind arouses joy, partakes of the joy of the supramundane; therefore, as the Blessed One said: "He produces joy from quietude, acquires coolness and becomes perfect gradually." And again, the Buddha declared to the bhikkhus: "At first I was a naked ascetic; I did not move my body or open my mouth for seven days and seven nights; I sat in silence enwrapped in bliss." This is the meaning, in the Noble Teaching, of "pleasant dwelling in the happiness of truth in the present life."

"Enjoyment of all objects through investigation" means that a yogin [meditator] acquires concentration and is not hindered by objects. Being pliant of mind, he is able to concentrate. He investigates the aggregations, the sense-spheres, the elements and others. He is well-disposed. Therefore, the Blessed One taught the bhikkhus thus: "Thus should you train yourselves. Everything depends on mind. Know this as it is."

"Acquisition of worldly knowledge" means that one having acquired concentration develops the five faculties of knowledge, namely: psychic power, divine ear, knowledge of others' thoughts, recollection of past existences, and divine eye. Therefore, the Blessed One has declared: "With concentrated mind one is able to change one's body at will. Thus one produces psychic power in the various modes."

"The attainment of perfection" means that one having a concentrated mind, although he has yet to reach the stage of the "learning-ender" [Arahant], may not fall back at all. One gains reward through concentration. One attains to "the form," "the formless," and to Perfection. The Buddha has declared: "Those who practice a little of the first meditation are able to join the retinue of Brahma. All such are born in such a world." These four benefits can be produced by concentration.

Obstacles to Concentration

How many states are obstacles to progress in concentration? Namely, eight states: lust, hatred, indolence, rigidity, agitation, uncertainty, delusion (dullness), absence of joy and bliss. All other evil and unhealthy states are obstacles.

Causes of Concentration

How many causes of concentration are there? Namely, eight states are causes: renunciation, nonhatred, brightness, sustained application of thought, gladness, those factors that arouse perception of the truth, and all skillful (healthy) states. These are causes of concentration.

On Approaching a Good Friend

Then how is concentration brought out?

If a man wishes to bring out concentration, he at first should approach a preeminent friend. Why? If, at first, when a yogin wishes to accomplish excellent concentration, he dwells apart from a good friend, he will not acquire steadfastness. In a Discourse it is said: "Maghiya bhikkhu partakes of deterioration." It is comparable to a man who sets out alone on a distant journey. None guides him. When a man sets out alone, he is like an elephant that is not guided by the goad. If, when a yogin practices, he listens to the discourses and instructions of a good friend, he is able to remove his many difficulties and get into the right method and practice. If he strenuously endeavors and strictly trains himself, then he is able to acquire excellent concentration.

Qualities of a Good Friend

What are the seven qualities? Lovable, esteemable, venerable, able to counsel well, patient, able to deliver deep discourses, and not applying oneself to useless ends.

What is "lovable"? Led by two kinds of practice, a man preaches well: dwelling together happily, having come to a mutual understanding and not abusing one another.

"Esteemable" means that one is tranquilized through the action of virtue, fulfills the protection of mindfulness, is not overdesirous, and does not speak much.

"Venerable" means that one is endowed with the merit of much learning and appreciates well the value of meditation.

"Able to counsel well" means that one considers thus: "Let my speech be lovable, esteemable, venerable and fruitful," and [one] benefits others and esteems the truth. Therefore, one restrains oneself from things that ought not to be done. Thus one observes to the end and does not forsake.

"Patience" means that one is like a saint, understands well, never hesitates in one's speech, and does not flatter.

"Able to deliver deep discourses" means that one well understands the real inner content of concepts and can convey them meaningfully.

"Not applying oneself to useless ends" means that one well understands the place [the true direction] of *kamma* [the power of moral conditionality].

These are the qualities of a good friend, who should be sought.

Sixteen Ways of Training in Mindfulness of Respiration

(1) and (2) "Breathing in a long breath, breathing out a short breath, breathing in a short breath, thus he trains himself." . . .

Knowledge causes the arising of nonconfusion and the object. What is nonconfusion and what is the object? The yogin gains tranquility of body and mind, and abides in mindfulness of respiration. The respirations become subtle. Because of subtlety they are hard to lay hold of. If at that time the yogin's breathing is long, he, through fixing, knows it is long. If the image arises, he considers it through its own nature. Thus should nonconfusion be known. And again he should consider the breaths, whether long or short (as the case may be). Thus should he practice. And again, the yogin causes the arising of the clear image through the object. Thus should one practice.

(3) " 'Experiencing the whole body, I breathe in,' thus he trains himself." In two ways he knows the whole body, through nonconfusion and through the object. What is the knowledge of the whole body through nonconfusion? A yogin practices mindfulness of respiration and develops concentration through contact (complete awareness of the rise and fall of the abdomen) accompanied by joy and bliss. Owing to the experiencing of contact accompanied by joy and bliss, the whole body becomes nonconfused. What is the knowledge of the whole body through the object? The incoming breath and the outgoing breath comprise the bodily factors dwelling in one sphere. The object of respiration and the mind and the mental properties are called "body." These bodily factors are called "body." Thus should the whole body be known. That yogin knows the whole body thus: "Though there is the body, there is no being or soul (a permanent entity)."

The Three Trainings

"Thus he trains himself" refers to the three trainings. The first is the training of the higher virtue, the second is the training of the higher thought (purified mind), the third is the training of the higher wisdom. True virtue is called the training of the higher virtue; true concentration is called the training of the higher thought; and true wisdom is called the training of the higher wisdom. That yogin by these three kinds of training meditates on the object, recollects the object, and trains himself. He practices repeatedly. This is the meaning of "thus he trains himself."

(4) " 'Calming the bodily formation, I breathe,' thus he trains himself." Which are the bodily formations? He breathes in and out with such bodily formations as bending down, stooping, bending all over, moving, quivering, trembling and shaking. And again, he calms the gross bodily formations and practices the first meditation, *jhāna*, through the subtle bodily formations. From there, he progresses to the second meditation, *jhāna*, through the more subtle bodily formations. From there he progresses to the third meditation, through still more subtle bodily formations. From there, he progresses to the fourth meditation, having ended (the bodily formations) without remainder. If he causes the ending of respiration without remainder, how is he able to practice mindfulness of respiration? Because he has grasped well the general characteristics, the image arises even when the respirations lapse. And because of these many characteristics, he is able to develop the image and enter into meditation (*jhāna*).

(5) " 'Experiencing joy through the object, I breathe in,' thus he trains himself." He attends to respiration. He arouses joy in two meditations, *jhāna*-s. This joy can be known through two ways: through nonconfusion and through the object.

(6) " 'Experiencing bliss, I breathe in,' thus he trains himself." He attends to respiration. He arouses bliss in three meditations, *jhāna*-s. This bliss can be known through two ways: through nonconfusion and through the object. The rest is as was fully taught above.

(7) " 'Experiencing the mental formations, I breathe in,' thus he trains himself." "Mental formations" means "perception and feeling." He arouses these mental formations in four meditations, *jhāna*-s. He knows through two ways: through nonconfusion and through the object. The rest is as was fully taught above.

(8) " 'Calming the mental formations, I breathe in,' thus he trains himself." He calms them (perception and feel-

ing) and trains himself. The rest is as was fully taught above.

(9) " 'Experiencing the mind, I breathe in,' thus he trains himself." He attends to the incoming breath and the outgoing breath. The mind is aware of entering into and going out of the object, through two ways: through non-confusion and through the object. The rest is as was fully taught above.

(10) " 'Gladdening the mind, I breathe in,' thus he trains himself." Joy means rejoicing. In two meditations, he causes the mind to exult. Thus he trains himself. The rest is as was fully taught above.

(11) " 'Concentrating the mind, I breathe in,' thus he trains himself." That yogin attends to the incoming breath and the outgoing breath. Through mindfulness and through meditation (*jhāna*) he causes the mind to be intent on the object. Placing the mind well, he establishes it. Thus he trains himself.

(12) " 'Freeing the mind, I breathe in,' thus he trains himself." That yogin attends to the incoming breath and the outgoing breath. If his mind is slow and slack, he frees it from restlessness. Thus he trains himself. If it is elated, he frees it from lust. Thus he trains himself. If it is depressed, he frees it from hatred. Thus he trains himself. If his mind is sullied, he frees it from the lesser defilements. Thus he trains himself. And again, if his mind is not inclined toward the object and is not pleased with it, he causes his mind to be inclined toward it. Thus he trains himself.

(13) " 'Discerning impermanence, I breathe in,' thus he trains himself." He attends to the incoming breath and the outgoing breath. Discerning the incoming and the outgoing breath, the object of the incoming and the outgoing breath, the mind and the mental properties and their arising and passing away, he trains himself.

(14) " 'Discerning dispassion, I breathe in,' thus he trains himself." He attends to the incoming breath and the

outgoing breath, knowing thus: "This is impermanence; this is dispassion; this is extinction—this is Nibbāna." Thus he breathes in and trains himself.

(15) " 'Discerning cessation, I breathe in,' thus he trains himself." Discerning many hindrances, according to reality, he knows: "These are impermanent, the destruction of these is extinction, Nibbāna." Thus with tranquilized vision he trains himself.

(16) " 'Discerning renunciation, I breathe in,' thus he trains himself." Discerning tribulation according to reality, he knows: "These are impermanent," and freeing himself from tribulation he abides in the peace of extinction, Nibbāna. Thus he trains himself and attains to bliss. The tranquil and the sublime are to be understood thus: All activities are brought to rest. All defilements are forsaken. Craving is destroyed. Passion is absent. It is the peace of blowing out [Nibbāna].

Of these sixteen, the first twelve fulfill serenity (*samatha*) and insight (*vipassanā*), and are discerned as impermanence. The last four fulfill only insight. Thus should serenity and insight be understood.

And again, all these are of four kinds. The first is that practice which leads to the completion of discernment. There is a time when one discerns impermanence through attending to the incoming breath and the outgoing breath. This is called the knowledge of the long and the short through practicing. Calming the bodily formations and the mental formations, gladdening the mind, concentrating the mind, and freeing the mind—this is called the arising of the knowledge of the whole body, bliss and the mental formations. "Experiencing the mind" means: "The completion of discernment." "There is a time when one discerns . . ." and so forth refers to the four activities which always begin with the discernment of impermanence.

And again, practice means attaining to a state (of meditation, *jhāna*) through mindfulness of respiration. This is practice. Through this mindfulness of respiration, one attains to the state which is with initial and sustained application of thought. The experiencing of joy is the state of the second meditation. The experiencing of the mind is the state of the fourth meditation.

And again, all these are of two kinds. They are practice and fulfillment. Such practice as is included within fulfillment does not cause decrease of the sixteen bases. Practice is like a seed; it is the cause of merit. Fulfillment is like a flower or a fruit, because it proceeds from a similar thing.

If mindfulness of respiration is practiced, the four foundations of mindfulness are fulfilled. If the four foundations of mindfulness are practiced, the seven enlightenment factors are fulfilled. If the seven enlightenment factors are practiced, freedom and wisdom are fulfilled.

The Four Foundations of Mindfulness

How is such a state attained?

The foundation of mindfulness which begins with the long incoming breath and the long outgoing breath is the reviewing of the body. That which begins with the experiencing of joy is the reviewing of feeling. That which begins with the experiencing of the mind is the reviewing of thought. That which begins with the discernment of impermanence is the reviewing of states. Thus one who practices mindfulness of respiration fulfills the four foundations of mindfulness.

The Seven Enlightenment Factors

How are the seven enlightenment factors fulfilled through the practice of the four foundations of mindfulness? If the yogin practices the (four) foundations of mindfulness, he is able to abide nonconfused in mindfulness; this is called the enlightenment factor of mindfulness.

That yogin, abiding in mindfulness, investigates subjection to ill, impermanence and phenomena; this is called the enlightenment factor in inquiry into states. Inquiring into states (*dhamma*) thus, he strives earnestly without slackening; this is called the enlightenment factor of exertion. Developing exertion, he arouses joy that is clean; this is called the enlightenment factor of joy. Through the mind being full of joy, his body and mind are endowed with calm; this is called the enlightenment factor of calm. Through calmness his body attains to ease, and his mind is possessed of concentration; this is called the enlightenment factor of concentration. Owing to concentration, the mind acquires equanimity; this is called the enlightenment factor of equanimity. Thus because of the practice of the four foundations of mindfulness, the seven enlightenment factors are fulfilled.

How are freedom and wisdom fulfilled through the practice of the seven enlightenment factors: The yogin who has practiced the seven enlightenment factors much gains in a moment the wisdom of the path and the fruit of freedom. Thus because of the practice of the seven enlightenment factors, wisdom and freedom are fulfilled.

All formations are endowed with initial and sustained application of thought according to planes. That being so, why is only initial application of thought suppressed in mindfulness of respiration, and not the other?

It is used here in a different sense. Discursiveness is a hindrance to meditation. In this sense, it is transcended.

Why is air contact pleasant? Because it calms the mind. It is comparable to the soothing of a heavenly musician's mind with sweet sounds. By this, discursive thinking is transcended. And again, it is like a person walking along the bank of a river. His mind is collected, is directed toward one object, and does not wander. Therefore in mindfulness of respiration, the transcendence of discursive thinking is taught.

The Immeasurable Thought of Loving-Kindness [*mettā*]¹

What is loving-kindness? What is the practicing of it? What are its salient characteristic, function and manifestation? What are its benefits? What is the procedure?

As parents, on seeing their dear and only child, arouse thoughts of loving-kindness and benevolence towards that child, so one arouses thoughts of loving-kindness and benevolence towards all beings. Thus is loving-kindness to be known. The undisturbed dwelling of the mind in this practice is called the practicing of it. To cause the arising of benevolence is its salient characteristic. The thought of loving-kindness is its function. Nonhatred is its manifestation. If a man practices loving-kindness, he is benefitted in eleven ways thus: Happily he sleeps; happily he awakes; he does not see bad dreams; he is dear to humans; he is dear to nonhumans; deities protect him; fire, poison, sword and stick come not near him; he concentrates his mind quickly; the color of his face is pleasingly bright; at the time of death he is not bewildered; if he attains not the sublime state, he is reborn in the world of Brahma [the gods].

The Immeasurable Thought of Compassion [*karuṇā*]

What is compassion? What is the practicing of it? What are its salient characteristic, function and manifestation? What are its benefits? What is the procedure?

As parents who on seeing the suffering of their dear and only child compassionate it, saying, "O, how it suffers!", so one compassionates all beings. This is compassion. One

¹ The following meditation subjects are referred to as the Four Immeasurables (*appamāṇa*). The last, equanimity, is attained in the fourth *jhāna*, meditative absorption or trance state. Strictly speaking the *jhāna*-s are not part of the meditative practice of mindful awareness.

dwells undisturbed in compassion—this is called the practicing of it. The nonmanifestation of nonadvantage is its salient characteristic. Happiness is its function. Harmlessness is its manifestation. Its benefits are equal to those of loving-kindness.

What is the procedure? The new yogin enters into a place of solitude and sits down with mind collected and undisturbed. If he sees or hears of a person stricken with disease, or a person affected by decay, or a person who is full of greed, he considers thus: "That person is stricken with suffering. How will he escape suffering." And again, if he sees or hears of a person of perverted mind and bound with the defilements, or a person entering into ignorance, or one, who having done merit in the past does not now train himself, he considers thus: "That person is stricken with suffering; he will fare ill. How will he escape suffering? And again, if he sees or hears of a person who follows demeritorious doctrines and does not follow meritorious doctrines, or of a person who follows undesirable doctrines and does not follow desirable doctrines, he considers thus: "That person is stricken with suffering; he will fare ill. How will he escape suffering?"

That yogin by these means and through these activities develops the thought of compassion for these persons and repeats it. Having by these means and through these activities developed the thought of compassion and repeated it, he makes his mind pliant, and capable of bearing the object. Thereafter he gradually develops (compassion) for an indifferent person and an enemy. The rest is as was fully taught above. Thus he fills the four directions.

The Immeasurable Thought of Appreciative Joy [*muditā*]

What is appreciative joy? What is the practicing of it? What are its salient characteristic, function and manifestation? What are its benefits? What is the procedure?

As parents, who, on seeing the happiness of their dear and only child are glad and say, "*Sādhu!*" [an interjection] so, one develops appreciative joy for all beings. Thus should appreciative joy be known. The undisturbed dwelling of the mind in appreciative joy—this is called the practicing of it. Gladness is its salient characteristic. Nonfear is its function. Destruction of dislike is its manifestation. Its benefits are equal to those of loving-kindness.

What is the procedure? The new yogin enters a place of solitude and sits down with mind collected and undisturbed. When he sees or hears that some person's qualities are esteemed by others, and that he is at peace and is joyful, one thinks thus: "*Sādhu! sādhu!* may he continue joyful for a long time!" And again, when he sees or hears that a certain person does not follow demeritorious doctrines, or that he does not follow undesirable doctrines and that he follows desirable doctrines, one thinks thus: "*Sādhu! sādhu!* may he continue joyful for a long time!" That yogin by these means and through these activities develops the thought of appreciative joy and repeats it. Having by these means and through these activities developed the thought of appreciative joy and repeated it, he makes his mind pliant, and capable of bearing the object. Thereafter he gradually develops appreciative joy for an indifferent person and an enemy. The rest is as was fully taught above. Thus with appreciative joy he fills the four directions.

The Immeasurable Thought of Equanimity [*upekkhā*]

What is equanimity? What is the practicing of it? What are its salient characteristic, function and manifestation? What are its benefits? What is the procedure?

As parents are neither too attentive nor yet inattentive toward any one of their children, but regard them equally and maintain an even mind towards them, so through equanimity one maintains an even mind toward all beings. Thus should equanimity be known. The dwelling undisturbed in equanimity—this is called the practicing of it. Nonattachment is its salient characteristic. Equality is its function. The suppression of disliking and liking its manifestation. Its benefits are equal to those of loving-kindness.

What is the procedure? That yogin at first attends to the third meditation, *jhāna*, with loving-kindness, with compassion and with appreciative joy. Having attained to the third meditation, *jhāna*, and acquired facility therein, he sees the severe trials of loving-kindness, compassion and appreciative joy. Liking and disliking are near. These (loving-kindness, etc.) are connected with gentleness, elation and gladness. The merits of equanimity lie in the overcoming of these severe trials. That yogin, having seen the severe trials of loving-kindness, compassion and appreciative joy and the merits of equanimity, develops equanimity toward a neutral person and makes the mind calm. Having developed and repeated it, he makes his mind pliant and capable of bearing the object. Thereafter, he gradually develops (it) towards an enemy and then towards a friend. The rest is as was fully taught above. Thus he fills the four directions. That yogin practicing thus attains to the fourth meditation, *jhāna*, through equanimity. In three ways he attains to fixed meditation, *jhāna*; through comprehending beings, through comprehending village-domains and through comprehending all directions.

PART II

Zen Meditation

ZEN is the Japanese term for the Chinese word, *ch'an,*
which in turn is a transliteration of the Sanskrit, *dhyāna.*
Dhyāna, in this usage, can be approximately translated as
meditation. Zen (or Ch'an) Buddhism, then is the development of the Indian Buddhist *dhyāna* or meditation tradition in China and Japan. Zen may be said to have begun
its existence as a distinct school of Buddhism from the
time of Bodhi-dharma, the first patriarch, who is reputed
to have come to China from India in the 4th century A.D.
Zen reached its apogee in China during the T'ang Dynasty
(618–907 A.D.) where it was decisively influenced by
Taoism and also by Confucianism. In Japan Zen discipline
had a great appeal to the Samurai or warrior class during
the Kamakura period (1192–1333 A.D.); yet, Zen was
even more important as a preserver of Chinese cultural
expressions which inspired or influenced many Japanese
artistic forms.

Meditation in Japanese Zen is known as *zazen* or "sitting
Zen." Many aspects of Zen meditation will appear similar
to the Theravāda Buddhism studied in the previous section; however, several unique aspects exist, especially in

Rinzai Zen, the school represented in the following chapters.[1] The best known is the use of the *koan* ("public document") or enigmatic conundrum as a problem to be concentrated upon during *zazen* and to be discussed with the Roshi or Zen master during special interviews known as *sanzen*. Hakuin Zengi's famous *koan*, "The sound of one hand clapping," for example, has become almost a colloquialism. Rinzai Zen is also noted for the seemingly idiosyncratic methods employed by the Zen master to provoke deeper realization and understanding. Many are the tales of the Roshi pushing a disciple off the porch into the mud or giving his nose a hard tweek, all in a seemingly irrational manner. The Reverend Nishimura's chapter on Zen training contains numerous illustrations of the activities of the Zen Roshi.

The following section on Zen meditation begins with a presentation of the historical development of Zen training. Then it moves to a discussion of *zazen* proper before concluding with a commentary on one of the most important texts in Zen Buddhism, *The Heart of the Perfection of Wisdom* (*Prajñāpāramitā Hṛdaya Sūtra*). Instead of offering simply a discussion of *zazen* which would have been necessarily repetitive of certain aspects in the preceding section, we have chosen to include materials of both an historical and philosophical nature. In this way we hope not only to complement but also to enlarge the dimensions of this study of Buddhist meditation. It should also be added that some parts of the following chapters will strike the reader uninitiated in Zen materials as odd, paradoxical or logically incomprehensible. Indeed, it would hardly be representative of Zen if it were otherwise!

[1] There are two major schools of Zen in Japan today, Rinzai and Sōtō. Although differences between them can be exaggerated, the Rinzai form of *zazen* stresses the use of the *koan* and *keisaku* or wooden stick as part of the mental and physical discipline.

5

Zen Training

The Reverend Eshin Nishimura, author of this chapter, has many perspectives on Zen: he is the priest of a rural Zen temple; he was trained at the famous Zen monastery of Nanzen-ji under Shibayama Roshi; and he is a teacher at Hanazono Buddhist University. His wide understanding of Zen is apparent in this chapter on Zen training. Rich in the lore of the Zen tradition it presents both the idea and actual faces of Zen which the Reverend Nishimura distinguishes as "Zen" and "Zen Buddhism" respectively. Several significant aspects of the development of zazen within the Zen traditions of China and Japan are emphasized. One of the most important is the dominating role played by the Zen master or Roshi upon whose wisdom and insight the progress of Zen training depends. The place of the koan in Rinzai Zen and the tension of the "Great Doubt" experience in Zen training are clarified. The chapter also points out that zazen is not confined to isolated periods of sitting meditation but is more of a total and pervasive attitude toward life which the periods of "sitting-zen" help to establish.

* * *

Buddhist Background for Zen Training

The Buddha was the person who released *zazen* meditation from traditional Indian asceticism and gave it a
more humane meaning. From its beginning, therefore,
training in Buddhism has had no connection with the so-
called asceticism often typifying mysticism in general. In
the Buddha's mind it is totally impossible to find perfect
humanity in the sacrifice of the physical body. Body and
mind are one and not to be separated. Freedom of mind
is possible only when the physical body finds freedom.

What the Buddha sought in his humane meditational
method was to discover the real self, completely free
from the external world of suffering but without escaping
from it. Buddhist meditation presupposes neither that the
self is totally separated from nor identified with the world.
Rather it aims to create a state of being beyond the distinction of self and world.

In Buddhist teaching, the absolute self which the Buddha sought is beautifully symbolized in "The Four Wisdoms of the Buddha-nature." When he awakened after a
long Zen meditation, the Buddha uttered, "How miracu-
lous it is to see that all beings in this world, without
exception, possess Buddha-nature! Man is unable to realize
it simply because of his ignorance!" To realize this innate
Buddha-nature by one's own self is to come to find the real
self which makes it possible for man and the world to
exist together. *Zazen* meditation is thought to be the finest
way to realize it.

The first wisdom of Buddha-nature is called "The Wisdom of the Great Round Mirror." As we know, a mirror
reveals its substance in its clear emptiness. If a mirror had
any content in itself, it would not be a mirror. The real
existence of a mirror exists in nonexistence. Behind the
paradoxicality of this statement is the affirmation that one

exists when he reflects the true nature of everything he sees. "When the autumn moon is reflecting in the quiet pond," reads a beautiful Japanese poem, "there exists neither consciousness to reflect, nor consciousness to be reflected; there is but one fact: the reflecting is of itself existence." This function of the mirror is none other than the substance of the mirror. In the same way, Buddha-nature, or the real self, does not have any form or content by itself. The ordinary self, which has a consciousness of ego opposing the external object, is not the real self, but a mere phenomenon in this finite world. The real self is the "original face existing before even one's parents were born." The real self is the formless self which is never formed. Because of its emptiness, a mirror can reflect absolutely any object which comes before its surface. A mirror does not refuse to reflect any object. In other words, on the surface of the mirror there is no selection, but all are equally accepted. This is the second wisdom of the mirror and is called "The Wisdom of Equanimity." This might be more functionally translated as, "The Wisdom of Equality." There exists no distinction between good and evil, big and small, beauty and ugliness, sacred and profane for the mirror. The mirror reflects such huge things as mountains and oceans. In the same way, it will reflect a tiny insect. The mirror accepts the repulsive feces as readily as a beautiful flower. In the same way the inborn Buddha-nature is impartial to all objects. Such an equality of acceptance is found in a baby's attitude toward an object. For him there exists no value judgment, definition or concept, all of which rest on man's dualistic orientation and intellectual interpretation of it. In the mind of a baby there is no distinction between himself and another. Man and the world are one. But the moment he begins to count "two," according to a famous Japanese mathematician, Kioshi Oka, a dualism arises in the baby's consciousness. As he grows he builds up a self-consciousness which separates himself from all other things, gradually dividing the world into good and evil, beauty and ugliness, long and short, young and old, and so on. These dualistic judgments are made merely from his egocentric standpoint and not from a universal view.

The same thing can be seen in man-made concepts or definitions. In a Zen text, there are many examples of dialogue between master and disciple. The master asks, holding the Zen stick, "What is this?" The disciple replies, "A Zen stick." "No, it is not," replies the master. "If it is not, then what is it?" The master answers with a loud voice, "A Zen stick!" The disciple's Zen stick was a simple concept taught by somebody else. When, therefore, it is denied, he is confronted with great difficulty in understanding it. For the disciple, the name of the Zen stick is the same as the substance of the Zen stick; therefore, when the master calls it a Zen stick, the name or label has no importance and may be replaced by the word "flower," if he so chooses. We must understand the famous phrase, "The mountain is ocean, and the ocean is mountain," in this light. It is perfectly clear: life-and-death dualism is a matter of conceptualization. If one really knows the single face beyond concept, absolute life exists even in the midst of death. In the same way, if one is living in dualistic conceptualizations of life, his life is at once death.

As on the surface of a mirror, only the object itself is reflected and not the concept or definition, so also in Buddha-nature, only the thing itself in the phenomenal world can be grasped. This might be called, "The Wisdom of Equanimity."

The third wisdom of Buddha-nature is called, "The Wisdom of Right Investigation." This investigation, in a way, seems to be contrary to the second. In the second wisdom, the mirror was characterized as impartial or equal. This wisdom was, so to speak, a state of absolute oneness, where the mountain is ocean and the ocean is mountain. But here we see an entirely different function of the mirror, in which, "The mountain is just mountain, and the ocean is just ocean." No mirror reflects a mountain as ocean and vice versa. In the mirror, good is good, and evil is evil; beauty is beauty, and ugliness is ugliness; long is long, and short is short. Such absolute affirmation is produced by the clearness of the mirror. In other words, absolute affirmation of the object is possible only when absolute negation of the subject (i.e., the mirror) is accomplished.

As in "The Wisdom of the Great Round Mirror," Buddha-nature is also clear. It sees each object clearly, as it is, without any change or alteration. But the ordinary self cannot accept the object as it is because of its egocentric judgment. The ordinary self is the self formed by self-consciousness, that is, the affirmation of the self. Objects, therefore, cannot be totally accepted and affirmed. The absolute formless self, which is the absolute negation of the ordinary self, is the real self which accepts the objective world in its absolute affirmation. The Zen master Dōgen, a founder of Japanese Sōtō Zen, comments as follows: "To study Buddhism is to study self. To study the self is to forget oneself. To forget oneself means to see the true self in all other things in the world. . . ." In short, man finds his own self only when he investigates all things in the world exactly as they are. When a Zen master is asked, "What is the real self?" he may demonstrate such a real self by replying with the phrase, "A flower is red, and a willow is green," or "The eye is horizontal, and the nose is vertical."

The fourth and final wisdom of the mirror is called, "The Wisdom that Accomplishes All that Should Be Performed." This wisdom implies a vivid function of the mirror that suddenly changes its reflection. The wisdom of the mirror, to accept everything clearly as it is, can only exist simultaneously with the wisdom of returning to emptiness at the moment its object is taken away. If some memory remains on the mirror, the next object cannot be reflected as it really is. Therefore, this immediate return to emptiness is the precondition for complete reflection of the next object.

The ordinary self tends to keep the memory of the object once it is printed on its consciousness and to judge the next object in relation to that memory. When different objects come to it, the consciousness perceives them in comparison with the former object already defined or conceptualized. Or, in the case that the same object appears repeatedly, consciousness tends to become accustomed to perceiving it and loses its freshness. But the real self, which is a formless self, is understood always to be empty like a mirror. To live one's life at each moment with full awareness is to live in the past and future at this moment. On the other hand, to live without full awareness of this present moment, with only memory and expectation, is not one's life at all; it is death.

Today people are very eager to acquire new experiences, to do different things and try to avoid doing the same thing, and this is taken to be the development of the human consciousness. But for the Oriental mind, this is not the way to find reality. In Oriental teaching, it is to concentrate the human consciousness on one thing which is not changeable, so that one might deepen it continually until this oneness becomes an entirely different value, called *satori* or *kensho*. *Zazen*, one of the most severe disciplines, which concentrates our fickle modern mind on the stillness of oneness, is, in this respect, the most direct path to the absolute awareness of reality.

These are the four wisdoms of the Buddha-nature. It is the real inborn nature existing in all beings. And this inborn nature is the very self which Buddha discovered and which his descendants have tried to discover for themselves through using the same method as Buddha. This is *zazen* meditation.

Premonastic Zen Training in China

According to historical record, Bodhi-dharma, the First Patriarch of Chinese Zen, was the first person to introduce the Buddha's heart to China, instead of simply bringing his teachings written in the form of scriptures, as all other Buddhist scholars had done. His poem illustrates his purpose in coming to China:

> A special transmission outside the scriptures,
> Not depending upon letters and words;
> Directly pointing at man's nature,
> Seeing into one's nature and becoming Buddha.

After arriving in China, he meditated in a small cave for nine years, until Hui-k'o came to him. Hui-k'o asked Bodhi-dharma to instruct him. Meditating facing the wall, Bodhi-dharma did not turn to him for three days and nights. Finally, Hui-k'o, standing in the snow to his knees, showed his eagerness by cutting off his arm and holding it up. Seeing it, Bodhi-dharma turned around:

"My soul is not yet pacified. Pray, master, pacify it," said Hui-k'o.

"Bring your soul here, and I will pacify it," replied Bodhi-dharma.

Hui-k'o hesitated for a moment, but finally said, "I have sought it these many years and still I am unable to seize it!"

"There, it is pacified, once and for all," so answered Bodhi-dharma.

In this way Hui-k'o was appointed the Second Patriarch of Chinese Zen. From this document we know that the Buddha-nature, the core of Buddha's teaching, is not necessarily realized through *zazen* meditation in sitting (*dhyāna*).

The central teaching of Bodhi-dharma is known as "The Two Ways and Four Practices." The two ways are theoretical and practical. In the practical way he includes four practices: the practice of *dharma*[1] with the voluntary acceptance of suffering, the practice of *dharma* with a deep understanding of *karma*[2] fate, the practice of *dharma* without desire, and the practice of *dharma* with selflessness. The theoretical way to *dharma* is established by these fourfold practices.

Here we must pay attention to the difference between Buddha's meditation (*tathāgata*[3] meditation) and patriarchal meditation in Chinese Zen. *Tathāgata* meditation is more speculative, conditioned, perhaps, by the mind set of the Indian people. For example, in the Buddha's teaching, a beginner is required to practice calmness and insight. There are five restraints of mind in the practice of calmness:

1. Meditation on the impurity of worldly life, in order to adjust the mind in regard to passion and avarice.

2. Meditation on mercy, in order to cultivate the idea of sympathy toward others and to stop the inclination to become angry.

3. Meditation on causation, in order to rid oneself of ignorance.

4. Meditation on the diversity of realms, in order to see different standpoints and to rid oneself of selfish views.

5. Meditation on breathing, which leads to concentration, enabling one to correct the tendency toward mental dispersion.

When one's faulty mind has been adjusted and calmness has been obtained, one proceeds to the next stage.

There are the four restraints of the mind in the practice of insight:

1. The impurity of the body is meditated upon and fully realized.

---

[1] *Dharma* is the Sanskrit of *dhamma* (Pāli). Here it refers to the truth as taught by Zen.

[2] *Karma* is the Sanskrit of *kamma* (Pāli) and refers to the fate one has achieved through his past actions in this and previous lives.

[3] *Tathāgata*, "thus-gone" is used here as a title for the Buddha.

2. The evils of the sensations are meditated upon and fully realized.

3. The evanescence or impermanence of the mind and its thoughts is meditated upon and fully realized.

4. The transience of all elements of selfishness is meditated upon and fully realized.

The details of this kind of speculative meditation practice are discussed in Part I of this book. The kind of gradual mental procedure involved seems to me to be typically Indian. Chinese patriarchal meditation, however, is more practical and is practiced in everyday tasks. Fulfillment of mental relaxation must be realized in moments of one's daily life. Also, the total existential crisis of man's being is crucial; and when this crisis becomes acute, it creates a breakthrough. Therefore, whenever a man hopes for a certain goal in the future and fails to achieve it, a crisis point arises. When Hui-k'o found nothing to seize, he was in the midst of an existential crisis. It was at this very moment that Bodhi-dharma pacified him.

Let me repeat the famous story of Hui-neng, the Sixth Patriarch of Chinese Zen. One day, his master requested each of the monks to present a poem showing his state of mind. The head monk, Shen-hsiu, read:

> This body is the Bodhi-tree
> The soul is like a mirror bright;
> Take heed to keep it always clean,
> And let not dust collect on it.

Hui-neng, who was not a monk but a layman working in the rice polishing cottage, secretly wrote a poem and hung it on the wall. It read:

> The Bodhi-tree is not a tree,
> The mirror-stand is not a stand;
> There is nothing originally,
> Where can dust collect?

Hui-neng won the appointment as the Sixth Patriarch for his insight.

Once, when Ma-tsu had sat cross-legged all day in meditation at the monastery of his master Nan-yüeh, he was questioned by his master:

"What are you seeking here sitting in this cross-legged manner?"

"My desire is to become Buddha," answered Ma-tsu.

Thereupon the master took up a piece of brick and began to polish it hard on a stone nearby.

"What are you working on so hard, my master?" asked Ma-tsu.

"I am trying to turn this into a mirror," replied the master.

"No amount of polishing will make a mirror out of brick, sir," retorted Ma-tsu.

"If not, then no amount of sitting cross-legged as you do will make a Buddha of you," said the master.

"What shall I do then?" asked Ma-tsu.

"It is like driving a cart. When it doesn't move, do you whip the cart or the ox?" asked Nan-yüeh. Ma-tsu made no answer. The master continued:

"Are you practicing this cross-legged sitting in order to attain *dhyāna* or to attain Buddhahood? If it is *dhyāna*, *dhyāna* does not consist in sitting or lying; if it is Buddhahood, Buddhahood has no fixed forms. As he has no abiding place anywhere, no one can take hold of him, nor can he be let go of. If you are seeking Buddhahood by sitting in this cross-legged manner, you are murdering him. So long as you don't free yourself from this kind of sitting, you will never arrive at the truth."

In Lin-chi Lu (The Record of Lin-chi), the record of the founder of Rinzai Zen, we read the following:

One day Lin-chi was sleeping while sitting in the *zazen* meditation hall. By chance, his master Ma-tsu came into the hall and saw him sleeping. With his Zen stick, the master hit the wooden railing in front of him. Acknowledging that he was his master, Lin-chi went back to sleep. The master struck the railing again and went back to the other *zazen* hall, where he found that a higher monk was doing *zazen* sincerely. The master said, "The young monk Lin-chi is doing serious *zazen*. Why do you waste your time?" The monk asked, "What do you mean by that, master?" The master struck the railing once and went away.

As you might know already from these documents, in the early days of Chinese Zen history, Zen meditation in a cross-legged position was a secondary matter. Actually, we do not see any record of sitting meditation in the early Zen texts. For example, in the *Platform Sūtra* of Hui-neng, the definition of *zazen* meditation is clearly made in the phrase, "Not to have any thoughts about the external world of good and evil, and not to move from one's concentration upon self-nature; that is called *zazen* meditation." It is quite understandable that real quietness should be kept in mind, and not in form. If real stillness exists only in the quietness of the sitting form, it will not work when a man comes from sitting meditation and returns to his noisy, daily life. More effective meditation has to be the kind of wisdom which is useful in daily life. And this wisdom is called *prajñā*-wisdom, which is identical to *dhyāna* meditation.

While *tathāgata* meditation is thought to be a gradual progression toward Nirvāṇa reality, patriarchal meditation is a way of instantly transforming the unreal into the real. The difference between these two approaches to reality reminds me of the familiar argument between Hegelian and Kierkegaardian attitudes toward the truth. Hegel intended to reach the truth by the dialectical method, and as is well known, the dynamic of his dialectic is characterized by thinking about the antithesis, rather than unifying the two poles into one synthesis. Consequently, each synthesis necessarily presupposes another antithesis. In other words, dialectical progress always remains open and has no end. Therefore, as Kierkegaard critically observed, Hegel's absolute knowledge is still a relative approximation; that is, merely the thing which is "higher than."

Kierkegaard's existential dialectic, on the contrary, is not a gradual but a sudden grasp of the truth. Instead of unifying the two poles, the individual must choose one of them. It is an "either-or" choice. Between the real and the unreal, there is no continuity, but a deep abyss, over which one must jump at the risk of his life. The truth attained in this way is absolute. There is no gradual progress but the end itself. In other words, the starting point is already the goal. For Kierkegaard, truth was not to be asked, "What?" but "How?" This attitude toward truth seems to me to be very near to the Zen approach to Nirvāna.

It is said that great doubt, great conviction and great will are the three crucial elements needed to achieve awareness of the truth. Here, so-called calmness or insight is secondary. The greater the doubt, the greater the awareness must be, as the bigger the mass of ice, the more water when it melts. The conviction is that all human beings have the same possibility of achieving great awareness of the truth. The will is necessary to pursue awareness until it is fully realized. When these three elements are fully unified and have come to their fullest development, doubt breaks down and is suddenly transformed into full awareness. This is *satori* awareness. The term "enlightenment" seems to me to be unsuitable for this breakthrough experience. It sounds too passive, as though awareness comes from outside.

Te-shan was a well-known Buddhist scholar, especially in his study on *The Diamond Sūtra*.[4] One day he was travelling with one hundred volumes of his commentary on *The Diamond Sūtra* on his back and stopped in at a small tea house to have a snack (the literal translation of the Chinese "ten-chin" is to feed the mind). An old woman asked him, "Since you are a great scholar of *The Diamond Sūtra*, you know it is written there, 'The past mind cannot be grasped, neither can the present mind be gained, and the future mind as well cannot be acquired. . . .' Tell me,

[4] *The Diamond Sūtra* ranks with *The Heart Sūtra* as the most widely read of the Perfection of Wisdom (Prajñāpāramitā) texts.

then, which mind are you feeding?" He could not answer this question, and as a consequence he burned all his commentaries and came to face the great doubt in this simple question. He was advised by this woman to resolve the question under Master Lung-t'an nearby. After many years, one evening when Te-shan was leaving the master's hermitage, the master said, "It is getting dark outside, so you ought to take a lantern with you." When Te-shan took the lantern from his master, the master blew it out, and at that moment Te-shan was awakened. Wu-men comments symbolically on this great doubt situation in the first chapter of *Wu-men-kwan (The Gateless Gate)* as follows:[5]

> With three hundred and sixty joints and eighty-four thousand pores throughout your body, you have to be concerned with the koan Mu. All day and all night you should devote yourself to it without any thought of nihilistic nothingness or being and nonbeing. In due course, you will come to the stage where you may seem to be drinking a burning mass of iron and are unable to disgorge it. Therefore, you sweep away all illusions and delusions which existed before, and gradually you arrive at a mature state, in which the outer and the inner self naturally become one. And you alone will know yourself, just as a dumb man cannot tell his dreams. But once this great doubt breaks up, its force will surprise heaven and move the earth. . . .

In many cases of mystical religion, meditation and prayer are done for the purification of oneself, so that one may come "nearer" to reality. But in Zen meditation, the notion of progress toward reality is a foreign concept. In this respect, Zen meditation would not stand in the line of mysticism or quietism. But even within the Zen tradition, the Northern school of Chinese Zen (the gradual awareness of Master Shen-hsiu) and the Sōtō sect of Japanese Zen, which asserts that *satori* awareness is always realized in the practice of Zen training itself, are quite different

[5] The *Wu-men-kwan* is one of the great *koan* collections of Zen Buddhism. In Japanese it is known as the *Mumonkan*.

from Rinzai Zen. Rinzai Zen, to which I belong, is unique, emphasizing *prajñā*-wisdom much more than *dhyāna* meditation. When we compare Rinzai Zen practice to Theravāda meditation practice, we realize that there exists in the former the characteristics of Sino-Japanese Buddhism.

Monastic Training in Japanese Zen

The golden age of Chinese Zen in the T'ang Dynasty (618–907) declined as time went on because of its encounter with traditional Chinese teachings, such as Taoism or Confucianism. The unique vitality which earlier patriarchs manifested was weakened at the time Zen was introduced into Japan by those who came to Japan from China, or by those who went to China to study it. In my opinion, Japan seems to have been the most suitable field in which such cultivated and sophisticated Zen could develop. Though China and Japan are neighboring countries, their ways of life and thought are quite different. The Chinese way of life and thought is dynamic and has a boundless expanse; the Japanese, on the other hand, is static and small in scale. This contrast comes from the differences in geography and climate of the two countries. Chinese people, for example, use tables and chairs, but the Japanese sit on the floor. Or, a Chinese poem will be large scale in form and scope, but a Japanese poem is usually small in scale, yet very sensitive. Haiku poetry well illustrates the characteristics of the Japanese mind.

Japan is a small group of islands surrounded by vast reaches of water. Though the land is small, Japan has a great variety of natural phenomena created by the surrounding oceans. Consequently, the Japanese people are naturally sensitive and artistic. This characteristic of the Japanese people was suited to the adoption of the highly cultured form of Chinese Zen. Those monks who came from and went to China brought various kinds of Chinese culture with them which were preserved and developed in Zen monasteries.

Another unique quality of the Japanese people is a passionate and energetic character. As a modern Japanese philosopher points out, this trait may be influenced by the islands' volcanic nature. It is this character trait to which the martial nature of the Chinese Zen of the Sung Dynasty (960–1127) appealed, a trait developed in North China when Zen Buddhists had to meet strong attacks from rising new religions. Japanese feudal lords used Zen to instill a martial spirit in the people.

Zen was accepted and adapted from China by the Japanese people. Lacking space here to discuss the changing modes of Japanese Zen during its history, this section will deal with several unique characteristics of Japanese Rinzai Zen training practiced in Rinzai monasteries and formulated by the great Zen master Hakuin[6] two hundred years ago.

THE MIDWIFERY METHOD. As I mentioned before, great doubt, great conviction and great will are the three conditions for entering Zen training. Without even one of these a man cannot obtain the desired result. When these three elements are fully matured, however, a man is at once in the state of true awareness. When a man comes to the point of desiring the total solution of his doubt, at that moment it is accomplished. This is a principle of Zen training. A monk's desire, therefore, must be tested first of all. Hui-k'o's story of cutting off his arm before Bodhi-dharma demonstrates this intent. In a Zen monastery a monk's desire is tested by having him remain in a bowing posture in the entry hall for two days and by meditating alone facing the wall in a tiny room for five days. This is too severe a test for those who have only a weak desire to practice Zen. As wise men know, a man

[6] Hakuin Zenji was one of the greatest reformers of Rinzai Zen. His commentary on *The Heart Sūtra* appears in Chapter 7.

can pull a cow to the river but cannot make her drink. The cow cannot be forced to drink and will do so only through her own volition. We know that many missionary religions attempt to draw people to their religion and find it impossible to make them accept it simply because they are coerced. Keeping a cow away from the river is the best way to make her drink the fresh and beneficial water by herself when the right time comes.

The midwifery attitude of the student is most typically shown in the education given to a disciple by his Zen master. The lamp of Bodhi-dharma was transmitted through the so-called indirect transmission. Direct transmission by the master is not the way to full understanding of the truth for the disciple. Since the *satori* awareness of Zen is totally existential, it cannot be transmitted from the outside, but must be realized from the inside. The task of the master is, therefore, to let the student be awakened by the *dharma* truth through his own efforts. The master is, in this respect, not a truth-giver, but a midwife to the man who seeks the truth. Therefore, it is quite natural that the reply of the master to the disciple's question cannot be an ordinary answer. The master's answer comes out of his own awakened personality; therefore, the answer is fully meaningful only when the disciple arrives at that state of awareness. The master should wait until the disciple, through his own endurance, is awakened. He should not lead his disciple; otherwise, the disciple will not achieve his desired end. Yet, when the disciple's effort is greatest, the master should not hesitate to encourage him. This delicate turning point is called *sokutakunoki* in Zen terminology. *Soku* literally means "the picking of the shell of the egg from the outside by the mother hen." *Taku* means "picking the baby chick from the inside." The two acts must be performed at the same moment. If *soku* and *taku* are not performed simultaneously, the baby chick will not hatch. And just as this mysterious act is performed through the innate wisdom of the chicken, so it is done through the Zen master's wisdom; therefore, choosing a right master is especially important in Zen.

THE KOAN. Today in Japan only Rinzai Zen (not Sōtō Zen) uses the *koan* extensively. The *koan* may be described as a problem which is given by the master to his student. It is not a mathematical problem which must be solved logically but a tool by which the student arrives at the right understanding of the truth. The use of the *koan* originally began at the end of the T'ang Dynasty in China when patriarchal Zen was declining. *Koan* literally means "public document." Public here indicates the universality of the truth which has been grasped by all the patriarchs. The *koan* is, therefore, a paradigm by which the Zen student reflects upon his state of mind. The unique acts of particular patriarchs, their dialogues with disciples or the most important events of their *satori* awareness have naturally been chosen for the traditional *koan*. In the early days of Japanese Rinzai Zen, these *koan*-s were divided into three groups: *richi*, or theoretical knowledge; *kikan*, or practical application; and *kojyo*, or ascendance. *Richi* comes mainly from the Buddha's words, as for example, "All beings have Buddha-nature." *Kikan* was taken from a partiarch's act or spoken word, such as striking with the Zen stick and uttering, "Kwatsu!" Another example would be Yün-men's famous phrase, "The mountain goes over the ocean"; or Daio's "A muddy ox flies in the sky, and a stone horse walks into the water." *Kojyo* is the group of *koan*-s by which the student can transcend the preceding stages of *richi* or *kikan*. Examples of this type of *koan* are the following: "The willow is green, the flower is red" and "The eye is horizontal, but the nose is vertical."

The *koan* system currently employed in Japanese Rinzai Zen monasteries was systematized by the great Master Hakuin, who revitalized Japanese Rinzai Zen about two hundred years ago. This system consists of eighteen hundred *koan*-s divided into five groups. After a student has passed through all the *koan*-s, he is still required to pass through *matsugo-no-rokan*, or the "final gate." After fifteen or twenty years of hard discipline using these *koan*-s, it is said that at most only one student out of hundreds can totally embody the Buddha's truth.

MEDITATION IN MOVEMENT. "A day of no work is a day of no eating," is a strict rule of the monastery. This phrase can actually be traced back to the Chinese Zen master Po-chang. The idea is typically Chinese and quite unthinkable in India. There are two possible reasons for this. First, the Chinese way of life is more active than in India. The Indian's speculative way of living is not acceptable to the Chinese mind which is more positive, concrete, individual, realistic and extroverted than the Indian mind, which is more negative, abstract, universal, metaphysical and introverted. This contrast between the Indian and Chinese minds was manifest when Buddhism was introduced into China. Even Nāgārjuna's philosophy of Emptiness[7] for example, was transformed by the Zen master Chao-chou (778–897) into the practical mood of Nothingness. The Buddha-mind is "a great compassionate mind" for the Indian, but for the Chinese it is a "a scoop of dried feces" or "three pounds of flax." Master Nan-ch'uan was once asked by Chao-chou, "What is Tao?" He replied, "The ordinary mind is Tao." A monk asked Chao-chou, "Why did Bodhi-dharma come from the East?" His answer was, "An oak tree in the garden!"

The second reason for the above rule may come from the actual way of the monastic life. When Chinese Zen became prosperous in the T'ang Dynasty, many monks gathered around the great Zen masters and established large communities. At the time of Master Po-chang (749–814), the monks, in order to maintain these communities,

---

[7] Nāgārjuna, who flourished in India in the second century A.D., is the founder of the Mādhyamika School of Buddhist philosophy which has had a decisive influence on Zen.

established communal regulations. The text of the Zen monastic regulations is known as *Po-chang Ch'ing-kuei,* and even today it regulates life in Japanese Zen monasteries. Hard daily tasks were required of the five hundred monks under Po-chang; in this way, meditation was important not only in sitting but in the form of hard work.

Moreover, since Zen Buddhism follows the Mahāyāna Buddhist tradition, it affirms that practices such as meditation should be included as part of daily life. For this reason Zen cannot be called simply quietism or mysticism. For the Zen Buddhist, real quietness is not gained in the opposite condition of noise and movement, but is beyond such relative states. Quietness of mind is really an absolute, so that even in noisiness real quietness can exist, if only the mind is quiet and vice versa.

Today in Japanese Zen monasteries monks are assigned daily tasks, such as cleaning the grounds or washing their clothes, cultivating the garden where they raise their food, chopping wood for fuel and begging in town for donations. While performing their tasks, the monks keep constantly in mind the statement, "Meditation in movement has a thousand times more value than meditation in sitting."

STRICT RULES. Rinzai Zen monasteries have been operated according to strict rules ever since Master Hakuin reformed the way of Zen monastic life. For some people, it may appear ascetic. For example, in the early days, the monasteries used a fireplace in the center of the meditation hall during the winter. We find the record of a special discourse by a Zen master on the subject of lighting this fire in old Zen documents. But today, monks are not allowed to have a heater or even to wear socks while walking in snow. Japanese Zen, in this sense, is a religion of discipline, through which man tries to change his personality. To become a Buddha, an awakened one, a man needs unusual discipline. To break through the ordinary self, a man must keep his whole being in a state of ulti-

mate tension, wherein any additional external force will
be sufficient to bring about a breakthrough. To the Japanese mind a similar thing happens when a man draws a
bow to its maximum tautness, where only the slightest
breath of air would be sufficient to increase the stress on
the bow to the breaking point. The following are examples
of these strict rules:

1. Monks should not leave the monastery on private
business.

2. Monks should not speak or laugh loudly; whispering
is also not permitted, especially in the meditation hall, the
dining hall and the bath.

3. Monks should not waste water. (Only three cups of
water, for example, may be used for washing the face.)

4. Monks should not move carelessly but must constantly distinguish between movement and stillness.

5. The taking of a bath and shaving of the head are
allowed only once every five days.

6. In a twenty-four hour period monks should eat only
three times and drink tea only twice.

7. Monks must be punctual in rising and in going to
bed.

8. No reading of or listening to anything other than
Zen texts is allowed.

9. At least twice a day a monk must consult with his
master.

10. Monks must beg every three days.

One week of intensive training (*sesshin*) is held monthly
throughout the year. In the summer the monks must rise
at three in the morning and perform *zazen* until nine in
the evening. The following is the daily schedule for this
special training period:

Rise	3:00 a.m.	Breakfast	5:00
Morning		Zazen	5:30
service	3:30 a.m.	Consultation	6:00
Zazen	4:30	Zazen	6:30

Master's discourse	8:00	Evening service	4:00
Consultation	9:30	Supper	4:30
Lunch	10:00	Zazen	5:00
Rest time	10:30 a.m.	Consultation	7:00
Consultation	1:00 p.m.	Zazen	8:30
Zazen	1:30	Retire	9:00

DEEDS OF SECRET VIRTUE. We know that a good deed is easy to perform in public, but it is difficult to perform in private. Such "secret virtues" are required of the monk in training his personality. Why is this so important? According to Oriental teaching, one may acquire merit when he performs a secret deed of virtue. In other words, if one does something with the expectation of reward, nothing will be received. In this context, we should recall the following story: When Bodhi-dharma came to China, the King of Wu interviewed him and asked, "I have built a hundred temples throughout the country and sponsored a number of priests and nuns. What kind of merit can I expect to receive?" Bodhi-dharma replied, "No merit." In this encounter with the King, Bodhi-dharma divined the King's inner motive and then departed. The idea that no reward should be expected for one's good behavior is central to Oriental moral teaching. "Think neither good nor evil." How one behaves is the substance of Buddhist moral law. Even if one behaves well, he will be wrong if he is conscious of doing good and evil. The deed, on the other hand, performed with no designation of good or evil is always absolutely good and pure.

So-called good behavior to the Chinese and Japanese mind is to follow the natural law and not to waste what is given by nature. Through such good behavior, one can be a man of virtue. In this sense, our deeds are not evaluated by human, moral judgment. Publicity, therefore, is not our concern. The above is the basic principle of the deed of secret virtue. In the monastery, monks are encouraged to practice this as a part of their personal training.

Two monks were on their way to a temple where they were going to ask a great master about the *dharma* truth. When they came to the river which flowed through the temple, they found the leaf of a vegetable floating on the water. On seeing it, they decided not to visit the master and turned away. This story demonstrates how important the idea of secret virtue is for monks.

One summer evening, the Zen master Gisan was taking a bath. As the water was too hot, he asked a disciple to bring some additional cold water. The disciple threw some of the hot water away and brought back a full bucket of cold water from the river. Seeing these acts the master scolded his young disciple very severely, because he had wasted the water, and said, "If you had given that water to the glory of the evening, it would have been very pleased and so also would have been the water. No matter how you train yourself in doing *zazen*, you will fail to become a man of virtue." At a later time, this disciple became a great Zen master and took the name of Tekisui, "a drop of water."

The biography of the famous Sōtō Zen priest, Santoka, records his deed of secret virtue. One day someone visited Santoka's hermitage. He served a meager supper to the guest. "Why don't you eat?" the guest asked. "I have no extra bowl, so I will eat later," replied the master. After they had finished their supper, Santoka cleaned his bowl with the water which he had used for washing the rice. After cleaning the bowl, he washed his body and the entire room, then at last used the water for the flowers in the garden. He was not a miser but a man who knew the gifts of nature. This kind of spirit and behavior toward nature is required of the monks in a monastery.

THE GREAT DEATH EXPERIENCE. As I mentioned before, the purpose of *zazen* is to break through the shell of the ego and realize the formless self which is identical with the whole universe. To this end, what must take place is a total revolution within the person involved. A gradual approach to reality is useless, as we have seen before. Decision, the will to jump over the abyss which lies between unreality and reality, is necessary. But a man must devote himself to achieving this goal at the risk of his life. Such an experience is possible through the use of the *koan*.

In a Japanese Rinzai Zen monastery, each monk is given a specific *koan*, according to the maturity of his mind. The first *koan* given to such a man is usually Joshu's "Mu," or sometimes Hakuin's "Sound of One Hand Clapping." Once, a monk asked Joshu, "Does a dog have Buddha-nature?" Joshu replies, "Mu!" To concentrate one's whole existence on Joshu's utterance is what is required of the monk. Twice a day or several times a day during the special training weeks, a monk must consult with his master, in order to demonstrate how much he has resolved the mystery of the *koan*. We are often surprised to see how many answers are possible for such an irrational question. But after all these possibilities have been shown to be inadequate by the master, the monk must naturally come to the stage where he realizes that there is no answer. He, therefore, hesitates to see the master without an answer and stays at his place in the meditation hall. But he is obliged to go to the master's room at the insistence of the elder monks. For the monk who has nothing to say in front of the master, the latter, often encouraging him in a harsh and scolding manner, has him return to the meditation hall. In this way the master and the elder monks cooperate in pushing the young monks forward. Such behavior is usually called, "The Deed of Great Compassion." It seems violent at the time, but later on the monk will be thankful for their encouragement which helped him to achieve the deepest awareness of reality.

The monk's doubt about the *koan* becomes a total, existential doubt, and the monk himself becomes a great mass of doubt. In this state he loses his consciousness of time and space, and of the subject-object dichotomy. All names, concepts, definitions, value and moral judgments are driven out of his consciousness. He loses even his consciousness of being. Therefore, this state is called, "The Great Death." His facial expressions dissolve, and his face becomes a mask. He cannot move or stand or eat by himself, a truly dangerous stage of existence. Some Zen masters, reminiscing, have described this experience in such terms as the following: "It was like sitting in the midst of a thousand-mile square mass of ice," or "It was like being in a completely black universe." This dark, dangerous stage of being is a crucial stage to pass through in order to prepare for the brilliance of the awakened state. This could be compared to a dark tunnel without which man cannot reach the opposite side of the mountain.

For this kind of experience, monks need the help of another person. Herein lies the significance of monastic life. There is no private room in the Zen monastery. Zen is, so to speak, group mysticism. The mind of the individual monk is polished by the others. *Sessa takuma*, literally "rubbing one another in order to become polished," demonstrates this aspect of the process of awakening. In Rinzai Zen monasteries, the monks sit facing each other in the meditation hall, while in Sōtō Zen monasteries, the monks sit alone, facing a wall. Here we see the uniqueness of Rinzai meditation. The master's task is the encouragement, rather than the instruction of Zen. He, therefore, tends to be harsh rather than mild; his compassion appears in the form of severe coolness toward the monk. "There should be no friendliness in the search for the *dharma* truth" is written on the Zen stick used to strike the monk for encouragement.

One day about fifty years ago a group of monks were walking single file back to the monastery. When they came to a hill and saw an old man drawing a cart up the slope, the youngest monk, who was at the end of the line, helped to push the cart. Just at that moment the master who was leading the group, turned around and observed the incident. Upon returning to the monastery, the master called this young monk to his room and said, "You are not a suitable person to practice *zazen*. Your mind is always moving about. You would do better to leave the monastery and do something else." The young monk was then thrown out of the gate of the monastery. The monk, however, was not such a simple-minded person as to give up this way of life. He continued to meditate at the gate for several days and nights. Finally he was allowed to return to the monastery. This is the story of one of the greatest Japanese Zen masters.

SATORI AWARENESS. The experience of *satori* awareness is the ultimate goal of monastic life. Every moment of monastic daily life points to this genuine experience. Therefore, a monk decides to stay in the monastery until his goal is fully reached. *Satori* experience is not a shallow psychological or emotional experience, but a total existential rebirth of the being. This kind of deep experience is only made possible by the absolute negation of the old being, when the great death of the old self is fully achieved. Absolute affirmation of the real, newborn self necessarily comes out of an absolute negation of the old self.

In the early days of Zen Buddhism in China, a monk often came to consult with his master for the first time filled with doubt. In other words, the monk was already in that darkness from which there is the full possibility of awakening. Thus one word or some small event was a sufficient catalyst for breaking up the darkness. Yün-men, for example, was awakened at the moment his master Bokuyu shut his temple gate to refuse him entry and broke his leg. Kyōgen was awakened by the little sound of a stone hitting the bamboo when he was sweeping the garden. Reiun was awakened by a camelia flower falling to earth. Jyakuyo was awakened when his master blew out the light of the lantern in the dark evening. Although all these events are small, their significance proved to be profound.

Japanese Rinzai Zen training is the reexperience through the *koan* of the great experiences of the Zen patriarchs and the realization of the real self in which all the transmitters of Bodhi-dharma have found reality. The deeper the man's darkness of mind, the greater his awakening will be. The more tightly a bow is drawn, the more easily it is broken by a single blow.

DISCIPLINE AFTER SATORI AWARENESS. The whole course of Zen training is divided into two parts: discipline upward and discipline downward. From the awareness of doubt to *satori* awareness is the former; the discipline afterwards is the latter and is much more important. *Satori* awareness is a universal experience and not uniquely different for each individual. Therefore, there is a great distance between the universal *satori* experience, occurring in the depths of the individual personality and the self-conscious existence characterizing most people. There needs to be a strong effort to integrate genuine *satori* experience into one's own personal character; otherwise one may be drawn back to one's former self. This effort is called *shonen sozoku* or "continuity of right thinking." This discipline is important to "remove the smell of *satori*." Shoju-rōjin, a Zen master of Hakuin's youth, speaks reminiscently of the difficulty in practicing *shonen sozoku*. He writes, "In my experience, it has been very hard to keep hold of the right thinking of *satori* awareness until I reached the age of eighty. But now I have come to find the ideal state of *satori* awareness where I need no effort to hold it, where, indeed, right thinking follows by itself." Confucius likewise says, "At the age of eighty, a man ought to be one who can behave however he likes, yet all that he does is within the law."

The Zen experience which is found in total freedom from any concept or definition or degree or name should also be free from even the Zen experience itself ("the stink of Zen"). In other words, we may say that a real saint cannot be distinguished from "the butcher, the baker, the candlestick maker." You may have seen the ten ox-herding pictures, a very rare Zen text detailing the progressive states of a seeker of truth. The last picture, which portrays the final stage of seeking the truth, is accompanied by the following commentary and poem:

> Entering the City with Bliss-Bestowing Hands
> His thatched cottage gate is closed, and even the wisest knows him not.
> No glimpses of his inner life are to be caught, for he goes on his own way without following the steps of the ancient sages. Carrying a gourd, he goes out into the market; leaning against a staff, he comes home.
> He is found in the company of wine-bibers and butchers; he and they are changed into Buddhas.
> Bare-chested and bare-footed, he comes out into the market-place.
> Daubed with mud and ashes, how broadly he smiles!
> There is no need for the miraculous power of the gods,
> For he touches, and lo! the dead trees are in full bloom.

The ideal state of Zen personality is beyond the distinction between the sacred and the profane. The absolutely sacred transcends the so-called religious value of sacred. In other words, the really sacred should exist in the midst of secularity. Therefore there is no problem of secularization or desanctification in Zen Buddhism. The highest reality is to be found in the midst of daily secular life, not in a place existing far away from the secular realm such as a church. It is for this reason that Zen meditation should be spread throughout the modern secular world. This is why it is said that meditation is more important in action than in quietness.

Role of Rinzai Zen Training in Daily Life

Since Japanese Zen Buddhism follows the line of Mahāyāna Buddhism, the idea of the Bodhisattva or the Buddhist Saint is the most central doctrine. In the Buddhist theory of the Ten Stages of Being,[8] the Bodhisattva is just one step lower than the Buddha. Originally, Bodhisattva was a title referring to Gautama, the historical Buddha, in his several previous lives in which he prepared to become the Buddha. He became the Buddha when he came to this world to live his final life. In the Mahāyāna tradition, all who practice Buddhism are called Bodhisattvas. A Bodhisattva, therefore, is a person who seeks upward to be a Buddha and yet remains in his Bodhisattva stage in order to save by "downward" discipline all sentient beings. "Those who practice *zazen* meditation must have great compassion in order to save all sentient beings" is the first creed for a Zen follower (cf. *Zazen-gi*). The wisdom of *satori* awareness and the compassion arising from *satori* should be one.

A man who has become aware must, therefore, both for his own sake and for the sake of other sentient beings, continue forever his downward discipline. We may suppose that it is because of this ideal of the Bodhisattva that Zen masters have created a unique Zen culture. The expression in daily work of the awakened personality is necessary, first, to perfect the personality of the master and, second, to force the people around him into an awakened spirit.

The expression of the inexpressible naturally creates a unique result. This is the essence of Zen culture. Zen

[8] The Ten Stages of the Bodhisattva way are described in the *Daśabhūmika Sūtra*. In the tenth stage (the Cloud of the True Norm) the Bodhisattva has all the powers and characteristics of a Buddha.

culture must be the expression of the inexpressible something which comes out of the awakened, selfless self. To understand this statement in any full degree, it is necessary to find the same state of mind which exists in the minds of the creators of the culture. However, we see today a misunderstanding of Zen culture. People tend to regard Zen as merely one type of culture. They like to call it "Zen culture" and even try to imitate its uniqueness. Because Zen itself is formless, there exists in Zen nothing so definite as to deserve the name of "Zen" or "Zen culture." The expression of the inexpressible and the form of the formless are only tentatively called Zen.

In this context, I would like to distinguish between Zen and Zen Buddhism as culture. Zen itself is a formless thing. Zen Buddhism is the social and historical formulation, determined by the history and climate through which Zen has been transmitted, of the formless. Zen culture at its beginning was created in the monastery in order to encourage the monks in their training. Dr. S. Hisamatsu[9] picks seven characteristics of Zen artistic culture and relates them to the essence of Zen.

1. non-symmetry	formlessness
2. simplicity	non-miscellany
3. nobility of starkness	non-definition
4. naturalness	no-mind
5. mysteriousness	bottomless
6. trans-secular	non-obstacle
7. quietness	non-movement

These characteristics of Zen culture function as a kind of *koan* for the monks who live surrounded by Zen arts to help them understand the deep meaning of Zen. Zen painting, architecture, gardening and all other aspects of Zen culture have been formulated in this way within the

[9] Dr. Shin'ichi Hisamatsu, former professor of philosophy at Kyoto University, is Director of the F.A.S. Zen Institute, Kyoto, Japan.

complexity of Japanese culture. Zen culture as we can see comes out of Zen and, thus, is an expression of Zen itself.

From my understanding of the Western tradition, culture seems to be thought of as separate from and transcended by religion. Philosophically speaking, the human consciousness starts with the precultural state, where the subject and the object are not yet distinctly separated. Man's self-consciousness is still not awakened. This is the world of sense where the objective world is reflected on through the senses. But, as soon as man begins to be aware of himself, the self-consciousness divides the world into a subject and an object. The objective world is thought to be a product of self-consciousness. By this act of the conscious self, man tends to objectify the outer, external world so much that his subjectivity is finally hidden behind his objectivity. This is the present condition of culture. Cultural values, like truth in philosophy and science, goodness in morality and beauty in art are all objectified objectivity.

Man, however, wants to recover his subjectivity from this subject-object dichotomy, and it is religion which serves man in the attainment of this highest state of consciousness. The value of religion is in its holiness. This value is not speculative but existentially real. It is in holiness that man identifies his religious feeling. Thus, in religion, man can recover his subjectivity in relationship to this absolute value. Religion is possible only when man overcomes his cultural conditioning. Here, then, is the basic conflict between religion and culture, religion and science, and the sacred and the profane.

In Zen Buddhism it is necessary for man to return to the state even before that of the precultural, in which even man's senses are no longer present. Such a state is almost like death itself; therefore, it is called the great death experience. And that moment when man is reborn from such a state into the world of the senses, but now with a genuine consciousness (Buddha-nature), is called the *satori* experience. This is Zen. It follows that our daily life should be the expression of an awakened consciousness and that there should be no conflict between culture and religion. D. T. Suzuki's[10] explanation, "In the first state of man's consciousness, mountain is mountain, ocean is ocean; in the second state mountain is ocean, ocean is mountain; and in the last state, again, mountain is mountain and ocean is ocean," is understandable.

Paradoxically, then, only because the self is absolutely negated in the great death experience can we transcend both the sacred and the profane and absolutely affirm our secular, daily acts in Zen. Today in the West, Christianity seems to be struggling greatly with the secular, but Zen is not having any difficulty because it creates in a positive manner meaning within the secular world. To live in this "secular city" we cannot deny nor concede to the secular. Thus, what we are seeking today must be the ability to live in this secular city by transcending it. We can have neither attachment nor detachment. Nonattachment seems to be the only possibility, and this attitude of nonattachment toward the secular is what Zen followers practice.

[10] D. T. Suzuki is the person most responsible for the interest in Zen Buddhism in this country. He has translated many Zen texts and written many books about Zen (e.g., *Introduction to Zen Buddhism, Manual of Zen Buddhism*).

6

Rules for Contemplation
in Sitting

The *Zazen-gi* (*On Zazen Meditation*) is a brief meditation manual going back to eighth century China. Its roots in the traditions of Buddhist meditation are much deeper, however, and the reader of the *Zazen-gi* will note similarities with the *Satipaṭṭhāna Sutta* of Theravāda Buddhism. In both cases there are instructions to withdraw to a quiet place, assume a meditation posture and begin by concentrating on respiration. The intention of this meditation practice is also similar in both texts, namely, to be aware of the arising and passing away of all phenomena. In the *Zazen-gi* such awareness gradually overcomes the "chain of becoming" and one naturally becomes "non-separate" or unified.

The chapter begins with the Reverend Eshin Nishimura's translation of the text of the *Zazen-gi* and then proceeds to a series of six lectures on the text by Mumon Yamada Roshi (see Acknowledgments) also translated by the Reverend Nishimura. These lectures point out that the *Zazen-gi* is still very much a part of the living tradition of Zen Buddhism in Japan.

Zazen-Gi

Bodhisattvas who study *prajñā*-wisdom[1] first must have deep compassion for all beings and deep longing to save all of them. They must practice *samādhi*[2] meditation with great care; and they must promise to ferry these sentient beings over to the other shore, refusing to practice *zazen* only for their own emancipation. Now, one needs to be free of distraction from external sense objects and of mental disturbances, so that body and mind are one and movement and stillness are not separated. Taking meals, one eats neither too much nor too little; sleeping neither too briefly nor too long.

When one wishes to begin *zazen*, he places a thick cushion in a quiet place, wears a robe and belt rather loosely, and puts all things about himself in good order. Then one sits with legs crossed in the lotus posture: First one places the right foot on the left thigh and then the left foot over the right thigh; or one may sit in a half-crossed position in which only the left foot rests upon the other thigh. Secondly, one places the right hand on the left foot, palm facing upward; then one places the left hand on the right palm so that the faces of the thumbs push against each other. Gradually one raises the body and repeatedly moves it backward and forward, to left and right, so that one may find a balanced sitting posture for the body.

The body should not lean to either side, not forward or backward. The bones of the hips, back and skull rest atop one another like a *stūpa* [or pagoda]. Also the body should not be so upright that someone else would feel

---

[1] *Prajñā* refers to the wisdom of enlightenment. To designate the special character of this wisdom the translator uses the term, *prajñā*-wisdom.

[2] *Samādhi* can be rendered in various ways, e.g. concentration. Here it refers to the kind of meditation practice suggested by the *Zazen-gi*.

uneasy seeing it. Keep ears and shoulders, nose and navel parallel to one another; the tongue should touch the upper jaw, both lips and teeth being closed; eyes should remain slightly open so that one avoids falling asleep. If one comes to *dhyāna*-meditation[3] its power is incomparable.

In the old days there was a monk of high attainment who always practiced *zazen* with his eyes open. There was also a Zen master called Entsu-zenji of Houn-ji who used to scold those who practiced *zazen* with eyes closed. He called them an "evil cave of the black mountain." A deep significance lies here. Only a man of attainment would know it. Once the physical posture has been well-ordered and the breath regulated, one must push forth the abdomen. One thinks not of good and evil; receiving into one's awareness each moment of illusion as it rises in the mind, then they disappear. Gradually forgetting the chain of becoming, one naturally becomes nonseparate. This is the core of the *zazen* method of meditation. In my opinion, *zazen* meditation is the most humane way to *dharma* truth.[4] Nevertheless, many persons become ill. This might result from lack of care in the practice of *zazen*.

If one were acquainted with its deep meaning, his body would be naturally relaxed, his spirit refreshed, his right thinking clarified, and the taste of *dharma* would deepen his mind. He would become quiet, clean, and joyous. Or, if he has awakened, he will be as the dragon in water or the tiger crouching on his mountain.[5] Or again, even if one has not yet reached this awareness, he has not wasted his energy—just as the man who blows on a fire with the help of the wind. In any case, one should follow his own judgment as to his level of awareness and never deceive himself.

[3] *Dhyāna* in Sanskrit (*jhāna* in Pāli) is often rendered as trance. Here it refers to the higher stages of *samādhi* meditation.
[4] *Dharma* (*dhamma* in Pāli) in this case refers to the truth as taught by Buddhism.
[5] The dragon and tiger are symbolic of extraordinary power.

Yet the higher one stands on the way, the more varied the evils which obstruct it—some enticing one ahead, others pushing one back. However, once awareness has been realized, all these obstacles cannot remain. The forms of evil are clarified in detail in such texts as the *Surangama Mahā-sūtra, Shikan Investigation* by the great master Tendai (538–597) and the *Text on Practice and Awareness* by the Zen master Keiho-shumitsu (780–841).[6] Those who would prepare their defenses against these evils must know of them in advance.

When one wishes to come out of meditation, he should move his body gradually; he should stand up deliberately, without hurry. After coming out of meditation, one should utilize skill in each moment to hold his *samādhi* power as carefully as a mother holds her baby. In this way *samādhi* power will be matured.

The practice of *zazen* is one of the most urgent needs of all men. If one has not achieved the complete quietness of *zazen*, he may find that he is helpless in the crisis situations of life. Therefore, to find the jewel one must calm the waves; it would be hard to get it if one stirred up the water. Where meditation-water is clear and calm, the mind-jewel will naturally be visible. Thus the *Vaipūlya-pūrnabodhi-prāpta* Sūtra says, "All Wisdom of non-attachment and clarity comes from *zazen.*" Or again the *Sad-dharma-pundarīka* Sūtra reads: "Let one's mind concentrate in silence and let it remain motionless like Mt. Sumeru."

It has been made clear that one can go beyond only by this quiet process; and it is only by one's *samādhi* power that one is enabled to die while sitting or standing in meditation. Even if one makes a life-long effort to become fully aware of truth, he still cannot avoid stumbling. How then can the lazy man who postpones *zazen* practice pre-

---

[6] The three texts are meditation Sūtras (Sutta in Pāli).

pare for *karma?*[7] Therefore, the ancestors have said, "If one has no *samādhi* power by which to conquer death, he must blindly return to the darkness and float eternally on the ocean of life-and-death." However, O my Zen brothers, read this text again and again so that both you and other beings may at the same moment attain real awakening.

LECTURES ON ZAZEN-GI
BY MUMON YAMADA ROSHI

I. *Everybody Is a Bodhisattva*

Today we are going to enter another rainy season meditation term which will last exactly ninety days. To live together through this meditation term in one place is our precious tradition which has been handed down through centuries in Zen monasteries since Buddha's time. As the most important text for those who begin to practice Zen meditation for the first time, I would like to read the *Zazen-gi* with you.

Originally this text was included in the *Po-chang Ch'ing-kuei* (a prospectus of Zen monastic life) compiled by Po-chang Huai-hai (720–814), a great Chinese Zen master. Later on it was scattered and lost but recompiled again during the Yüan dynasty (1280–1368). Therefore, our present text is not necessarily Po-chang's original, and the author is unknown. However, for a Buddhist school like Zen which asserts *zazen* as its prime principle, this text relating the *zazen* method is the most important.

First of all, *za*, in Chinese literally means to sit, and Zen comes from the Sanskrit term *dhyāna* which actually means to contemplate. Therefore, *zazen* means to contemplate in sitting. Recently somebody asked me, "Is it useful to practice *zazen* even for a layman?" I replied, "No, since man is an animal, for him to walk is more

[7] *Karma* (*kamma* in Pāli) refers here to a person's fate determined by his own actions.

normal. However, it is rather doubtful if we see around us a man who is walking in the true sense. Are not many people simply walking from force of habit? Are they not moving simply by drawing and extending their legs? Though they seem very busy in their daily life, how many people are walking their own ways with a deep investigation into life?"

"At the time of World War II, I heard a funny story. Somebody saw many people standing in queues awaiting their turn and thought that there must be something rare. After a long while he found himself waiting for somebody's funeral ceremony. If one enters college because others do, or marries because the other does, his life will not be his own. To avoid such a stupid way of life, man must stop himself to discover the right way to advance. To stop and think quietly in such a way is nothing but *zazen*." My answer seemed to satisfy my guest, and he left delighted.

Then what does one think of while sitting quietly? What he should think of is his real self who sees, listens, laughs and cries. To think "Who am I?" is *zazen*. The result is the realization that not to think is the best thinking. In other words, the thing which one does not need to think of at all is his real self. This is exactly what the Japanese Zen master Dōgen once said: "Think what you do not think." You might then say, "If one does not need to think, then why practice *zazen*?" But this is not correct. The mind is not so simple. It is filled with so-called instinct, habit, thought, intellectual judgment and so on. These do not comprise the real self, but they delude the real self by arising from somewhere like a cloud or fog; therefore, they might be called illusion or ignorance. Clarifying such a mind by quiet sitting, we will find the real self where there is no fog of illusion nor any cloud of ignorance. To live brightly, correctly, and vitally in this realized true self is Zen itself. For this purpose, *zazen* is the best way to acquire this quiet thinking and clarified mind.

There are four meditation postures: walking, standing,

sitting, and lying down. The sitting posture is the most quiet of these four. To sit, thinking quietly, clarifying the mind, entering the state of no-mind where we do not think of anything will be called *zazen*. The ancient people said, "Not to think anything is the only training for being in Buddha." To sit on this very ground is training in identifying the self with the whole universe. The Chinese character for sitting is symbolized by two men who are sitting on the ground. In the Western tradition heaven seems to me to be the secret place of God, the earth, dirty and sinful. However, in Oriental religion we find the light of the Buddha in sitting on this dirty earth. To grasp the wisdom of emancipation amid the dust and suffering through sitting is *zazen*.

Gi literally means rule. The rules for *zazen* have been handed down to us by our ancestors who found the best through their long experience.

> Bodhisattvas who study *prajñā*-wisdom first must have deep compassion for all beings and deep longing to save all of them. They must practice *samādhi* meditation with great care; and they must promise to ferry these sentient beings over to the other shore, refusing to practice *zazen* only for their own emancipation.

"Bodhisattvas who study *prajñā*-wisdom" are nothing more than we Zen trainers seeking for the wisdom of awakenness. All those who begin to have the upward desire to discover the truth and simultaneously the downward desire for service to all mankind are, without exception, Bodhisattvas. Mahāyāna Buddhism, that is to say, the way of the Bodhisattva, is a so-called layman's Buddhism. Its core is the lay people who are to be saved in the midst of daily life in society, business and home. You will usually see Bodhisattvas with long hair wearing such decorations as necklaces, earrings or bracelets. This actually symbolizes the Indian aristocratic image by which we recognize these Bodhisattvas as the symbol of lay people.

Among the Bodhisattvas we see that only Jizō[8] has a shaved head. He is known to be the Bodhisattva who incarnates himself in all six worlds of living beings—the worlds of hell, evil, animals and so on—in order to save even those who are suffering from deepest agony. Such people in extreme agony would find their savior more certainly in a saint with a shaved head who has thrown away his desire than in one who is enjoying his luxurious secular life. In this respect, a Bodhisattva *priest* is also required. As you might know, saint Shinran (1173–1262), the founder of the Pure Land faith in Japanese Buddhism, never took off his priest's robe or surplice though he strongly supported lay Buddhism.[9]

All who promise to seek the wisdom of upward awakenness and to serve all human beings are without exception Bodhisattvas. Those laymen and women who join our *zazen* are also Bodhisattvas—Bodhisattvas who study *prajñā*-wisdom.

In the Buddha mind there are the two aspects of wisdom and compassion just as the sun shines making light and heat. To seek for *bodhi* (wisdom of awareness) upward is to train oneself to seek Buddha's wisdom, and to save the sentient being downward is to practice Buddha's compassion. We cannot realize the Buddha's wisdom unless we are awakened to it by ourselves, but Buddha's compassion is possible to have in our own selves whenever we desire it. It is wonderful to know that "Compassion is not far from us. It is here in our hands whenever we want to practice."

My master Seisetsu Roshi used to say, "We Zen brothers who are wearing monkish robes with *shukin* belt and covered with surplice can be compared to the gift wrapped

---

[8] Jizō, the Japanese form of the Bodhisattva Kṣitigarbha, is especially venerated as the protector of children.

[9] The Pure Land School (Jōdo Shin Shu) founded by Shinran is the largest of the traditional Buddhist sects in Japan today. It flourished along with Zen in the Kamakura Period.

up with special paper and tied with a ribbon to present ourselves to Buddha. This style itself is the worshipping style for all human beings. Therefore, you must care for such a body as that which is not yours any more." In this way, you must have great devotion to dispel all human suffering. In short, this is the Bodhisattva's vow: "Though there are innumerable sentient beings, I vow to save all." When one utters such a great vow, he at once achieves his real awakening. He is already Buddha or Bodhisattva although he has not been awakened yet.

Seisetsu Roshi was studying under his master Ryoen Roshi, at Tokko-in temple in his youth. One day Seisetsu Roshi was scolded by the master who said, "Such a dishonest man as you would be better off to make a pilgrimage to the secret Buddhist places in Shikoku island. (There are eighty-eight secret places in Shikoku island even today.) He started to make his pilgrimage and one day came to the bridge called Toyo-no-hashi (Bridge of Ten Nights) which is said to have been built by the ancient Buddhist saint Kōbō-daishi.[10] There is a custom that travelers must take off their straw sandals whenever they cross it. But the young monk Seisetsu, considering that he had exactly the same qualities as the saint, walked over it with sandals. When he reached the other side of the bridge, he found the notice-board on which saint Kōbō-daishi's poem was written as follows:

> Suffering people passing over from their life-travel,
> The bridge so busy that one night seems as ten.

Reading this, tears welled in his eyes and he turned back to cross the bridge barefoot. It is important to note that he was so innocent. Dōgen Zenji, the founder of Japanese Sōtō Zen, writes,

[10] Kōbō-daishi (774–835) was one of the founders of Shingon Buddhism in Japan during the Nara Period.

Even though I might not become Buddha because
  of my ignorance,
I vow to save all others since I am a priest.

In this way, those Bodhisattvas who study *prajñā*-wisdom,
whether priest or layman, must first of all have great compassion to save all sentient beings, even though they are
innumerable, and to make of them Buddhas.

To practice *zazen* must not be for one's own self but for
all human beings in this society. It should not be done
only for the comfort of oneself, much less for one's success
in life. To do *zazen* for such a purpose will cause you to
fall into hell and be charged by the lord of hell for every
meal you have ever eaten.

II. Movement and Stillness Are Not Separated

[For the achievement of emancipation through Zazen]:
Now, one needs to be free of distractions from external sense
objects and of mental disturbances, so that body and mind
are one and movement and stillness are not separated. Taking
meals, one eats neither too much nor too little; sleeping
neither too briefly nor too long.

When one wishes to begin *zazen,* he places a thick cushion
in a quiet place, wears a robe and belt rather loosely, and
puts all things about himself in good order. Then one sits
with legs crossed in the lotus posture: First one places the
right foot on the left thigh and then the left foot over the
right thigh; or one may sit in a half-crossed sitting position
in which only the left foot rests upon the other thigh.
Secondly, one places the right hand on the left foot, palm
facing upward; then one places the left hand on the right
palm so that the faces of the thumbs push against each other.
Gradually one raises the body and repeatedly moves it backward and forward, to left and right, so that one may find a
balanced sitting posture for the body.

The body should not lean to either side, not forward or
backward. The bones of the hips, back and skull rest atop
one another like a *stūpa.*

Now we come to the state where the way of *zazen* is taught. First of all, when we start *zazen*, we have to discard all that is connected with our sense organs and intellect. We have to give up everything around us. There are various lengths of *zazen* training: a ninety-day retreat, a one-week session, two hours a night, ten minutes after washing one's face in the morning and so on. In any case, you have to forsake everything except doing *zazen*. You have to forget all those matters of official business, of home, of social relations, of the world situation; and about love or hate, joy or sorrow, loss or gain.

You may complain about doing such a leisurely thing in your busy life. But *zazen* is a big undertaking which changes sentient beings into Buddha. It is as revolutionary as holding the whole world in one's own hand or to grasp the freedom to choose either to die or to revive. It is not easy. Bodhi-dharma has written:

> Not concerned with outer things,
> Without having any troubles inside;
> If one's mind is like a wall,
> He would at once be in Tao (Truth)

Cutting out all overwhelming secular relations, not having stormy waves inside one's mind, if a man can be in the state of mind like a firmly founded wall, he will grasp the great Tao which he has never found before. The sixth patriarch of Chinese Zen, Hui-neng, once defined *zazen* by saying, "Not to have any consciousness of good or evil outwardly is called Za (sitting); not to move from seeing self-nature inwardly is called Zen."

In this respect, it follows naturally that when the mind moves the body follows, and when the body sits quietly then the mind at once sits in peace. For body and mind are not separated; they are one. It is abnormal for mind and body to move in different directions, or the mind to move when the body is quiet. It is said, "When man eats a meal, he is required to identify with the meal." In the same way, when he works, work itself works; when he does *zazen, zazen* itself meditates. This is what the text means by, "Movement and stillness are not separated."

I know a master of Utai (chanting of Nō dance texts) in Kyoto. He is widely known today, but in his younger days he had a difficult time. He used to be a Christian but later began to do *zazen* at the monastery. He has told me that when one starts to sing the Utai, one begins with the word "Korewa." The word "Korewa," therefore, is the key word in the Utai, and upon hearing it one may judge the ability of the singer. As soon as the singer is able to identify with this word, he starts to sing. To train for singing Utai, my friend practiced *zazen*. . . . He also says that the highest state of Nō dance is Zen itself. Nō dance is nothing but *zazen* in motion. There exists an unmoving thing in the movement itself. In other words, what is not moving is moving. This is the spirit of Nō dance where there is no separation between movement and stillness. In the same way, the art of tea and Zen is one; the art of sword and Zen is one. You must train yourself for this oneness in your work in the garden, begging in town, in standing, in sitting, in sleeping and in awakenness.

Concerning meals (in the monastery), it is said in the Gokan-no-ge (five-line vow said at mealtime) that to eat good medicine (i.e., a meal) is only for the healing of the slender body. If a meal is taken as medicine, we must partake of it in correct measure in time and quantity. Originally, in the Buddhist precepts a snack was not allowed. From lunch of one day to breakfast of the next morning monks were allowed only liquid refreshment but not solid food. My teacher under whom I studied Tibetan Buddhism in my youth kept this strict rule throughout his life. For doing *zazen*, nighttime is most suitable for achieving *samādhi* (concentration). But if one takes a meal in the afternoon, blood vessels become disordered, causing drowsiness and difficulty in reaching *samādhi*.

Sleep must also be carefully controlled. Neither too

brief nor too long a period of sleep is good. We are required to take the middle way in every case. Buddha explains this truth with a beautiful example saying, "Strings neither too taut nor too loose can sound a beautiful tone."

Now when one begins *zazen* a quiet place is best. Though the great Zen master Daito-kokushi in his poem recommends a noisy place such as on a big bridge, this practice would be possible only for the mature. Beginners might be inversely controlled by the exterior disturbances, and passers-by would not be thought of as mountain trees as Daito-kokushi writes. Upon finding a quiet place, situate a thick cushion as comfortably as possible for the length of time you wish to sit. Dress or belt should be worn loosely, yet with dignity. In his autobiography, Kodo Sawaki Roshi relates a humorous experience which happened in his youth at his master's temple. One day all the disciples left the temple except one young monk, Kodo, himself. Having nothing to do he entered a small closet and practiced *zazen*. About that time the old maid of the temple came to the closet, opened the door and was so surprised to see him there meditating that she began to bow deeply again and again. Kodo thus realized how noble the *zazen* posture must appear. *Zazen* posture, having dignity, is nothing but the Buddha himself.

(To practice *zazen*) we must sit in a cross-legged posture (lotus posture). The Chinese word, *kekka fuza*, literally means folding the legs showing the soles of the feet. First of all, put the right foot on the left groin (the root of the thigh), then the left foot on the right groin so that both legs are crossed tightly. This is called *kekka fuza* which is a perfectly immovable posture. This position, however, is rather hard to maintain for the beginner because it may cause cramps. In such cases, *hanka fuza* is allowed. This is only a half crossed legs posture. Either leg can be put on the other. The posture in which left foot is placed on the right thigh is called *kissho-za* (Sri-sitting posture), and the opposite is called *gōma-za* (Māra-defeating sitting posture.[11]

After the legs have been fixed, put the right hand on the crossed legs and the left palm on the right palm, making a small round circle with the thumbs pushing against each other. Next, raise the body quietly and move it forward and backward, to left and right several times to fix the central axis of the body. Then sit upright, expanding the backbone as much as possible. Our teachers compare this to the bamboo that is so straight that a stone dropped from the top of it reaches the bottom without any interruption. The perfect posture of *zazen* creates an isosceles triangle with legs and backbone forming a ninety degree angle. We have to be very careful not to bend too far forward nor too far backward. In this way *zazen* posture hopes to resemble a *stūpa* by piling up hip bone, backbone and skull, one on top of the other.

In India after the Buddha's death eight *stūpa* (or pagoda) were built in eight districts to be worshipped as a symbol of the Buddha. . . . In Burma and Thailand the pagoda is considered to be most holy. In China and Japan there are many outstanding pagodas made of wood, stone and marble of three or five stories. When we investigate the framework of the five-story pagoda, we are surprised to discover its layered structure balances by hanging from a central axis from the top of the pagoda instead of being built up from a stone base. For this reason these pagodas have stood a thousand years in countries of frequent typhoons and earthquakes. Our human life should be like that. If we are free from all disturbances from the outer world and the inner world, we might remain apart from all attachments, necessarily progress to the world of Nirvāṇa, and grasp eternal life. This is *zazen*.

---

[11] These terms are formal designations. Śri is a title meaning lord. Māra is the name of the Buddhist equivalent of Satan.

III. To Open the Eyes

The body should not be so upright that someone else would
feel uneasy seeing it. Keep ears and shoulders, nose and navel
parallel to one another; the tongue should touch the upper
jaw, both lips and teeth being closed; eyes should remain
slightly open so that one avoids falling asleep. If one comes
to *dhyāna*-meditation, its power is incomparable.

In the old days there was a monk of high achievement who
always practiced *zazen* with his eyes open. There was also
a Zen master called Entsu-zenji of Houn-ji who used to scold
those who practiced *zazen* with eyes closed. He called them
an "evil cave of the black mountain." A deep significance lies
here. Only a man of attainment would know it. Once the
physical posture has been well-ordered and the breath regulated, one must push forth the abdomen. One thinks not of
good or evil; receiving into one's awareness each moment of
illusion as it rises in the mind, then they disappear. Gradually
forgetting the chain of becoming, one naturally becomes
non-separate. This is the core of the *zazen* method of meditation.

Zazen requires a perfect posture, correct and orderly,
yet it should not be too strained. It is not recommended to
throw the head so far back so that others may feel uneasy
seeing it. Since it is said *"Zazen* is the *dharma* teaching of
comfort," it should be done in a totally relaxed and comfortable position. However one must make the body erect
by extending the backbones directly upward. Ears and
shoulders should be parallel, nose and navel also. But it
would be almost impossible to keep nose and navel in one
line unless one's abdomen is extended outward as much
as possible. "The tongue should touch the upper jaw."
The author of the text is very careful about even such
small parts of the body. It is true that every part of the
body should be correctly positioned, otherwise correct
zazen cannot be expected. Lips and teeth should be closed
tightly. Eyes should remain slightly open so that things
only three feet ahead will be seen. People might suppose
that with the eyes closed, one could reach calmness more

easily; however, that is wrong. Closing our eyes, our mind fills with illusions and is emptied of quietness. Also we might easily fall asleep. Our patriarchs taught us to open our eyes as much as possible in *zazen* just as the picture of Bodhi-dharma, the founder of Zen Buddhism, shows us. We have never seen a picture of Bodhi-dharma with his eyes closed. Even though visual distractions occur, you should always be free from them, letting them go as they arise. If you were to become accustomed to *zazen* with your eyes closed, *zazen* would be ineffective when your eyes were opened, especially in busy places. On the contrary, if you train your *samādhi* power through open-eyed *zazen*, wherever you happen to be, you will not lose your power of meditation.

The sentence, "In the old days, there was a monk . . ." cannot be found in the original source of the old text. It may have been added when the present text was written. Entsu-zenji of the Houn-ji Temple is the Dharma-uncle of the Soseki-jikaku Zenji Zen master who is known as the author of the present text. . . . This Entsu-zenji used to criticize closed-eye *zazen* as an "evil cave of the black mountain." According to the world view of the ancient Indian people, at the center of the universe is a mountain called Sumeru surrounded by four lands in each of the four directions. Our world is located in the Southern land and, as a magnet, points to the North, which is the center of the universe. They also believed that two mountains supported the central mountain, Sumeru, between which was an entirely black area where evil spirits dwelt. This area is called the "evil cave of the black mountain."

The author of the text warns us from thinking that practicing *zazen* in a dark place where nothing is seen or heard is most relaxing. It is, rather, likened to falling into the "evil cave of the black mountain." Therefore, Rinzai Zenji, the Zen master Lin-Chi, founder of Rinzai Zen, says, "You must be frightened of the evil cave of the black mountain." This dark place is not the area of the awakened at all. It is the midst of the ignorant. You cannot achieve real *kensho* (seeing the Buddha nature) unless you break through this dark place. "Deep significance lies here. Only a man of attainment would know it."

The above has outlined the way to sit. Next we must regulate the breathing. To regulate breath is quite an important item in *zazen*. The ancients said that every man can understand breath so that the control of breathing is extremely important.

My master, Seisetsu Roshi, used to relate the following episode. In his youth, when practicing *zazen* in the night on the veranda of his Zen master, Ryoen Roshi, who had already retired, he was called by the Roshi, "There must be a dead rat on my mosquito net. Take him down, please." On taking down the net, a rat slipped off. "What happened to it, Roshi?" he asked. The master explained, "While I was sleeping, this rat came up to my mosquito net and made me feel short of breath. I knew this happened because his short breath was controlling my own. I tried to follow him at first, and then gradually adjusted the pace of his breath to mine. Finally I stopped my breath so that the rat who had been following my breath might cease to breathe, losing his consciousness. Since this rat is not dead but has only lost his consciousness, put him away somewhere." I think this episode is illustrative of the *samādhi* power gained from *zazen*. To attain such power we must control our bodily posture and breath. The Japanese pronunciation of the term for "long life" is exactly the same as of the term for "long breath." It shows us how important it is to have long breathing in our daily life in order to achieve long life. Irregular breath will not give us long life.

Concerning the breath, there are four ways of meditation explained in the Tendai texts.[12] They are *fu, zen, ki,*

[12] Tendai is a sect of Mahāyāna Buddhism in Japan with headquarters on Mt. Hiei outside of Kyoto. It was especially powerful during the Heian Period (794–1185).

soku. Fu implies snorting breath. This is not good. *Zen*
means purring breath which is also not good. *Ki* means disordered breath, sometimes too fast, sometimes too slow.
Lastly, *soku* means the most perfect breath which is continuous and quiet as if it were faint breath. We have to
shape our breathing into such quiet, long breaths. The
ancients made a strenuous effort to practice such breathing.
Some of them even placed a feather on their nose while
meditating.

With the body and breath controlled, start *zazen* in a
relaxed way by softly concentrating your strength in your
abdomen. We must now control the mind or, as the text
states it, "Think not of good and evil." It is, however,
unimaginably difficult to control the mind. The Buddha
said, "The mind is like a venomous serpent, a wild animal,
or a sworn enemy." You might think that sitting in such
quiet circumstances nothing arises to disturb the mind;
but it is not so. The quieter the circumstances become,
the more disordered the mind may grow. So many things
appear one after the other. Even the great Hakuin Zenji
confessed that while he was doing *zazen*, he remembered
such a small event as his lending a few bowls of rice and
beans many years ago to the next door neighbor. It is
strange that we remember the things we do not usually
even consider. In the meditation hall only the sound of
the bell and wooden clappers enter through our senses, but
many things arise in the mind to be considered. We come
to realize how much man thinks about the unnecessary;
how corrupted man's mind is. Our mind is polluted like a
muddy ditch from which marsh gas constantly springs.
We cannot imagine what will appear or spring up. It is
a mass of delusion, and, therefore, it is to live our daily
lives without knowing that the mind of each individual
is corrupted. Buddhism calls this dirt-encrusted mind
ālaya which means an accumulation of subconscious
images. . . . To cut away this mass of delusion with the
sword of *prajñā*-wisdom so that we may discover the

bright mind of the real self is called controlling of mind.

As the text says, we are not allowed to think good or evil, advantage or disadvantage, love or hate. This no-mind state where nothing exists is the right posture of the mind. Dōgen Zenji says, "Think nonthinking." He recommends controlling the mind, pointing to the real self which is the mind of nonthinking. As it is said, "Whenever a thought comes to mind, be aware of it." In this way, we let the illusions or delusions come as they arise in order to awaken the state of no-mind which is the true mind. For this purpose, the ancients explained, "Have no illusions" or chanted the name of the Amida-Buddha and the name of the Kannon Bodhisattva . . .[13] In Zen Buddhism we also throw away all illusions by concentrating our mind on the problem the *koan* suggests. Since illusion and delusion have no substance, just like a cloud or mist, they will disappear if we do not cater to them. Therefore, the text says, "Be aware of illusions, then they will disappear." Letting all illusions be as they are, concentrate all your mind on the *koan*, day and night, without any dualistic consciousness. Then, naturally, the inward and outer worlds, self and universe, subject and object, become one. In due time, the event we have sought is realized, yet it cannot be explained. At that moment we experience the inexpressible comfort of spiritual freedom, and the unique taste of *zazen* springs up from the deep.

This experience is not yet *satori*-awakenness; it is not yet "seeing nature" or "becoming Buddha." In the *Mumonkan*, an old Zen text called the "Gateless Gate," it is said,

Once breaking through [the mass of great doubt] as if with the sword of General Kwan, one gains the great freedom at the juncture of life and death to kill the Buddha when he

[13] The Amida-Buddha is the Buddha of the Western Paradise and is the principal object of devotion of Buddhists of the Pure Land sect. Kannon or Avalokiteśvara is the Bodhisattva associated with Amida.

meets him, to kill the patriarch when he meets the patriarch and so receive the freedom of enjoying the situation wherever he may stand.

We must have such a breakthrough experience where we realize real subjectivity and real freedom. There man becomes the lord of the world and there evolves his creative life of destroying-and-creating freedom. . . .

Zazen is, in this way, more than control of posture, breath and mind, but also, in a wider scale, circumstances, family and, finally, society. Therefore, *zazen* is not easily accomplished.

IV. Spirit Is Opened

In my opinion, *zazen* meditation is the most humane way to *dharma* truth. Nevertheless, many persons become ill. This might result from lack of care in the practice of *zazen*.

If one were acquainted with its deep meaning, his body would be naturally relaxed, his spirit refreshed, his right thinking clarified and the taste of *dharma* would deepen his mind. He would become quiet, clean, and joyous.

Zazen is to return to the most normal, natural state of both body and mind; the state of greatest ease which is perfect emancipation from all suffering, namely, the state of Nirvāṇa, where neither life-and-death nor suffering-and-comfort nor love-and-hate dichotomies exist. Yet, people usually think of *zazen* as a sort of strict, ascetic discipline [and] Zen monastic life is considered one of dark gloom disconnected with ordinary life. This is wrong. . . . The life of a Zen monastery is really the paradigm of democratic life.

The reason we gather here is to seek the noblest, surest and highest purpose of human life. We are engaged in the creation of the highest immaterial culture for human beings; therefore, we practice *zazen* with the pride and joy of performing a secret vocation among many other people. But, in undergoing such a precious discipline as *zazen*, some people contract diseases because of a lack of

care concerning *zazen* practice, or because of their unnat-
uralness in doing *zazen*. *Zazen* must be done with oneness
of body and mind, movement and stillness. If the mind
were truly empty, the body would be also empty. Then
how could this emptiness contract disease?

If you conduct *zazen* with a deep understanding of this
present text, your body will be naturally relaxed and your
spirit refreshed. The ancients thought that everything in
the universe consisted of four elements: soil, water, fire,
and air. The human body contains them also. Bones, teeth,
nails and so on belong to the soil element. Blood, saliva,
gastric juices and other components forming most of the
human body belong to the water element. Temperature
is a fire element. The movement of hands, legs, and eyes
are caused by the strength of air. And it is believed that
each element has one hundred and one diseases. Therefore,
four hundred and four diseases are numbred as man's
diseases. In doing *zazen*, however, these four elements are
so naturally harmonized that no diseases exist. Fire tends
to flow upward, water downward; however, by concentrating all our bodily strengths into the abdominal region,
fire flows down so that the legs may receive heat; also,
water flows up so that the head may cool. In this way
good health is maintained, the spirit is kept clean, and a
smile remains on your face. No mist of delusion nor haze
of illusion remain, and the mind becomes clear like the
blue sky. This is what the text says, "Right thinking is
clarified." All matters of sorrow, joy and anger become
clear and right thinking in and of themselves.

In due time, we begin to embody the so-called taste of
zazen or taste of *dharma* [truth]. By that the spirit becomes
fresh so we can deepen the state of *zazen*. As it is said,
"An inch of sitting makes an inch of Buddha," or "One
day's sitting makes one day of Buddha." The taste of
dharma is deepened gradually by continuity of short *zazen*
experiences. Some of you must have had a hard time as
beginners in doing *zazen*, but it is a great [joy] to see your

personality already change in one week. This is good evidence of the fact that your spirit has become pure, and right thinking has arisen.

The feeling which is gained after doing *zazen* is inexpressibly comfortable. The Japanese term "clean-comfort" is surely a most suitable word for this feeling. It is rather different from what is experienced in other religions when man receives merit from outside of himself. It is the feeling of happiness which springs out of the depth of one's being. Those who do *zazen* must develop this deep feeling. Buddhism is not active today due to the lack of this profound experience. Buddhist priests lack this vital feeling as well as laymen. How can such a religion develop? New rising religions are of a low grade in principle, but the people belonging to them are filled with spirit. . . . Orthodox Buddhists lack this experiential dimension. You might know that every Buddhist scripture is concluded with the phrase, "Hear the Buddha's sermon, bow to the Buddha with deep joy and return home." Why do those who read this scripture not possess any profound feeling? You who do *zazen* must have deep joy. Work hard in order to experience this great joy which is nothing but the significance of life itself.

V. *Like Dragon in Water*

Or if he has awakened, he will be as the dragon in water or the tiger crouching on his mountain. Or again, even if one has not yet reached this awareness, he has not wasted his energy—just as the man who blows on a fire with the help of the wind. In any case, one should follow his own judgment as to his level of awakenness and never deceive himself.

Yet the higher one stands on the way, the more varied the evils which obstruct it—some enticing one ahead, others pushing one back. However, once awareness has been realized, all these obstacles cannot remain. The forms of evil are clarified in detail in such texts as the *Śūraṅgama Mahā-sūtra*, *Shikan Investigation* by the great master Tendai

(538–597) and the *Text on Practice and Awareness* by the Zen master Keiho-shumitsu (780–841). Those who would prepare their defenses against these evils must know of them in advance.

When one wishes to come out of meditation, he should move his body gradually; he should stand up deliberately, without hurry. After coming out of meditation, one should utilize skill in each moment to hold his *samādhi* power as carefully as a mother holds her baby. In this way, *samādhi* power will be matured.

One inch of sitting makes one inch of Buddha. If we sit while an inch of incense burns, our spirit naturally becomes clean, much more so, of course, if we continue our *zazen* for long years under the right instruction of *Zazen-gi*. It is, however, the mere merit of *zazen* and not yet the awakening which is the final purpose of Buddha-dharma. It is not yet *kensho*, seeing the Buddha-nature. Only when vital life comes out of the state of pure subject-object oneness do we see real *kensho*. Even if we are not yet awakened, we can taste the clean, comfortable state of mind by which we feel bodily emancipation and spiritual clarity. How much more wonderful it is to add the taste of *kensho*. In the *Mumonkan*, it is written, "[Once we see the real nature] we may go with successive patriarchs hand in hand, seeing together with the same eyes and listening with the same ears. Is this not delightful?" We can see things with the same eyes as those of Buddha's or Bodhi-dharma's. Or we can listen to the something with the same ears as those of the patriarchs. This means that we have now attained the wisdom of Buddha. Or, simply, we have become Buddha himself.

When Hakuin Zenji broke through himself by listening to the dawn temple gong in the far distance, he jumped for joy like a mad man every day for a week. It is easy enough to understand his feeling—not only having the same eyes as Buddha but walking with him hand in hand. It is undoubtedly bliss . . . to get up every morning with

Buddha and sleep with him at night. What a wonderful life.

Not only that, but now a man grasps the oneness of life extending over the universe. He is now a lord of the earth. His majesty is therefore comparable to a dragon in the water or to a tiger crouching on his mountain. Even if a man were not yet awakened, he would soon arrive at *kensho* unless he were to quit the sincere practice of *zazen*. He will soon have the great joy of *satori*-awakenness like the fire which is gained by blowing with the help of the wind. Therefore, you need not be frustrated nor too hasty.

"One should follow his own judgment as to his level of awakenness and never deceive himself." This is a very important line. To be honest is the most important quality in the practice of *zazen*. We must suffer absolutely. No deception is allowed in seeking one's real nature. I am not a clever man at all. So I took two or three times the energy of others to discover the right answer to each *koan*. I devoted my time to sitting itself without trying to work anything out through my intellect. But this strict discipline became the most useful thing for me today to resolve my daily problems.

A *koan* is a very strange thing which is automatically resolved whenever we enter the great death experience. The answer itself comes to us instead of us answering it. It is really the voice of heaven or revelation. Only when we turn a dial in ourselves does the answer appear. *Zazen* is nothing but turning this dial; that is to say, to die in the midst of *koan*. Not to be able to find the answer to the *koan* shows the lack of this great death experience. I never tried to solve a *koan* through the intellect. On the contrary, I tried to throw away my intellect for those twenty years of my youth. I cannot help saying that it is a miracle to see the answer upon giving up the intellect. Shinran, the founder of the Jōdo Shin sect of Japanese Buddhism, was still studying under his master Honen in Kyoto when an argument occurred among the disciples about the depth of faith in Amida-Buddha. Young Shinran asserted that the master's faith and his own faith were exactly the same in depth. The others said that they were different. Master Honen judged them saying, "My faith is given from Amida-Buddha, so is Shinran's. Therefore my faith and Shinran's are the same. If some of you say they are different, then you will not be able to enter the Pure Land where I will enter."

The same thing can be said about the answers of a *koan*. If it is what is resolved through the intellect, each answer would be different. But the real answer of a *koan* comes from the other side as an answer from heaven in the *samādhi* state of mind, so they must be one and the same. Among the answers of such patriarchs, as Kanzan and Hakuin, and of novices, there is no difference in completeness. The most important thing is to grasp the state of absolute conviction which is never swayed by another's opinion. . . .

The more *zazen* is practiced, the more disturbances come to appear on the way to awakenness. There are two kinds of evil disturbances. One is that which disturbs us by too much stimulation of emotion or will, and the other is that which bothers us by opposition to them. In both cases we are disturbed in our path to *dharma* [truth]. Even in the monastery a monk may become famous among the laymen belonging to the monastery and lose his original determination and purpose by being entertained by them. . . . Other monks, on the contrary, may be forced to forego the monastic life. . . . Both cases should be avoided. The text says, "Only when awareness is realized," so we must keep awareness always [before us] allowing no obstacle to remain, and in due course the awakened self will become the everlasting Self.

In doing *zazen* you will see *makyo*, the so-called evil state of mind, but you should not be controlled by this disturbance. You may see various kinds of psychological images in your *makyo* state such as images of Bodhisattvas, dreamy feelings as if you are being drawn down into a dark hell or flying in space. All these appearances are but phenomena of the *makyo* state, and you should not be disturbed. You have to give all your effort to concentrating on the *koan* and keeping awareness intact. Since these warnings are given in old meditational texts like the *Sūrangama Mahā-sūtra*, *Shikan Investigation* taught by Tendai, and the *Text on Practice and Awareness* written by the Zen master Keiho, those who anticipate such emergencies would do better to read about them ahead of time.

When you intend to come out of *samādhi* ecstasy, you must be very careful even though it is difficult to enter the *samādhi* state inside the meditation hall. . . . To come out of *samādhi* move very slowly, for in *samādhi* breath quiets almost to the point of disappearing. If you were to move quickly, it might easily cause illness. First, move the tips of your fingers or chafe your hands and feet; then, gradually raise your whole body. Even after coming out of *samādhi*, you have to be careful not to lose your *samādhi* power by concentrating your entire energy in your abdomen. It should be done without any negligence as a hen warms her eggs or as a mother holds her baby. If you are negligent to any degree, you will suddenly return to the beginning, and *samādhi* power will not have been developed.

VI. To Seek for the Jewel

The practice of *zazen* is one of the most urgent needs of all men. If one has not achieved the complete quietness of *zazen*, he may find that he is helpless in the crisis situations of life. Therefore, to find the jewel one must calm the waves; it would be hard to get it if one stirred up the water. Where meditation-water is clear and calm, the mind-jewel will naturally be visible. Thus the *Vaipulya-pūrnabodhi-prāpta Sūtra* says, "All wisdom of non-attachment and clarity comes from *zazen*." Or again, the *Saddharma-pundarīka Sūtra* reads:

"Let one's mind concentrate in silence and let it remain motionless like Mt. Sumeru."

It has been made clear that one can go beyond only by this quiet process; and it is only by one's *samādhi* power that one is enabled to die while sitting or standing in meditation. Even if one makes a life-long effort to become fully aware of truth, he still cannot avoid stumbling. How then can the lazy man who postpones *zazen* practice prepare for *karma*? Therefore, the ancestors have said, "If one has no *samādhi* power by which to conquer death, he must blindly return to the darkness and float eternally on the ocean of life-and-death." However, O my Zen brothers, read this text again and again so that both you and the other beings may at the same moment attain real awakening.

"The practice of *zazen* is most urgent," so says the text. There are six main practices to Nirvāṇa among the Bodhisattva's vows. They are: (1) giving, (2) obeying the precepts, (3) endurance, (4) making an effort, (5) meditation and (6) wisdom. Among these six practices, meditation is the most central and urgent. We have to practice it first. In his poem on *zazen*, the great Zen master Hakuin writes:

> All the Pāramitās [perfections] such as giving and obeying
> the precepts
> And those practices such as chanting Buddha's name, confession and discipline and many other good deeds
> Are included in meditation.

When we chant the name of the Buddha, the real meaning of chanting exists only where the chanting person and the Buddha whose name is chanted are not separated but unified. This is actually nothing but meditation.

Confession is to remember and confess sins which have been done in the past, but no matter how sin is confessed, it will be no more than delusion. What we have to do in penitence is to return to the pure, original mind which existed before sin was ever committed. Therefore, in the

Buddhist scripture it is written, "When you intend to confess, do *zazen* to see the real features [of one's self]. All sins are like frost dew and will be easily dispelled under the sun [of vision]." To do *zazen* and see one's real features is the best penitence. . . . For the son who runs away from home it is not real penitence to repent outside of his home. The best penitence is for him to come back to his home. In the same way, no matter how penitent we are in leaving our original nature, we will be hopeless until we return to the home of our real nature. . . .

The sixth patriarch Hui-neng defined *zazen* thus: "to be free from outer form and to have inner order." This means that *zazen* is, outwardly, to forget all bodily shape and feature and to identify the self with the outer world, and at the same time, inwardly, to have the steady spirit which is never controlled by the outer world. *Zazen* meditation is urgent to daily social life. An actor would not be a good actor unless he forgot himself and identified himself with his role and controlled his ambitious mind. The same thing can be said about an athlete who identifies himself with the sport itself, or about a musician identifying himself with music. All these are possible only by the power of *zazen* meditation.

Not so many years ago, the Zen master Goyu Morita suffered with a carbuncle on his back and could not lie down. Therefore he used to sit in *zazen* for twenty-four hours. He underwent an operation, and though he refused anesthesia, no expression of pain showed on his face. This affords a good example of the power of meditation which an ordinary man cannot attain easily. If we do not keep such power with us in daily life, we will be at a loss in the face of crisis. The famous poet, Dokan Ota, was pierced by a spear. . . . Holding the spear, he made a poem which goes, "Life is not so precious for me now, since I know that it has already been lost." Reciting this poem, he peacefully died. This is also one of the powers of *zazen* meditation. None of us are sure when we face death; therefore, we must be prepared for this crisis.

"To find the jewel, one must calm the waves; it would be hard to get it if one stirred up the water. Where meditation-water is clear and calm, the mind-jewel will naturally be visible." Most people would jump in the water if a jewel were dropped into a pond and stir up the water until it became too muddy to find anything but stones or tiles. But a wise man would never do such a foolish thing. He would wait for the water to become calm so that the jewel might naturally come to shine by itself. Zen discipline is the same. The more you try to know Zen principles by book-learning or questioning, the farther you move from Buddha-nature. If you try to reach awareness by sitting without wondering, however, the jewel of Buddha-nature will begin to shine by itself; and you will realize the real self for which you have been searching.

Zazen meditation is the most direct way to the truth of Buddhism. Instead of wandering in thought, you must sit with your whole being, forgetting all intellectual searching. In the *Saddharma-puṇḍarīka Sūtra* it is said, "Let one's mind concentrate in silence and let it remain motionless like Mt. Sumeru." If you practice *zazen* in this way, you are already in the world of Buddha while amid sentient beings. This is called the "direct entrance into the Buddha stage in one jump." If you want to become Buddha by removing suffering, it will be entirely impossible. You have to jump into Buddha's world suddenly. This is why Zen Buddhism is called the "teaching of sudden awareness," and for this purpose we need *zazen*. . . .

It is very difficult to live our short lives which last for only about seventy years and in which we meet many failures. . . . If we spend our time leisurely without any effort to be delivered from suffering, we will not be free from the so-called turning wheel of the six worlds. Therefore, our elders strongly emphasize and command us to cultivate *zazen* power before we reach the end of life. Those who practice *zazen* must practice in strength with the correct instruction given by the Zen text of *Zazen-gi* in order both to save themselves and all other sentient beings.

7

Perfection of Wisdom

Hakuin Zenji (1685–1768) is considered the second founder of the Rinzai Zen sect in Japan and is one of the most important religious figures in the Tokugawa Period (1603–1867). He was a poet and painter but is best known as a Zen master of mystic intensity and a religious reformer who brought Zen to the common people. The following commentary is Hakuin's exposition of the *Prajñā-pāramitā Hṛdaya Sūtra* (*The Heart of the Perfection of Wisdom*), one of the most important texts of Mahāyāna Buddhism, especially Zen. It is customarily chanted at the end of *zazen* sessions in the Rinzai tradition. The text is brief in the extreme but is said to represent the quintessence of the Prajñāpāramitā literature which is basic to the Zen point of view. The pithy, almost incomprehensible nature of *The Heart Sūtra* makes a commentary on the text essential. Hakuin's commentary, in poetic style, is, itself, extremely difficult to grasp. The Reverend Eshin Nishimura has added footnotes to his translation but even with their help the reader may sometimes find himself groping for meaning. Such a response is part of Hakuin's intention as he makes clear in the conclusion. One outstanding virtue of the commentary's enigmatic expression is the mental frustration it produces—much like the frustration of the *koan* exercise in *zazen*. The commentary, then, deserves to be pondered in its own right and not read simply

as a document to clarify the *Prajñāpāramitā Hṛdaya Sūtra.*
Indeed, in itself it offers an exercise in *zazen!*

* * *

A translation of the text in its entirety does not precede
the commentary since several English translations are
readily available (e.g. Edward Conze, *Buddhist Wisdom
Books*). The commentary is entitled, "Hakuin Zenji's Venomous Commentary on the *Prajñāpāramitā Hṛdaya Sūtra,*"
as edited and proofread by the monks at Sendai[1] Monastery and begins with the following introduction:

> A blind old man of the cave of wisteria vines came back
>   naked to his humble house and made himself at home.
> What a miserable man Fu-ta-shih[2] is! See, he loses the
>   castle which he occupies.
> Do not say, "Cold and no taste!" Even one meal would be
>   enough to erase your hunger forever.
>
> By cutting down all the wisteria vines in the universe
> To bind up all the monks in the world,
> I hope you attain such total liberation
> as great eagles playing with a lotus stem.

Hakuin's introduction is then followed by his comments
on words or phrases of the Sūtra, itself, including the title.

Mahā

This Sanskrit term is freely translated "large."

What is it?! Nothing in the universe can be compared
with this. Most people mistake it to mean big and wide.

The superior man loves wealth, yet he knows the right
way to use it.

Would you show me the small kind of *prajñā*-wisdom?

[1] Sendai means "not to become Buddha." There are two kinds
of Sendai: one is not to become Buddha because of ignorance;
the other results from the Bodhisattva ideal of not becoming
Buddha until all sentient beings have been saved.
[2] Fu-ta-shih was a famous Chinese priest (496–569) who collected all the Buddhist scriptures into one building to form the
first great library of Buddhist texts.

The uncountable number of universes
In a drop of dew on the thin hair of an animal,
Three thousand worlds like a bubble in the ocean;
The pupils of insects existing on the eyelashes of the
mosquito
Never stop their play with the world.

Prajñā

This Sanskrit term is freely translated "wisdom."

Everyone possesses this by nature and does so in its
entirety.

A fellow who plays with mud will never find the ultimate.

Without leaning over the precipice, how can man reach
the truth?

What does the proverb, "Do not cut your nails under the
lamp!" mean?[3]

Even though you let the surveyor measure length, do
not let the snail cultivate the stony field.

Both ears are as though deaf, the eyes as if blind;
The universe loses its body at midnight;
Even Śāriputra[4] is unable to realize it.
A limping Persian has passed by the wharf!

Pāramitā

This word is translated freely as "arriving at the other
shore." Then, where is this shore?

Do not dig into the earth to find blue sky! The shrimp
can never escape from the basket no matter how hard he
tries.

The treasure is close at hand! Take one more step!

The fisherman in his boat strips the water from his wet

---

[3] The proverb originates in the Chinese classics where a Zen
master uses it to mean doing a dangerous deed. Hakuin might
mean that unless this proverb is correctly understood, man
cannot use *prajñā*-wisdom.

[4] One of the Buddha's great disciples noted for his wisdom.

line. Even the enlightened monk will secretly feel melancholy.

Who is the man standing on this shore, the great earth?
How pitiful it is to stand, in ignorance, on the undulating shore!
If a man does not slay his consciousness once,
He will have to continue his hard training eternally.

Hṛdaya

This has never had a name, but someone made the mistake of putting a name on it. Gold dust in the eye must be a nuisance.

Symbols such as priests' robes and beads must be dust on the truth. Then what is this?! Many people pick up horse's bones.[5] The reason why monks do not know the truth originates in their belief that there is an underlying consciousness. The source of endless life-and-death!

The ignorant call it Buddha.

How clear the mind never to be gained!
The long sky is swept clear.
To the meditating platform colder than iron
Moonlight comes with fragrance through the small window.

Sūtra [Scripture]

"Thus have I heard: At one time Buddha stayed. . . ."
Toh![6] Who are you opening and shutting the scriptures?
Many people seek golden scripture in the dustbin.

One skin of a lily bulb.
At Pippala Cave,[7]

---

[5] This saying refers to a story about a boy who goes to a battlefield to find the bones of his dead father, but brings back the bones of a horse by mistake.
[6] "Toh!" is an ejaculation often used in Zen dialogues.
[7] The place where five hundred disciples of the Buddha wrote scriptures from memory.

This Sūtra has not yet been written.

Kumārajīva[8] has not even a word to translate;

Ānanda[9] can never hear the Buddha's teachings.

The wild goose from the south standing on the beach in snowy reeds,

The mountain moon is so bright and clear it looks slender,

And the cold cloud seems to drop.

No matter how many Buddhas appear in this world,

They can never correct it, even with one word.

Avalokiteśvara

Bodhisattva in Potalaka.[10] Mahāsattva in everyone! There is no body in bondage between heaven and earth.

Man does not owe his actions—spitting or shaking a shoulder—to any other person's help.

Who can bind you?

It is a common action to scratch the Buddha's neck with one's left hand. How can a man avoid touching a dog's head with his right hand?

Grasping, walking: man needs no help;

He accumulates sin only by thinking.

If you throw away all of your love and hatred,

I will admit that you are the living Avalokiteśvara.

Bodhisattva [Wisdom-Being]

Between the terms "two *yāna*"[11] and "Buddha," the term "Bodhisattva" is hypothetically placed.

[8] A founder of Chinese Mahāyāna Buddhism. Of Indian birth, he is noted for his translation of several hundred Buddhist texts into Chinese.

[9] One of the ten great disciples of the Buddha.

[10] Name of the mountain where the Bodhisattva Avalokiteśvara lives.

[11] They are Śrāvaka-yāna ["Hearer-Vehicle"] and Pratyeka-buddha-yāna ["Isolated Buddha-Vehicle"]. Both are inferior ways of self-discipline to gain *satori* awakening. The Bodhisattva-yāna stands above both of them.

Being on the way, yet having never left home; having left home, never on the way. If a man could take the Four Great Vows[12] away, it would be the same as "The superior man taking eight out of ten."[13]

Jumping out of the cave of selflessness and formlessness,
To float up and down on the life-death waves of the *karma* ocean;
Save us, compassionate Bodhisattva of Mercy!
Countless incarnations are still not enough.

Practice

What did you say? Trouble has come! To sleep in the night, to run in the daytime, to empty the bowels; floating clouds, running water, falling leaves, scattering petals.

If a man doubts them, he will fall into hell. Nevertheless, if a man does not doubt them at the risk of his life, he will be subjected to greater trouble.

What are such actions as grasping and walking,
Or eating from hunger and drinking from thirst?
If a man takes any thought of them
It will be the same as killing Hun-t'un by removing his eyes.[14]

Deep Prajñāpāramitā

Toh! It is like making a wound by gouging out beautiful skin. For what purpose is *prajñā*? Here it is deep and

[12] The Four Vows based on the Gaṇḍavyūha Sūtra are as follows:
"However innumerable beings are, I vow to save them;
However inexhaustible the passions are, I vow to extinguish them;
However immeasurable the Dharmas are, I vow to master them;
However incomparable the Buddha-truth is, I vow to attain it."

[13] Here the notion is that eight out of ten is complete.

[14] Hun-t'un (chaos) died seven days after his good friends had kindly removed his eyes to make him look handsome (a tale from Chuang-tzu).

shallow! Is *prajñā* therefore like water of a river? Try to point out a *prajñā* which is deep and shallow. You are so stupid that you would buy a chicken of Ch'u![15]

It is called shallow to seek emptiness and deny form,
It is called deep to complete form and find emptiness.
If a man uses either form or emptiness to speak of *prajñā*,
He is like a lame tortoise wanting to catch a flying bird.

Time (the time when)
Again it has gouged its beautiful flesh! It exists from *kalpa*[16] to *kalpa*.

The sharp sword gleams with cold brilliance.
Jewels heaped up on an emerald plate.

Old soot swept up yesterday;
New Year's rice cake made tonight.
The pine with its root, orange with leaves—
We are waiting for our guests with new clothes.

Perceive
Cakravāda eye[17] has no dust. Do not blink in the air filled with lime dust. What is this Being?

The whole universe is the pure eye of the Śrāmana (monk). It is exactly what Hsüan-hsia speaks of.[18]

In the eye of a destructive insect, an ant turns a stone mill;
A spider makes a web in a grain of rice.
Pure Land, this world, and Hell—
How obvious the mango on the palm!

[15] From the Chinese classics. A man of Ch'u sold a chicken instead of a phoenix at an expensive price to a man who wanted to present it to the king.
[16] A period of time beyond calculation.
[17] A strong, clear eye.
[18] A Chinese Zen master (835–908).

The Five Skandha-*s are Emptiness.*[19]

An (imaginary) tortoise having a tail—how could she erase her traces?

Form is like the Cakravāda Mountain,[20] sensation and perception are like a diamond sword, volition and consciousness are like the *nyoi* treasure.[21]

Recognizing the five *skandha*-s which exist externally,
Man is subjected to beauty and ugliness.
It is like bubbles floating on the water,
Or a flash of light brushing the sky away.

To be delivered from all sufferings and miseries

The reflection in the guest's cup is not that of a snake originally.[22] In a dream, there is obviously three worlds.

After awakening, the great thousand worlds are complete Emptiness.

Two demons push a door against each other.
They both strain with their whole body;
After a long struggle, at last comes the dawn.
How ridiculous! Originally they were friends!

Śāriputra

Toh! What kind of superiority does the Śrāvaka Ārya[23]

---

[19] The five *skandha*-s are the aggregates of form, sensation, perception, volition and consciousness. Form belongs to the material world and the other four to the nonmaterial.

[20] The mountains surrounding the world in Indian cosmology.

[21] A Japanese term meaning, "as mind likes." *Nyoi* treasure might mean the treasure from which any jewel can be obtained and which the mind desires.

[22] The complete story is as follows: A man asked his friend, "Why haven't you come to see me for such a long time?" His friend replied, "Last time, when you served me wine, I saw a snake in the cup and seeing it I got sick." The man said, "It must have been the reflection of the snake painted on the ceiling." Hearing this, the friend was no longer sick.

[23] The "Worthy Hearer" who hides his Bodhisattva virtue and lives his life in the secular world to save all sentient beings.

have? Even the Buddha and the patriarchs would implore for their lives.

How does the Śrāvaka Ārya manifest his (Bodhisattva) virtue and outer (Śrāvaka) appearance? Does Śāriputra forget that he was embarrassed when he could not return to the male state at Vimalakīrti's room.[24]

His wisdom being the deepest in Jetavana,[25]

His brother stood in awe of him from the moment of his conception.

With deep devotion to Avalokiteśvara, he composed this Sūtra.

Teacher of Rāhula,[26] son of Śāri.

Form is not other than Emptiness, Emptiness is not other than form.

A bowl of the most delicious food has been soiled by the feces of two rats!

Even a splendid meal can not please one who is already full. It is like seeking water by brushing away the wave.

The wave is water.

Form does not intercept Emptiness, but is Emptiness; Emptiness does not destroy form, but is form.

On the truth that form and Emptiness is one,

A lame tortoise, putting on cosmetics, stands in the evening breeze.

That which is form is Emptiness, that which is Emptiness is form.

What an old piece of furniture this is! How stupid to teach a monkey to climb a tree! These are the tools which

---

[24] The story is found in the *Vimalakīrti Sūtra*, a beloved Zen text: When Śāriputra argued with an angel, he was changed into a female by her and was unable to transpose himself back into the male condition.
[25] An early Buddhist retreat center.
[26] Siddhartha Gautama's son. When he was nine years old, he is reputed to have become a monk and studied under Śāriputra.

have been shown at the shop for the last two thousand years.

The fisherman in his boat strips the water from his wet line.

The bush warbler's song comes with the breeze;
The peach flower blooms in the warm smoky day.
A group of pretty girls
Wearing flowers on their beautiful dresses.

The same can be said of sensation, perception, volition and consciousness.

It is like lying down in the wild weeds! If a man does not become afraid when he sees a monster, the monster will disappear by itself.

What a ridiculous figure a snowman in the sunshine! I have never seen such a monster in myself.

Such as earth, wind, fire and water is the trace of a flying bird;
Man's body and mind are the flowers of illusion.
The stone woman[27] throws away her reed and squares her thin shoulders.

A muddy water buffalo kicks the waves and shakes his angry tusks.

Oh, Śāriputra, all things here are characterized by Emptiness.

Man creates flowers, rubbing his eyes. There is nothing originally. Why does man not want to seek Emptiness?

It is like scattering feces on the clean ground.

Earth, mountain, river are like mirages;
Hell and Heaven, a town on the ocean.
Pure Land and this world, the brush of a tortoise tail;
Life, death and Nirvāṇa, the horns of a hare.

---

[27] The image of the stone woman and muddy water buffalo point out that the truth taught here cannot be explained by a rational concept.

They are not born, not annihilated; not tainted, nor immaculate; do not increase, do not decrease.

How fresh this is! But is it true? What does it mean that all things are not born, not annihilated? I hope you (Buddha) are not teasing us.

Man's arm does not bend outward.

The pupil responds according to the object,
The echo gives response to a call.
There is no stain in the secular world,
There is no immaculate image in Buddha land.
Eighty thousand teachings are lacking in anyone,
Three thousand temples are included in a speck of dust.
A young man takes a nap at Han-tan;
A man enters Nan-k'o to become a Lord.[28]

Therefore, in Emptiness

Foxes' holes and dead men's graves make many men fall down. The deep dark hole! It should be feared!
More than one hundred freezing, starving monks
Are celebrating the New Year holding old fans,
Hanging Bodhidharma's image on the wall,
Arranging a plum branch in a vase.
Coldness does not make the bush warbler open its mouth.
The warmth of fire fills the whole meditation hall.
The mountain yams wrapped in straw are presented.
The decorated festival cake is given.

There is no form, no sensation, no perception, no volition, no consciousness.

Why grasp at an illusory dream or an empty flower?
Throw away gain and loss, affirmation and negation!

Trouble comes from too much care.

By making all things Empty, what do you (Buddha) want to do?

---

[28] Reference is to a Chinese fable which teaches that life is nothing but a short dream even though it may have the outward appearance of success.

A calm, clear, empty, nonsuffering place—
Mountain, ocean, land are nothing but name.
When the mind is opened, it is divided into four;[29]
When form is integrated, it is reduced to one.
Mind and form are nothing but the voice of echoes.

*No eye, ear, nose, tongue, body, mind; no form, sound,
smell, taste, touch, object; no* dhātu[30] *of vision, till we
come to no* dhātu *of consciousness.*

There is eye, ear, nose, tongue, body and mind! Therefore there is form, sound, smell, taste, touch and object, too.

Autumn sky, spacious field; nothing passing by but a
man I do not know riding over there.

Six sensations, six objects occur;
No organs, no six sufferings.
Organ, object, sensation become the eighteen *dhātu*,
As one bubble on the ocean.

*There is neither ignorance, nor extinction of ignorance
neither old age and death, nor extinction of old age and
death.*

Scattering pearls on the beautiful curtain! Even if pearls
are hidden in the shabby begging bag, the wise know they
are treasures.

The water the cow drinks becomes milk; that which the
snake drinks becomes poison.

Into the midst of such deep clouds that man cannot
penetrate, there is a twelve-story tower where a hermit
lives.

Occurrence and destruction of the twelve chains of
causation;

[29] That is, the four noncorporeal aggregates: sensation, thought,
volition, consciousness.
[30] The Sanskrit term means "constituent part." The ancient
Indian peoples analyzed material and mental existence into
constituent parts or elements. One of the classical lists is the
eighteen *dhātus*.

That which occurs—the Sentience; that which is destroyed—the Saint.
This state of mind the Pratyekabuddha intuits;
Yet all are nothing but dust in the eye.
Dust in the eye! Who can grasp it?
Esteem the perfect teaching of Buddha!
If man realizes the teaching at its depth,
He can transcend the body of leper or fox.

There is no suffering, no rising, no annihilation, no path.
Seeing twinkling jewels on the night curtain, the ignorant man takes up his sword.
Salt in the water, or glue in the paint!
A snowy heron in the snowy field, or a bush warbler on the flowery branch.

Four deep-red, burning irons
Running with straw-sandals beyond the midnight cloud.
Suffering, arising, annihilation, path,
Nothing to do with Buddha's teaching.
Ajñāta-kaudinya, Bhārdi, and Mahānāman[31]
Found their old selves burned up at once.
Do not say the Buddha scooped up shrimp and clams at Migadāna;
He waits secretly for a man of Mahāyāna instinct.

There is no knowledge, no attainment.
Again a trick of the dead! Many people misunderstand these words, blinking in their coffins.
Although the man painted on the paper is obvious to see, he never responds to our call.

Burning black fire with black light;
Heaven and earth in chaos lose their reality.
Mountain and river in the mirror cannot be observed;
The entire cosmos is brokenhearted in vain.

---

[31] Three of the five disciples to whom the Buddha preached his first sermon in the Deer Park at Benares.

Bodhisattva: because there is no attainment.

Throw away! This is just like asserting innocence by holding on to what has been stolen.

Following and adapting to every occasion, yet staying always at the stage of Bodhisattva.

If man cannot realize "three-eight-nine,"[32] he will be subjected to suffering of mind on every occasion.

Bodhisattva, Mahāsattva!

He is called the sentient being with the great mind.

Entering Hell, he suffers in place of sentient beings,

Behaving spontaneously, he waits for no invitation;

Vowing never to remain at the low state of enlightenment,

He tries both to seek the higher attainment and to save sentient beings.

Even if the universe were destroyed,

He makes himself eternally keep his vow toward the good of all.

Because he dwells depending on the Prajñāpāramitā.

Ugly! Ugly! If a man finds he depends upon even a small teaching, he should vomit it immediately.

The severe cold of Yu-chou is endurable, but the hottest weather of Chiang-nan cannot be endured.[33]

Even if it is said that the Arhat has greed and anger,

A man should not say the Bodhisattva depends on *prajñā*-wisdom.

If a man finds something to depend upon,

That cannot be freedom, but bondage.

[32] Refers to the following Zen story: Zen master Po-yün Shou-tuan, in his youth, visited Master Yang-ch'i Fang-hui. The Master was out and his mother was in the temple. Po-yün asked the old mother, "Do you have a true eye?" The old woman replied, "If a man cannot realize three-eight-nine, he will be subjected to suffering of mind on every occasion."

[33] This analogy reiterates the point that one should not even depend on the *Prajñāpāramitā*.

The Bodhisattva's *prajñā*-wisdom is not special.
It is as free as a gem which is rolling on a tray,
Neither foolish nor wise, neither superior nor common.
I grieve that man adds legs on a dragon in painting.

*There are no obstacles, and therefore no fear, and going
beyond perverted views.*

This is not an amazing matter. What is supernatural
power but carrying water on the shoulder and gathering
brushwood.

Turning my head there was the setting sun on the west
side of my dwelling.

Not mind, not nature, not Nirvāṇa;
Not Buddha, not patriarchs, not *prajñā*.
The ten *dharma-dhātu*, burning iron hammer
Smashes the cosmos, and makes it empty.
Opening its mouth, there the sound of a roaring lion,
And all animals are afraid.
Making the body appear in various ways like a magician,
It has no difficulty changing its body according to the
situation.
Seeing the wound on the left shoulder of Mistress Li,
The Taoist burned moxa on the right leg of her servant.[34]
Perversion, illusion, and fear,
Are just one drop of water falling into a valley.
Ch'ih wore a novel costume when he was made to go
to Ch'i.
Li's coffin had no decoration when he died.
Waking a napping priest to tell him
That children broke a fence and stole a bamboo shoot.

---

[34] This line comes from the following Chinese story: The mother
of Mr. Li, a great merchant, once had a great swelling on her
left shoulder. She sent her servant to a Taoist magician for
treatment. Since the magician knew the old lady would dislike
having moxa burned on her shoulder, he burned on the leg of
the servant and, thus, healed the swelling. Hakuin points to
the freedom the man of wisdom has to do what he pleases.

He finally reaches Nirvāna.

The holes into which a man falls increase in number year after year. The tricks of the dead! It is as meaningless as a worn-out sandal.

The real disciple of our school holds quite a different view.

A father hides his son's fault; the son hides the father's.

Citta[35] which all sentient beings have
Is just the Nirvāna which Buddhas have.
The wooden chicken stands on the coffin holding an egg;
The earthenware horse following the wind goes back to his home.

All the Buddhas of the past, present and future depending on the Prajñāpāramitā.

Pushing a good thing, a man makes it bad. Almost all people want to change themselves into another's skin and bones. But the original face which has no powder is best and unique.

Boiling water has no cold part!
Prajñā-wisdom makes all Buddhas.
All Buddhas perform *prajñā*-wisdom.
Subject and object are as one yet two.
A crane is crowing in an old windy nest.

Attain to the highest, perfect enlightenment.

Do not hammer a nail into Emptiness! Even if a bull is delivered of a calf, Buddhas can never realize enlightenment by means of *prajñā*-wisdom.

Why not? Because *prajñā*-wisdom and enlightenment are not two (different things). Or even if there were a oneness which a man could get, it could not be the Truth.

There is such a great fire that even the Buddha would lose his life if he went near enough to look at it.

---

[35] *Citta* means "consciousness" or "mind"; "heart" in the sense of center of consciousness.

Even if an otter climbed a tree to catch a fish,
The Buddha could never realize enlightenment by means
of *prajñā*.
To say that the Buddha attains *prajñā*
Is the same as saying that the Arhat has a wife.

Therefore, one ought to know that the Prajñāpāramitā
is the great Mantram (Dhāranī).[36]
Selling water at the river's bank.
Do not admire the lacquerware which was thrown away
at Ho's hermitage.[37] When the Chinese character is copied
three times, it is easy to confuse it with another, for
example, crow may become horse. Or it is like a merchant
who cheats us by selling cheap merchandise.
Do not step on anything white when you walk in the
night; it will necessarily be either water or a stone!
Respect the *mantram* which is man's own nature.
A hot, burning iron is changed into sweet drink.
Hell, this world, and Heaven,
Become a spot of snow falling into a fireplace.

The Mantram *of Great Wisdom*
Do not say "Mantram of Great Wisdom!" If a man
breaks this bumpkin stick (ordinary self) once, the universe becomes a mass of black. The cosmos loses its color,
and the sun and moon swallow their brilliance.
It is like filling a black lacquered bowl with black soup.

"Mantram of Great Wisdom," perfect at birth;
The light of wisdom fills the whole universe.
The endless ocean of man's sin
Is like a bubble on the water or a flower in the eye.

[36] A magical incantation. In Japanese Buddhism it is used
largely by the Shingon school.
[37] In China there was a shrine called Ho where a Taoist was
serving the gods. He threw all the used bowls away in the
river after each meal was served to them. When the people
living at the bottom of the mountain picked them up, they
were all uselessly damaged.

The highest Mantram

How about what is under the feet? Take out the lowest *mantram* for me.

Like the beauty of the falling leaf in the autumn rain, so the yellow field and the cloud in the glow of evening.

The highest, the most noble, the primary,
Even the Buddha or Maitreya[38] is his servant.
It is possessed originally within everyone;
And is only realized through a man's absolute death.[39]

The peerless Mantram

Prajñā-wisdom has been divided into two! Where is the undivided one? Who says there is no difference between above and below, nor among the four directions?

Seven flowers broken into eight. Te-yün's old gimlet[40] has come down from the peak of Miao-fen mountain many times.

Carrying snow to fill the well by employing a foolish saint.

Old plum tree in the cold;
It bursts into bloom with the spring rain.
Its shadow changes according to the moon;
Its unseen smell comes with the spring breeze.
The branch covered by snow in winter
Is covered now by many flowers,
In spite of the cold.
How admirable! It blooms earlier than any other.

[38] The Buddhist savior who will come into this world in a future *kalpa*.
[39] The real self transcends all concepts or definitions and, therefore, is formless. In this sense such a defined or conceptualized personality as Buddha or Bodhisattva is at a lower stage.
[40] Te-yün's old gimlet means the matured personality of Master Te-yün which is not shining but very sharp.

Which is capable of allaying all pain
To seek the core of the lily's bulb by taking off the skin;
To whittle around a square bamboo or to pull the fur off
a carpet.
Nine times nine equals eighty-one.
Nineteen and twenty-nine meet each other and yet do
not hold out their hands.

If a man realizes *prajñā*-wisdom,
The whole universe will blow away like ashes.
Heaven and Hell will become old pieces of furniture,
Buddha Land and Pandemonium are smashed to pieces.
The bush warbler blends with the snow singing a
beautiful song,
The black tortoise climbs up the candlestick wearing a
sword.
If a man wants to achieve such a state of mind,
He must sweat all over his body, once.

It is truth because it is not falsehood.
Precisely this is a great falsehood:
An arrow has already passed by!
What are you in contact with throughout the day?

Ch'i-yen killed three faithful retainers,
Su-wui deceived a couple of generals,
Shunning a tiger by imitating a chicken,
Selling dog's meat by hanging up a sheep,
Seeing the people's obedience when one points at a deer,
Killing the step-child by using a wasp,
Tao-chu killed Yü-nu,
Chi-hsin surrendered to the king of Ch'u,
Eating charcoal and hiding oneself under a bridge,
Throwing down an ornamental hairpin and crying beside
the well,
Putting the lord's corpse on a palanquin with a bream,
Breaking the father's teeth and presenting a bitten ear,
Fixing the bridge in the daytime,

And going through Ch'en-ts'ang in the night—
If a man could see through all of them,[41]
The sharp sword in the casket would shine.

This is the Mantram *proclaimed in the* Prajñāpāramitā.
What is it which has been shown to this point? It is as
though one hates wine and yet serves it to another.

The delicious taste of wine does not come from drinking
many cups. If a man does not come back for ten years, the
path he has walked will be forgotten.

Holding up one after another;
Piling up snow on the snow pile;
There is no place where a man can escape [from *prajñā*].
To whom do you [Buddha] serve so much wine after a
man is drunk?

It proclaims as follows:
Why do you repeat it again? How do you understand a
fisherman's singing or woodman's chanting?

Or what about the singing of the bush warbler or the
warbling of the swallow?

Do not try to divide the bubble from the water in the
ocean.

Twenty-four poems of seven characters to a line;
Four more poems of five characters added to them.
They are not written for noble priests
But for monks who are in discipline.
If you [students] do not find the way to enlightenment
There must be a bottomless pit of words.
Do not say these poems are too difficult to understand
But know you have no true eye to read them.
If you find what you cannot know
Quickly bite it and devote your body to digesting it.
If you digest it with the sweat of your brow

[41] All these lines refer to an old Chinese story about famous
stratagems.

Your bondage will be rooted out by the seventeen hundred [*koan*].

Once I saw the ultimate one through hard discipline
And had experienced the dissolution of my body.

To dissolve this body
Is the same as a lion who earns his dignity by hard discipline.

Fortunately, we Zen students have this spiritual experience
[And] we should strive our best for it.

Nowadays people abandon this way as if it were dirt.
Who can save this way in such a crisis?

I do not like to study it as literature in my old age
But want to produce worthy people.

One monk is satisfied with simply being awake;
Another one only argues about the words of others.

Shih-ma, a great Chinese scholar of the Sung Dynasty,
Because he lacked a true eye,

Whenever he faced a hard *koan* of the patriarchs
Said, "Our patriarchs make us suffer with difficult words."

Confess your *karma* of the five sins:
Your sin against the Buddhist Law is not shallow;
There are many such kinds of men in this world.

Also it is quite surprising to see that Zen is degenerating:
If you understand the mind of our patriarchs,
You would be blind as they said.

If you comprehend your situation,
All the words of the patriarchs are clearer than a mirror.
All contemporary students are careless:
One uses the mouth, another uses emotion.

If you think transmission can take place by paper or mouth,
The stage of our patriarchs is far away from you.

Oh! Young students! Forget yourselves!
[And] make the flower of truth bloom.

O Bodhi, *gone, gone, gone to the other shore, landed at the other shore,* Svaha!

It is easy to serve a superior man but difficult to please him.

Haze and ducks fly together, autumn river and long sky are identical in color.

It is raining on both the southern and northern village. The bride is facing her mother-in-law, the old man is feeding his grandchild.

The winter of the year of Enkyo-kōshi (1744)
My students cooperated in copying this.
Each character is worth ten Mon;
All characters used here amount to two thousand.
Their purpose is to try to keep my talk nonsensical.
I cannot help feeling happy to see it;
Therefore, here I wrote this poem,
To thank your kind minds.
Finishing my poem, I pray and say as follows:
Even if the cosmos is destroyed, my hope is endless.
I admire the charity of *prajñā*-wisdom
And spread it to the universe.
I devote myself to the Buddhas of the three worlds,
Also to our patriarchs in the world,
And all demons who guard Buddhism
And all the gods who live in our country.
My hope for the students of my monastery
Is that you will go through the gate of enlightenment quickly
So that your pure mind may shine brightly
And every evil in your mind may go away,
And that you do not rest until you have saved all sentient beings.

Responses to
Buddhist Meditation

In the Prologue a brief description of the structure and goals of the Meditation Workshop held in the January 1969 term at Oberlin was set forth. Yet, such a description can hardly do justice to the impact of the experience on the students involved. As a remedy to that lack and as a fitting conclusion to this study of Buddhist meditation which grew out of the matrix of that experience, a number of excerpted participant reports are herewith included. Each member of the project was required to submit some kind of written response at the end of the experiment. These responses varied from a paragraph length statement to a multipaged diary. The reports selected are not intended to represent a correct or necessarily exceptional response to the meditation experience, nor are any of them meant to be a model. Indeed, one might argue that the period of training was so brief as to call into question the value of including them at all. Nevertheless, from the standpoint of providing an adequate descriptive account of the workshop in Buddhist meditation, they add substance to an outline of the organization and conduct of the experiment.

I

After serious thought I've decided to attach the daily
journal in hopes that you may find it useful even though
I have some misgivings about it. There is the obvious
difficulty of trying to translate expressively and yet hon-
estly and objectively into verbal form experiences of an
essentially nonverbal nature. Also I thought and agonized
over too many of the entries, playing with words in trying
to be descriptively honest until much of the spontaneity
was probably bled out of them. Keeping the journal itself
became a stumbling block to meditation during the Zen
training because I began to think about, analyze, and
compare everything that was occurring in terms of how I
was going to record it later. In being committed to the
pattern of scrutinizing my experiences on a daily basis,
sometimes I had the feeling of not seeing the forest for
the trees. Perhaps in retrospect some time hence, I will be
able to see this experience as a whole and articulate just
how it touched me—for I know it did not pass lightly
over—and was part of my own religious quest and process
of becoming a person. But from the perspective I have
known, I can at best examine the parts to see how they
have contributed to the ineffable whole. . . .

During the period of Theravāda meditation, I felt a
center of calm spilling over into all aspects of living which
I had experienced before but never with such continuity.
The time to be introspective and to develop awareness of
what was going on within and without me was invaluable.
To a certain extent so was the detachment from emotion.
But I was afraid of giving up the capacity to surge with
powerful feelings. . . . Though I never really experienced
an enlightened realization of impermanence, suffering, and
no self in meditation, I became intellectually aware of
their worth as concepts and was continually applying them
to everything I experienced. I think I became a bit more

self-understanding and self-accepting, both of which are basic to healthy relationships with other people.

The Zen experience of being thrown out to sea with nothing specific to look for as in the Theravāda pattern was extremely frustrating. It was much more difficult not to expect anything perhaps because it took me almost until the final session to recognize the sort of intrinsic value in the discipline, which was readily apparent in the calming development of awareness of Theravāda training. I got caught in a dilemma of trying to choose between concentration and awareness, assuming that they were mutually incompatible. For a long time I didn't really feel that I was meditating at all but rather doing a great deal of fruitless thinking in an uncomfortable position. I wanted very much to feel into the Zen meditation because it seemed to be so much more accepting of individualization and human emotion. There have been moments when I have faced, not a dark night of the soul, but crisis moments when no rational answer was possible.

—On this first day of meditation, I didn't have much problem with pain except between sessions when changing positions, but my mind was like a wild animal raging from one disjointed thought to another. Attention to the breathing was completely lost in the chaos. This disturbed me even though the instructions had been not to deliberately shut out anything. Part of the frustration stemmed from the fact that I was quite sleepy and so not alert enough to try to maintain awareness of everything happening within and without me.

—Today I made the discovery that it is literally possible to sit back and watch the thoughts come and go just as it is possible to watch breath movements rise and fall. I was pleased with myself at being able to trace the links within the mental tangents back to their trigger points (e.g., sound of toilet flushing, twitching in the eyelid), some of which seemed ridiculous. In the first session when we were to notice the up and down breath movements and the distinction between the movement and our awareness of it, my fascination with tracing the thought processes was so overpowering that I wasn't paying much attention to breathing. Later when we were to try to be aware of the rising, duration, and cessation of both the up and down movement, a strong sensation of circular motion developed, and there were moments when the distinction between the physical aspect and the awareness was starkly clear. After the session I was ecstatic with the day but at the time retained a degree of passivity even in the midst of the "insight" experiences.

—Several of us meditated in Chao Khun's room for forty-five minutes. The experience today was one of great calmness. There was a feeling of what I will have to call detachment, for lack of a more accurate way of expressing it, in sitting back and watching the breathing and flickering thoughts without working at maintaining concentration on the breathing or tracing back the thoughts. At one point toward the close of the fleeting session the euphoric feeling became one of height, of being above myself and looking down.

—The initial stiffness in the knees and ankles soon disappeared without my having to direct full attention to it, and I was able to maintain relatively uninterrupted awareness of the three-part breathing movements for a few minutes. The rising movement was usually more pronounced. I first noticed my attention beginning to wane when realizing that I was mentally counting—arising, duration, falling—for both up and down movements without truly being aware of an accompanying physical movement. While intellectually recognizing impermanence in all this, I found myself thinking about it and then daydreaming (usually sparked by external sounds when bothering to trace the tangents back to their sources) without truly experiencing anything. My mind was slothful. It did not fight the daydreaming but was slow in becoming aware of it. In the second session I lowered my level of aspiration to maintaining awareness of the distinct physical movements and then to the difference between awareness and the actual movement. There were moments when the distinction was clear. The time passed quickly without anxiousness for the end of the session.

—Chao Khun turned us loose on our own, feeling that we'd had sufficient previous instruction. Today the movement in the abdomen was most pronounced rather than in the chest as it usually is so I directed my attention there. Found myself quite passive, even withdrawing from the seemingly increased noise. My mind did not jump about as much in its usual scrambled way or desire to dwell on memories, but a couple of times I caught myself quite involved in pure fantasy. This would disappear as soon as my attention was turned fully to it but would resume when I became bored with following the breathing. In connection with the fantasy I was aware of a slight feeling of pleasure which was unusual. Ordinarily I feel emotionally neutral during meditation. During the second part there was more wandering of the mind rather than fantasy. Also I experienced a feeling of coldness which became strong enough to cause shivers although it didn't seem so much within the body as enveloping it and wasn't uncomfortable.

—Most of the way through the first session, my mind seemed clear. It was also energetic and refused to be confined to awareness of breathing only. I could view the mental gymnastics detachedly, tracing the links back to their sources in some cases. Awareness was also clear regarding physical sensations (slight twitching of facial muscles, ringing in the left ear, etc.). I became acutely aware of a sharp pain in my left hip socket. When attention was focussed on this area, it seemed to spread throughout the leg and lower side while increasing in intensity. This caused an uneasiness (because such a strong pain had never arisen before, and the method of coping with it didn't seem to work) which might have accelerated into panic if the end of the session hadn't come shortly. Evidently this "blew my mind" for the opening stretch of the second part; my thoughts were tangled and crowded. The will to sort them out just wasn't there. Gradually the mind became a bit calmer. As attention was directed to the three-part breath movements, the familiar feeling of circular motion grew which seemed this time to be trying to jar or pull away from the physical body but which couldn't get completely free. At one point there was a sensation of swinging around to "view" myself as part of the group. None of the figures were really sharply defined as human but were only vague in outline. This may have been pure fantasy—I couldn't tell.

—Today in the initial moments, my awareness seemed sharper than usual and focussed easily on the breath movements. But then, perhaps out of pride that it seemed to be going so well or out of subconscious desire to have a good day since this was the last official meditation with Chao Khun, my mind began to be very capricious and the pain in my right leg became strong. After the 11:00 chimes sounded and I knew we were to break soon, the session was a total loss. Both legs were hot and in the pins and needles stage. I kept thinking, "Man, is this killing me! Why doesn't the session end?" In the other half, I maintained awareness of breathing for a little while and then seemed to settle into some kind of strange emptiness which wasn't sleep . . . maybe some kind of stupor. There was a sensation which can only be rather inadequately described as a slight weight on the brain. This sensation remained relatively unbroken until the end of the period which did not startle me.

—For a solid forty-five minutes I felt very alert for the most part, and at the same time pleasantly tranquil. At first I was preoccupied with the breathing and other physical processes going on within. For a time, the slight undulating movement of the torso seemingly caused by a strong heartbeat was compelling enough to become the

object of meditation. Then my thoughts took the center of
attention. The mental process was less like a hurricane and
more like a train of thought which could be watched dis-
interestedly even when people or memories of events ordinarily arousing strong feelings entered my consciousness.
The fact that I remained passive did not bother me as it
has sometimes before. Sensitivity to sounds was sharp, both
external ones and those associated with my own body.
There was also a new sensation of prickly warmth throughout the whole body. Toward the latter part there was an
experience of seeing colors and shapes which seemed to be
moving rapidly, similar to the experience when one has
been leaning heavily on the heels of the hands with closed
eyes.

—In this first day of Zen meditation practice my excitement, curiosity at the newness of the experience, the more
disciplined form, and the emotional reaction (some fear,
shock, disturbance) to hearing others being smacked with
the stick kept my attention and alertness keen throughout
the entire period. Up to the time Nishimura began walking
around to correct us, my mind remained concentrated on
counting the breathing. I never lost count although when
I tried to draw out the breaths they were shakier, my head
began to feel very light and empty, and concentration was
not quite so solid. There was no conscious attempt to
deliberately shut everything else out, but nevertheless I
was aware of my mind straying only briefly from counting.
When the first person was struck, I became very disturbed.
My own breathing speeded up, and I winced at the impact
of the blows. Then as other meditators were "encouraged,"
my agitation grew less . . . I became calm again until he
came down my row. There was a momentary conflict
between wanting to find out what the blows would be like
and fearing what they might be like which dissolved with
the realization that there was no real need to ask for the
stick for encouragement then because my attention had
not been slack. After the session I had the feeling that I'd

worked hard but not that I had meditated, at least in the sense of Theravāda meditation.

—My legs were very painful at first. Distractions seemed much greater today, especially sounds in the building. Counting the breathing became quite mechanical and would continue even while my mind was off on a tangent. Sometimes when the number ten was approached, my attention would suddenly come back to focus again with the realization that counting had gone on without mindfulness. The general feeling was one of attempted concentration, not meditation. The physical discipline seemed a barrier to awareness. The first time Nishimura used the stick it very much startled me, but subsequently the disturbance was not as great as yesterday. When he passed me, I asked for the "encouragement" without fear or hesitation. The blow was heavy—yes. But I almost wanted it to be; it was a good pain. It was very easy to sit perfectly erect after that. The tingling was a reminder. The walking phase didn't seem like meditation at all but rather a welcome break from sitting. During the last long segment my attention became caught up in the pattern of light and dark on the floor which shifted in configurations, something like watching clouds. Faces and head shapes were the most frequent patterns emerging.

—There was a certain feeling of calmness in the beginning. Still, there was not a very strong feeling of detachment, perhaps partly due to the fact that my eyes were open and I "saw" myself as part of a physical environment. Though the counting was lost only a few times, much of the time it was not being done mindfully. I got very hung-up today in *thinking*: about how things were going, how it compared to yesterday and to Theravāda, what I should remember to write in this journal, whether or not I should be trying to concentrate exclusively on the breathing, and in being concerned about the fact that I was thinking. I probably should have asked for the stick today, but Nishimura had whacked the two people in front of me, so at the time I didn't need it for alertness and hesitated, knowing he doesn't want to overuse it. The walking meditation was the best part. Breathing came naturally and was easy to keep track of. There was no anxiety, no pressure about keeping up. A feeling almost of disembodiment became strong at one point. I noticed it, was pleased with it, and lost it; then it arose again and lasted longer.

—My senses were seemingly a little sharper than usual, picking up smells and temperature changes as well as the usual inner and outer sounds. There also seemed to be more moments (at least up through walking meditation) when there was a feeling of detachment from sense perceptions although not from mental processes. My mind wandered considerably today, though I did maintain the counting, with some total breakdowns and many lapses of attention, throughout the session. Some of the wandering was thinking—which didn't bother me as much as it had yesterday—some playing with memories, and mostly daydreaming. I asked for the stick and was surprised at how much it hurt. Though it helped as far as holding the physical pose, it didn't really aid the meditation because I became wrapped up in thinking about the pain (how much it hurt, why it stung more than last time, and whether or not my frame of mind had influenced by reaction, etc.) not simply noticing it. The first part of today's session followed the general pattern of mechanical counting, daydreaming, thinking, and being bothered by thinking except that pain was the predominant sense impression. After the walking meditation when Nishimura gave someone the first blow, I was very much startled and completely lost track of the breathing. Then, partly still being confused by the question of whether or not I should be concentrating or being "aware," I seriously began to wonder why I was sitting there enduring the ache in my hip joint and struggling to do exactly as I was told. I just sat there and forgot about the breathing while the room echoed with subsequent blows and was disturbed because I had been detached neither from my body nor my mind nor could even be certain that that was desirable anymore—and waited for it to end.

—The concentration versus awareness dilemma continued unresolved but was not quite so traumatic. Maintaining real concentration on the breathing was a very elusive thing—conscious effort to do this only seemed to make it more difficult. The disembodied feeling arose again during walking meditation. I enjoyed it and tried to sustain it. The blows of the stick were as they had been the first time—sweet pain. But at the end of the period I did something I had not done before; I gave in to the ache in my legs in a sudden impulsive desire for relief, which the change of position did not bring. Then I had to wait out the last few seconds washed over not only by the continuing physical pain but also by guilt and disgust with myself. . . .

—I wanted today to be a "good" day, especially since it was the last session ever with Nishimura. But at first I could not force myself by sheer willpower to overcome sleepiness. I would catch myself not just preoccupied with thought fragments and bits of memories, but really involved in thinking about them. It seemed that whenever I had resolved this time to give full attention to the breathing I became caught up in thinking about something else. This didn't greatly disturb me but was faintly disappointing. Walking meditation was a welcome relief in the struggle and to my cramped legs also. Nishimura's words of reminder that this was our final time together and his admonition to pour all possible energy into it caused me to decide, though I don't think consciously, to concentrate everything on the sitting posture itself. For the first time there was a real satisfaction in the discipline of sitting itself and an acceptance of the value of doing simply that. Of course there were still flickerings of thoughts and memories through my mind, but neither this nor the fact that I wasn't maintaining constant awareness in counting the breathing ruptured the calmness. The blows of the stick were not sharp and painful but a definite reinforcement of my efforts at sitting. I was conscious of a feeling of exhilaration in these final minutes.

II

We practiced two kinds of meditation: that taught by a monk of Theravāda Buddhism, and meditation taught by a Zen priest. The month was divided into two parts, with the Zen meditation coming second. We meditated for an hour and a half each weekday, and had two afternoon discussions per week. I found that I had different reactions to the two types of meditation.

The Theravāda meditation caused me to consider the concept of self. It is interesting how relevant to modern psychology are the teachings of Buddhism. The analytical breakdown of self into five aggregates (physical phenomena, sensations, perceptions, mental formations, and consciousness) gives one somewhat the same perspective as does studying physiological psychology. One realizes in the process of analysis how rigidly one clings to the belief that one is a separated entity "I," and how conditioning has narrowed one's mind to not accepting outside influence. The impact of this sort of analysis is in the freedom to change it opens up. Even if to change means merely to recondition oneself in different ways, one now has the will to choose in which ways one wants to be conditioned.

Physical pain proved to be a good catalyst for starting this analysis. On the first day it was very uncomfortable. My feet began to go to sleep, and this frightened me. But by forcing myself to look at the pain objectively as perception by a brain of sensations in a foot, the attitude "I am in pain" could no longer carry as much strength as it had before. I remembered a diagram which I had seen in a psychology book of the sensory areas in the cortex. The diagram showed that different parts of the body have different sizes of corresponding sensory areas in the cortex, thus causing relativity of sensitivity in different parts of the body. I tried to see if I could discover this fact subjectively through observance of the pain I was feeling, since it had struck me how much Buddhist thinkers had discovered about the mind in this fashion.

Looking back at the end of the month, I think that the greatest value of the Theravāda meditation is in the type of discipline which it develops. In order to control one's mental processes, one must first develop what Chao Khun calls "bare attention." I began observing the thoughts and feelings I was experiencing. It is amazing how much trivial thinking goes on in the course of an hour. Unless one can learn to control one's mind, one cannot focus one's consciousness, and a great deal of energy is dissipated. One morning while practicing this observance, my mind seemed to divide itself. Part of it was detached, doing the observing. It was a state of awareness of my body as a combination of physical phenomena. However, I still could not explain who or what was doing this observing, so I could not say that this was any liberation from "I." It was merely a changed perspective toward "I." According to Chao Khun, the way to erase concepts is to become aware of them. But it seems to me that there would be an infinite number of such stages of consciousness: being aware of your mind; being aware of being aware of your mind; etc.

While the initial reactions were positive, toward the end of the week I began reacting against the meditation. I think I understand that attachment brings suffering, since all attachment is to things which are impermanent. What is obvious is one's fear of death. Yet this knowledge can take one in different directions. One is the belief that happiness is the absence of suffering, which would lead to the aim of detachment which Chao Khun taught. The other is accepting the fact that happiness and suffering are interdependent. I cannot see any freedom to be gained in following meditation to its ultimate end, because this seems to be an attachment to nonattachment. . . .

The Zen meditation affected me differently. The Theravāda made me think in analytical terms about the self. The Zen made me think about time and the external world. Intellectually the Zen was more exciting. I felt that the ideas were not ones which, if I followed them to any great degree, would force me to remove myself from the things which I find meaningful.

The Zen meditation was stricter than the Theravāda. One must arrange one's mat and possessions neatly before one begins to meditate. This is because one must be organized to have a clear mind, but it also reflects the belief that one's inner world is the result of interaction with the external world. On the first day, after our walk around the room between the two sitting sessions, Nishimura stopped by my mat and fixed my shoes neatly. I had left them disarrayed. In that one simple act he pointed out to me this important belief.

The significance of the incense, bell-ringing, and back-whacking, helped make me aware of the present moment. . . . In the beginning this appealed to me, but I soon found that an awareness of the present made me want to leave the meditation room and do something active with my mind. When I did try to meditate, the fact of external discipline proved to be a negative force. The Theravāda meditation threw me on my own. The discipline had to come from within. In the Zen meditation I found myself correcting my posture for Nishimura's benefit, rather than for my own. I think this reaction points out the importance in education of making a student realize that discipline and creative thought must come from within oneself, and not from or for an external source. . . .

III

During the period of Theravāda meditation, it seemed that my main obstacles in practicing mindfulness were my inability to suppress mental conversation with myself, a tendency to create imaginary visual phenomena while my eyes were closed, and the impulse to react to the physical pain of sitting. For the entire first week it was all I could do to keep from moving during the first half of each day's meditation; by the end of the second half, it was usual for me to have rocked forward and backward a few times to relieve the tension in my back and legs or used my hands to keep my legs in position. Looking forward to the moment when we could unfold our legs made me very conscious of the passage of time, and I could estimate quite accurately the number of minutes left until then. Meditation was then, among other things, an exercise in endurance.

Gradually I found that a certain amount of freedom from this expectancy and the impulse to react could be achieved. This may have resulted from physically adapting to the half-lotus position as much as anything. However, there were occasions when my usual sense of orientation in space and time would be lost. More than once there was the vague impression of having shrunk. Sometimes there was a sensation of slow rotation in one direction or another. Once, while I was trying to be aware of my sensations and thoughts, they seemed to acquire the attribute of occupying a finite volume surrounded by a tangible space in which sensation and thought did not exist. These and similar phenomena provoked my curiosity and provided my first real distraction from the pain of sitting and daydreaming.

The "best" session I had came toward the end of the second week. For some reason a mild sensation of disembodiment, such as described above, came over me almost immediately after the start of meditation. It gradually subsided, leaving me in a very quiet frame of mind. A tingling sensation suffused my face, and I became acutely conscious of all physical sensation occurring at the time. I found myself in the role of a spectator to, rather than a participant in, these sensations and was able to sit without adjusting my position at the end of the first half-hour and for the rest of the hour in addition. Toward the end, it was very difficult to maintain the role of the spectator, but by trying very hard to examine qualitatively the sensations I was experiencing, I was able to keep from becoming the "participant" and reacting.

Following that session the realization came upon me that the impressions of disembodiment and scaling-down occurring during meditation were among the terrifying aspects of a certain nightmare I used to have when I was very young. Up until this realization, I could never figure out what had been so frightening about those dreams, because they had been very abstract. But I have recognized the experiences to be exactly the same.

When we began Zen meditation, my consciousness was dominated by the awareness of the sitting position and the shock of having a steady input of visual information through half-opened eyes. Having to attend to the alignment of the mat, position of my body on the mat, and position of legs, arms, hands, head, teeth, and tongue made it possible to have a much more extensive awareness of the conditions of my sitting than I had had during the Theravāda meditation. Consequently, the pain of sitting, although still strong in my consciousness, was not nearly as much of a problem.

Gradually, however, the freshness of this type of sitting experience wore off, and simply being aware of my position became almost as much of a distraction as the pain had been before. Some mornings I would feel all askew or off balance, and would unconsciously tense my muscles to keep from leaning or toppling over. I was more conscious of just seeing than I was of what I saw; I think my eyes automatically de-focused. I still could not keep my brain from generating thought after thought, and concentration on breathing was very difficult. While walking in meditation, I was not so aware of thoughts, but walking itself took a fair share of my attention.

I asked for the stick every day, and in so doing conditioned myself to being struck without anticipation and fear of pain. The sensation of actually receiving the blows would momentarily blot out everything else from my consciousness, but for the most part I was able to remain a spectator to sensation.

Toward the last few days, I began to lose what Nishimura calls "the fresh consciousness." The impact of the stick kept me alert, however; and even though meditation itself was not exciting, the significance of the project began making itself felt on the level of intellect. . . .

In retrospect, I must concede that the notion of a Self, an "I," never disappeared from my head. Even in trying to analyze what I did actually experience, it is impossible to avoid the use of the forms "I thought—" and "I felt—" or "I experienced—" and so on. Perhaps this is the evidence of the conditioning effects of language and thought forms upon each other. Also, I could never completely obliterate the impulse to react toward even low levels of pain; I was merely able to keep from responding to it. But if I haven't been shaken out of my Western state of mind, I have been shaken up inside it. I feel very ill-at-ease about my observations and judgments, even those in this paper. Just the intellectual understanding I have of how subjective and conditioned they are has caused me to doubt to the point of hesitating in my decisions regarding what to do with myself and how to do it. Felt doubt is a curse upon the doubter; he can only resolve it by making an unwarranted assumption of the type he has come to question, or by finding some independent, nonsubjective variable that is beyond questioning. Contemporary American life patterns leave little middle ground; it is very difficult to ease into the second path by degrees. It is all the way or not at all, so the pressure is toward dropping the question.

IV

At first it is exciting to sit quietly in a novel position, for thirty-five minutes at a time. With eyes closed I begin to concentrate totally on my breathing, feeling it enter and leave my body, noticing the movement of my abdomen, noticing my mind's response to the process. Sounds come and go; someone next to me stirs, children's cries from outside reach my ears; but bent on total concentration I try to do as Chao Khun says: to notice the sounds, to watch them, then to let them go and forget them. As the silence continues, my legs begin to ache, and my feet are falling asleep. Suddenly all I can think of is the signal from Chao Khun to open my eyes and relax. When it comes, I am surprised and somehow wish I didn't have to come out of myself. But the period is ended. Chao Khun reads to us of the Buddha's advice to his disciples, of insight, of total awareness.

Thus the mornings of Theravāda meditation continue; on some days I find periods of genuine stillness of mind, short-lived but nonetheless real. On some days I find myself totally incapable of concentration, and I open my eyes frustrated and discouraged. The original novelty of the experience is wearing off, and I am aware of the incredible amount of perseverance and intense mental work which goes into real and worthwhile insight meditation. But even when concentration is most difficult, I find it somehow easier for my mind to accept the exercises and words of advice which Chao Khun gives to us. I have seen, for example, how fickle is my mind's interpretation of sensations; when my legs begin to ache, I have simply to become totally aware of the pain and it quickly disappears. I move at my own pace, practicing the exercises given us by Chao Khun. He watches us, calmly and peacefully; he is distant, but so obviously at peace. . . .

I am becoming used to the daily sessions, and my success in the morning has a direct effect on the rest of the day as the awareness I am developing begins to extend into the other hours of each day.

Two weeks later we enter the meditation room for the first day of practicing *zazen*. We are anxious to begin, to compare the Zen experience, under the strict guidance of the Reverend Eshin Nishimura, with the Theravāda experience. We sit in four straight lines, attempting perfect posture as Nishimura explains the importance of this to us. Thus *zazen* begins; it is quite different from the meditation of Chao Khun.

I am sitting as motionlessly as I can. I concentrate on my breathing as before, but in a different manner and with different results, although the results are harder to understand. Nishimura walks in front of me quietly; I touch my palms together. He stops; we bow to one another, and I bend over. He strikes me hard on the back six times. We then bow to one another again, and I resume the posture as he continues down the line. The blows force my mind back into an extreme intensity; the ritual and structure of the sessions are like an ever-present pressure to compel me to continue to struggle with my own consciousness. It is very difficult.

During the afternoons and in the discussion groups, we talk, sometimes seriously, sometimes not. Nishimura is a joyful man, and he finds it hard, I think, to conceal his joy and his irrepressible sense of humor. It is, perhaps, a disadvantage during the meditation sessions, because he is supposed to be very strict, but we always know he loves us, and we him. The sessions continue—some successful, some not. Sometimes Nishimura yells at us and tells us we are wasting our time; perhaps we are. . . .

V

—Three quarters of an hour with no break, concentrating on breathing. He said we could change positions if the pain became unbearable, so I found myself spending most of the time wondering if my discomfort could be classified as unbearable, or if I should try to stick it out. Actual meditation on breathing very poor. During practice later in the day my concentration was a little better. For a short time I had a peaceful floating feeling, but after it passed I had a difficult time trying to keep from being attached to it.

—Attachment to nonattachment, this is one of my main difficulties. During meditation I sit there trying to become enlightened, trying to find peace of mind, trying to feel and understand no-self. Chao Khun says the important thing is to recognize these feelings, then they will disappear.

—First half hour, concentration and mindfulness better than usual, although especially near the end of the period I was, as usual, impatient for it to end. During the second half hour I felt what seemed to be a deeper state of meditation. My breath became more shallow, I felt I was focusing almost full attention on it. I had a clear awareness of sounds, as well as other sensations. Sounds were only sound, was the thought which kept recurring, and this thought made me feel peaceful and somewhat ecstatic. I wanted to open my eyes so that I could enjoy seeing as much as I was enjoying hearing.

—Worst meditation period so far. Impatience, discomfort, no ability to concentrate. After the first five minutes I desperately wanted to go to the bathroom and could think of nothing else for the next hour and a half. Knowing that the only way to rise above the physical discomfort was by meditating with my full attention was no help whatsoever.

Intense desire to quit meditating altogether, mixed with almost as strong a desire to try again tomorrow and do better.

—First day of *zazen* meditation. Environment, body, mind, must all be in order. When he started walking around carrying his stick I was terrified, in spite of, or because of, knowing he would hit only those who asked to be hit. I knew the only way to get past my fear was to ask to be hit. It didn't hurt as much as I had expected, but I did not feel it helped me to concentrate better. I find it easier to practice *zazen*, because the formality of the situation makes it clearer exactly what you can and cannot do. But Theravāda appeals more to my intellect.

—The sound of the stick interfered strongly with my meditation. Every time I saw out of the corner of my eye that someone was going to be hit, I would cringe until I knew it was over and I could relax again. Worst of all was when he hit Nancy, who is my friend and was sitting across from me, even though I knew she had asked to be hit. . . .

—I became aware during meditation today of how much more calm and peaceful I am and how much less restless than I was at the beginning of meditation. I am not even aware of wanting to change my position now, while I used to be unable to keep still. My mind is not so restless, and not so often waiting for the final bell. . . .

—At first, great difficulty in breathing. I tried to breathe deeply but I felt as though I wasn't getting enough air. Then my breath became shallow; felt as though I hardly needed to breathe at all. Feeling of head being cut off from legs, with no body in between, and this made it impossible to imagine my breath going down all the way to my feet, as we were supposed to do. This feeling lasted until we began walking meditation, when breathing and emotions returned to normal. Time seemed to go much faster than usual; little feeling of waiting for period to end. In fact, I was really surprised when it was over. I feel as though I am finally *beginning*. I wish the monks were not leaving tomorrow.

—Became more aware of how I enjoy sitting for itself, rather than just using it as a means to enlightenment. It seems to bring a feeling of peacefulness, of being more at one with what is around me. I plan to continue after winter term ends.

VI

The present is that moment occurring just between the remembered instant and the anticipated one. A mind untrained in the awareness of the present can barely imagine totally becoming into this moment. But the fallacy lies only in the consideration of self as an entity extended in time; certainly this "self," diffusing its consciousness of concentration away into the past and future, cannot conceive of focusing its awareness into a single nonextended instant.

Consider an event that happens so quickly that it can only be identified in time by its divisions of time into before and after. The purpose of meditation can be seen as an attempt to train the mind's self-apprehension to be the instantaneous event which always occurs at that instant which is neither before nor after, otherwise known as the present. The untrained mind, habitually extended in time, can imagine this process as an intellectualization; it will then remember itself imagining in the previous instant and must recreate the imagining in the perpetually recurring present. Repeatedly and continually knowing itself as in this instant becomes a process of training the mind's powers of concentration and awareness. At the very beginning of the training the duration of concentration will be infinitesimally small; but, like any other artistic skill, it will improve with practice.

Improvisation on a musical instrument is an activity

made possible by the mind's apprehension of the vibrations that occur between accident and plan. In some sense this might be a description of any event of experience of the human condition; I find it appropriately analogous to my personal meditation experiences of last month. For I cannot speak of realizations and discoveries as meaningful intellectual events in the sense in which I would have intended these words a month ago. In fact it is the very distinction between description and intellectualization that has been dissolved, so that any real understanding of events around and within the residence of what I call my consciousness can only stand in terms of experiential activities. Absolutely anything and everything might be anticipated by the imagination; yet an actual event is simply the merging of the infinite with the infinitesimal.

Three experiences stand out in my mind that occurred in the first two weeks, practicing Theravāda meditation. On the third day I was meditating alone in the evening, attempting awareness of impermanence. Following the arising, existing, and passing away of each individual breath, I achieved for a period of time a balance between mindfully perceiving this impermanence and that of the pain of full lotus position (which at other times was too great for me to bear). In this manner I sank deeper into a state of conscious active peace. Suddenly I became aware of loud shouts and laughter in the hall outside my room; then came sounds of people running; a door slammed, and silence was again as before. In this event was a realization of the object of meditation in the three worlds instantly before me, and as I became the utter truth of impermanence of noise, breathing, and pain, that self-conscious seer was no more.

I dislike retelling these experiences as their description seems fated to sound overdramatized. Afterwards they were more like dreams than the cosmic, earth-shaking events they appear to be on paper. Somehow I prefer to regard them as artificially manufactured events originating in my subconscious mind which attempted to reward me for my hours spent in an uncomfortable position. This psychological explanation seems appropriate in the light of how significant I considered these events to be.

Five days later I was sitting with the group frustrated in the first half of the session at being unable to keep my mind from wandering. It was after the break, in the second half, that I was able to localize awareness at the borders of my mind and hold it there. The effort at concentration was so great that I could perceive only the tails of events just as they would leave and enter my mind. In this realm of timelessness I held fast to my position. Trying to focus on and identify one of the blurry images fleeting past my vision, I suddenly realized that I had in fact grabbed on to the tail of an entering blur, and my point of consciousness was swept with it into my mind. I could no longer tell if I was still holding on to the original event, for in every conceivable direction images surrounded me, moving incredibly fast and continually appearing and disappearing. Then, just as in a dream, all this faded into mist, and out of the soft humid cloud Chao Khun's quiet voice cut clearly through, ending the meditation period: "Okay."

The third experience was less spectacular, but no less significant. It was the next day, again in the second half of the session. For the last twenty minutes or so of the period I sank into a deep peace that was more silent than either waking or sleeping, with no consciousness of anything whatsoever, until I heard Chao Khun's voice. Again, I only realized what had been happening as an event I had experienced when his voice brought me out of this state.

Certain basic elements in the differences in approach between Zen and Theravāda Buddhism make it difficult to draw a meaningful comparison between the impressions of the first fortnight and those of the second. My reactions in meditation were similarly divided in both methods: about half of the sessions were simply frustrating, and the other half rewarding in some way. It is interesting that the most intensely rewarding sessions came during Theravāda meditation, and that the most intensely depressing times were after a frustrating session in Zen.

From the very beginning of the Zen experiment I enjoyed the ascetic formality and the discipline in posture and physical self-control. My reaction toward it was generally more positive while actually meditating, and more negative during the rest of the day; and the general experience was more existential than intellectual. Sometimes I would feel extremely happy and live ecstatically from moment to moment, and other times I would be very depressed and dissatisfied with myself; yet I would never think about any reason for feeling one way or another— I would just feel it. . . .

The strongest effect of the past month is the dissolution of the conflict between understanding and working, in the realization that the two are synonymous. . . .

Meditation is a process of stilling the usual daily concerns of the conscious mind and focusing one's attention on the question of one's being. . . .

Wisdom is a freedom from distinctions between understanding and not understanding. . . .

Selected Bibliography on
Meditation in Theravāda
and Zen Buddhism

Chang, Garma, C. C. *The Practice of Zen.* New York: Harper & Row, 1959. A study of Zen that includes discourses on Zen practice and a survey of Buddhist meditation.

Conze, Edward. *Buddhist Meditation.* New York: Harper & Row, 1956. A collection of texts on Buddhist meditation divided into four sections: devotional exercises, mindfulness, trance, and wisdom.

Dhammasudhi, Sobhana. *Insight Meditation.* 2nd ed., London: Committee for the Advancement of Buddhism, 1968. An explanation and interpretation of Theravāda meditation by the head meditation teacher at the Vipassanā Centre, Surrey, England.

Humphreys, Christmas. *Concentration and Meditation.* Berkeley: Shambala Press, 1969. An introduction to Buddhist meditation by the president of the London Buddhist Society and one of the principal interpreters of Buddhism to the West.

Kapleau, Philip. *The Three Pillars of Zen.* Boston: Beacon Press, 1967. An absorbing study of Zen meditation by the head of the Zen meditation center in Rochester, New York, who spent twelve years practicing in both Rinzai and Sōtō monasteries in Japan.

Luk, Charles. *The Secrets of Chinese Meditation.* London: Rider & Co., 1964. This study of Chinese meditation contains two chapters on meditation in the Zen (Ch'an) tradition.

Mahasi Sayadaw. *The Progress of Insight*. Kandy (Ceylon): Buddhist Publication Society, 1965. An exposition of the practice of mindfulness by an eminent Burmese meditation teacher.

Nyānaponika Thera. *The Heart of Buddhist Meditation*. London: Rider & Co., 1962. A lucid interpretation of the meaning of meditation in the Theravāda tradition together with an anthology of texts. Written by a German monk living in Ceylon.

Muira, Isshū and Sasaki, Ruth, F., *The Zen Koan*. New York: Harcourt, Brace and World, Inc., 1965. A study of the history of the development and use of the Koan in China and Japan.

Shibayama, Zenkei. *On Zazen Wasan*. Kyoto, 1967. An interpretation of Hakuin Zenji's "Song of Zazen" by the Zen master of Nanzen-ji in Kyoto, Japan.

Soma Thera. *The Way of Mindfulness*. Kandy (Ceylon): Buddhist Publication Society, 1967. A translation of the *Satipaṭṭhāna Sutta*, the principal meditation manual of Theravāda Buddhism, together with notes from two classical commentaries.

Suzuki, D. T. *The Training of the Zen Buddhist Monk*. New York: University Books, 1965. One of the few descriptions of life in a Zen monastery by the principal interpreter of Zen to the West.

Suzuki, D. T., Fromm, Erich, and De Martino, Richard. *Zen Buddhism and Psychoanalysis*. London: George Allen and Unwin, Ltd., 1960. Fromm's essay, in particular, provides an interesting psychological interpretation of Zen practice.

Vajirañāna, Paravahera Mahāthera. *Buddhist Meditation in Theory and Practice*. Colombo (Ceylon): M. D. Gunasena & Co., Ltd., 1962. An exposition of Buddhist meditation based primarily on the classical text, the *Visuddhimagga* of Buddhaghosa.

Glossary

Abhidhamma. "Higher Teaching." Also refers to the third
    division of the Theravāda canonical writings, which
    contains writings of a philosophical and psychological
    character.

Amida. The Japanese form of *Amitābha* ("infinite light"),
    one of the most venerated of the Mahāyāna *dhyani* or
    nonhistorical Buddhas who rules over the Western
    Paradise known as the Pure Land.

Anattā. No-self; the nonessential nature of mundane exist-
    ence. Together with suffering (*dukkha*) and imperma-
    nence (*anicca*) it composes the three salient charac-
    teristics of existence in Theravāda Buddhism.

Ānāpāna. Inhalation and exhalation. In the scheme of
    Theravāda meditation this term usually appears as
    ānāpāna-sati or mindfulness of respiration.

Anicca. Impermanence; transience; flux. One of the three
    salient characteristics of existence in Theravāda Bud-
    dhism.

Anubodha. Awakening; recognition; perception. From the
    same root word as the title, the Buddha, the
    Awakened One.

Anupassanā. Looking at; contemplating. Theravāda medi-
    tation teaches the importance of simply observing the
    elements of existence (*dhammānupassanā*).

Appamāna. Boundless; without measure. In Theravāda
    Buddhism the term has a technical reference to the

Four Unlimiteds acquired through meditation. They are: *mettā* or love; *karuṇā* or compassion; *muditā* or sympathetic joy; and *upekkhā* or equanimity.

Arhat. A "worthy one." In Theravāda Buddhism the Arhat is the highest stage of sanctification before the realization of the ultimate goal of Nirvāṇa.

Avijjā. Ignorance; without knowledge. The state said to to characterize most worldlings.

Avalokiteśvara. One of the most important Bodhisattvas or "wisdom beings" in Mahāyāna Buddhism. Although venerated widely throughout East Asia, Avalokiteśvara is particularly associated with Amitābha, the Buddha of the Western Paradise.

Āyatana. One of the classifications of elements of sentient existence in Theravāda Buddhism. It refers to the six sense organs together with their corresponding sense bases (e.g., the eye and visible objects, the ear and sound, etc.).

Bhavāṅga. Becoming; continuity of consciousness. Rendered by some translators as "stream of consciousness."

Bhikkhu. A "beggar"; the term used to designate a Buddhist monk in Therevāda Buddhism.

Bodhisattva. "Wisdom being"; a Buddha-to-be who vows to save all sentient beings prior to his own realization of Nirvāṇa. Particular Bodhisattvas such as Avalokiteśvara come to be worshipped as saviors in some forms of Mahāyāna Buddhism.

Citta. Mind; consciousness; the heart of conscious life.

Dharma (Dhamma in Pāli). One of the most important terms in the vocabulary of Buddhism. It has a wide variety of meanings including fundamental constituent of being, natural law, moral law, teachings of the Buddha.

Dhātu. Basic element. May refer in particular to the four elements (earth, water, fire and wind), or to physical elements, or to the elements of sense consciousness.

Dhyāna (Jhāna in Pāli). Trance state; state of mental absorption. Often a part of the conventional formula of four or eight levels.

Diṭṭhi. View; point of view; belief. *Sakkāyadiṭṭhi:* the false

teaching of a belief in a soul. *Sammādiṭṭhi*: complete
or true teaching.

Dukkha. Suffering; ill; unsatisfactoriness. One of the three
salient characteristics of existence.

Indriya. From the Sanskrit meaning "belonging to Indra."
In Theravāda Buddhism came to mean controlling
principle or directive force.

Jhāna. See *dhyāna.*

Karma (*Kamma* in Pāli). Act; deed. Often refers to the
Law of Karma, a law of moral retribution. *Kamma-vipāka*: the law of action and reaction.

Kāya. Body. Used in a variety of compound words in various Buddhist schools. *Kāyapassaddhi*: tranquillity of
body or the senses.

Kensho. Seeing into one's nature; consequently seeing into
the Buddha nature. Often used interchangeably with
satori in Zen Buddhism.

Koan. "Public document." In Zen it refers to a baffling
statement or verbal conundrum intended to confound
logical reasoning and point to ultimate truth.

Makyo. An evil state of mind threatening the Zen meditator who has not yet experienced *kensho.*

Maṇḍala. Circle; a symbolic place marked on the ground
for the performance of a sacred rite.

Nāma-rūpa. One of the earliest definitions of the major
components of sentient existence in Buddhism. The
reference is to the elements of the body (*rūpa*) and
mind (*nāma*).

Nirvāṇa (*Nibbāna* in Pāli). The Summum Bonum of Buddhism. The ultimate goal to be achieved; a state of
perfect wisdom and equanimity.

Prajñā (*Paññā* in Pāli). Knowledge; wisdom. Often regarded as higher or emancipating knowledge. *Prajñā-pāramitā*: perfection of wisdom.

Pāramitā. Mastery; perfection; supremacy. One of the supreme virtues of the Bodhisattva (e.g., compassion,
wisdom).

Paṭicca-samuppāda. Conditioned arising. Refers to a conventional twelve-fold formula beginning with ignorance and ending with old age and death.

Prāṇāyāma. Restraint of breath. One of the "limbs" of Yoga.

Pratyekabuddha. One who has won enlightenment by himself and does not share his wisdom with others. In Mahāyāna Buddhism he is considered to be lower than a Bodhisattva.

Rinzai. Japanese for the Chinese term, Lin-chi, after the name of the famous Zen master by the same name (A.D. ?–867). Rinzai Zen is one of the two major schools of Zen in Japan today.

Samādhi. Concentration; focusing the consciousness.

Samatha. Tranquillity. An important result of the practice of meditation.

Sampajāna. Clear comprehension. Often appears together with *sati* or mindful awareness as twin aspects of insight (*vipassanā*) meditation.

Saṁsāra. "Flowing together." Refers to the constituents of existence flowing together in the process of rebirth.

Saṁyojana. The ten fetters binding man to the wheel of rebirth. Conventionally enumerated as belief in a self, doubt, attachment to rites, sensual desire, ill will, desire for form objects, desire for formless objects, pride, mental unrest, and ignorance.

Saṅkhata. "Put together"; compounded and, hence, conditioned. Refers to the mundane world of existence. Opposite of *asaṅkhata,* the uncompounded or Nirvāṇa.

Sanzen. Interviews by the Zen master with his student for the purpose of having the latter present his views on the *koan* he is studying.

Sati. Mindfulness; awareness. *Sammāsati*: full or complete awareness. *Satipaṭṭhāna*: foundation of mindfulness; an important text in Theravāda Buddhism is called the *Satipaṭṭhāna Sutta.*

Satori. The Japanese term for the experience of enlightenment or full awakenness.

Sesshin. A period of intensive meditation training in the Zen tradition held at periodic intervals.

Shonen-sozohu. Continuity of right thinking. A term used for the training following *satori.* Often referred to as "downward training."

Sīla. Moral virtue; morality; ethics; rules of proper behavior. In Buddhism moral virtue is both a prerequisite for meditation practice as well as one of its concomitant factors.

Sōtō. One of the two major Zen sects in Japan today. In numbers of adherents it exceeds the Rinzai sect.

Śūnyatā. Emptiness or Void. A designation of the real nature of things in the Mahāyāna tradition. Made important in the *Prajñāpāramitā* texts and developed by the Indian philosopher, Nāgārjuna (second century A.D.).

Sūtra (*Sutta* in Pāli). "Strand"; used to designate a particular text in Buddhism, e.g., *Prajñāpāramitā Sutra.*

Taṇhā. Thirst; desire; craving. The condition of being which characterizes most worldlings.

Tathāgata. "Thus gone." A title given to the Buddha as one who has crossed over to the farther shore or Nirvāṇa.

Vedanā. Feeling; sensation. One of the five aggregates of existence in the Theravāda classification of the five factors of human life.

Vijñāna (*Viññāṇa* in Pāli). Principle of consciousness; knowledge, especially discriminating knowledge. Sometimes contrasted with *prajñā* or intuitive knowledge. *Ālaya-vijñāna:* storehouse consciousness or the eighth consciousness.

Vipassanā. Inward vision; insight; insight meditation.

Zazen. "Sitting Zen." The term for meditation in the Zen tradition.